Sex Roles,
Life Styles,
and Childbearing

Sex Roles,
Life Styles,
and Childbearing

Changing Patterns in
Marriage and the Family

John H. Scanzoni

THE FREE PRESS
A Division of Macmillan Publishing Co., Inc.
NEW YORK

Collier Macmillan Publishers
LONDON

The Free Press
A Division of Macmillan Publishing Co., Inc.
866 Third Avenue, New York, N.Y. 10022

Collier Macmillan Canada, Ltd.

Library of Congress Catalog Card Number: 74–28939

Printed in the United States of America

printing number

1 2 3 4 5 6 7 8 9 10

Library of Congress Cataloging in Publication Data

Scanzoni, John H
   Sex roles, life styles, and childbearing.

   "This investigation was carried out under contract
no. 70-2192 from the Center for Population Research,
National Institutes for Child Health and Human Develop-
ment."
   Bibliography: p.
   Includes index.
   1. Family—United States. 2. Family size.
3. Sex role. 4. Birth control—United States.
I. Title. [DNLM: 1. Family. 2. Family planning—
United States. 3. Life style. 4. Marriage.
5. Sex. HQ536 S283a]
HQ536.S34   301.42′0973   74-28939
ISBN 0-02-927720-5

Contents

Preface

THIS IS A STUDY of 3,100 husbands and wives living in ten cities, representing five states. The cities include Chicago and Springfield in Illinois; Detroit, Grand Rapids, and Muskegon in Michigan; Columbus, Springfield, Cincinnati, and Cleveland in Ohio; and Evansville in Indiana. It was sponsored by The Center for Population Research of the National Institutes for Child Health and Human Development. Professional interviewers from National Analysts gathered the information from a sample that includes not only both sexes but also a high proportion of blacks, working wives, and younger persons.

Much speculation exists as to whether what people believe about male–female roles has any effect on family planning and on population trends. Up until now, there has been little systematic investigation into the question of whether sex or gender role norms really affect having or not having children. In this book, an analysis is made of the sex role norms of husbands and wives, which shows how these norms affect such things as the number of children persons intend to have, the age when people marry, effectiveness in using contraceptives, wife employment, and so forth. Moreover, an examination is made of how these gender role norms are related to religion, age, race, education, marital satisfaction, and economic satisfaction. We try to discover how these kinds of factors operate with sex role norms to influence fertility control.

A major conclusion of this study is that persons who hold more modern, egalitarian sex role norms do indeed behave in such a way as to have smaller families. In this way, wives become freer to pursue their own interests—mostly within the occupational realm, but elsewhere as well. Younger persons, for example, seem to hold more egalitarian sex role norms than do older persons; and this may be one part of the explanation of the sharp decline in births in the early seventies.

As far as identifying future population trends is concerned, we need to pay close attention to sex role norms. Certain groups who for one reason or another react against egalitarianism for women may begin to increase their reproduction. It is not inconceivable that the United States or other modern nations could follow the lead of either Rumania or Argentina in eliminating abortions or in banning the pill. Thus, wives who were most motivated by sex role norms to hold down family size would be the most likely and able to do so.

The further importance of sex role norms lies with their implications for continued population growth in the Third World as well as in poverty areas in the United States. In these situations, it seems apparent that even the most sophisticated technology is not sufficient by itself to slow down population growth. The study reported in this book suggests that changes in gender role norms are necessary as well.

In short, this study is about how the sociology of marriage affects the sociology of reproduction. The kinds of roles that men and women want to play both in and out of marriage influence fertility control and family size on the micro level, and subsequently population growth itself on the macro level.

Acknowledgments

THIS INVESTIGATION was carried out under contract No. 70–2192 from The Center for Population Research, National Institutes for Child Health and Human Development. Many thanks are due to the excellent staff at the Center—especially its director, Jerry Combs, and Wendy Baldwin and Duff Gillespie—for their support of this project from its inception. Ellen Liff, of National Analysts, and Martha McMurry contributed heavily to design of the measuring instruments. Craig MacPherson and Lois Downey were invaluable as programmers during various stages of data analysis. Criticisms and comments of various drafts of this manuscript were supplied by a variety of persons, including J. Mayone Stycos, Jonathon Kelley, and Phillips Cutright. A final version was read in great detail and criticized in very helpful fashion by Kenneth C. W. Kammeyer. Finally, I want to thank Art Iamele, my Free Press editor, for his confidence in the project and his patience during the various stages of manuscript preparation.

J.S.

Sex Roles,
Life Styles,
and Childbearing

Chapter 1. Introduction and Perspective

THE QUESTION OF WHY PEOPLE HAVE BABIES is amusing and simple-minded at the same time that the answer is unclear, complex, and profound.[1] As the world enters the last quarter of the twentieth century and prepares for the twenty-first, this answer could take on ominous implications. Some contend that it already has—that bourgeoning population growth, especially among developing nations, is a threat to man's continued existence on this planet. This book does not focus on the consequences of population growth, nor could we possibly consider all the factors that contribute to that growth. Instead, our interest lies within the area of human fertility —and, still more specifically, in the motivation to have children.

SOCIETY AND FAMILY

Our interest in this issue stems directly from a long-standing concern with the linkages between the economic-opportunity and the family systems in modern society. Heretofore our investigations have centered on linkages mediated through the status and role of husband. For example, we have looked at the impact of the work roles of clergymen on family interaction in the context of commitments to church and sect orientations (Scanzoni, 1965). We have also traced some of the ways in which the husband's occupational performance influences husband-wife cohesion and marital stability, and we have also seen how economic resources influence structure and process within black families (Scanzoni, 1970 and 1971).

In all of these and similar studies by others, the wife role, although theoretically significant, has not revealed its prime import in any direct linkage to the larger society. Whereas the husband's behavior is significant in both the occupational and the conjugal settings, the wife's has been generally significant only within the latter. Wives have of course worked, and in some cases they have been the mainstay of the family's social and

1

economic well-being. But the predominant structural arrangement has been one based on role specialization in which the husband has generally occupied the provider role while the wife occupied the familial role of "expressive hub" or "socioemotional leader." Not that such an arrangement is intrinsically fixed nor "functionally requisite." In another place we have analyzed how since 1800 marriage has evolved into the present patterns of specialization and discussed how in the future it may continue to evolve into patterns based on role interchangeability (Scanzoni, 1972).

Indeed, one of the issues clarified in this book is the extent to which the traditional pattern of marital role specialization is or is not persisting in American society. However, a necessarily related issue is of far more major concern here, that is, the degree to which variation in marital role structure is associated with family fertility. Our premise is that if there is any significant change in marital role structure it would be in the direction of lessening role specialization and increasing role interchangeability. Specialization is the result of the husband's unique participation in the opportunity structure. Interchangeability would mean that the wife would have access to the opportunity structure and to occupational achievement equal to that of her husband as a person, in the same sense that blacks seek access equal to that of whites. For there is nothing inherently "white" or "masculine" about modern opportunity structures that is necessarily inimical to equal participation by nonwhites or married women.

This type of change of marital structure would not necessarily eliminate linkages to the economic system that exist under role specialization. Instead, it would both expand and modify them. Marital processes would become even more complex, yet they would still depend on understanding linkages between economic and family structures. But if interchangeability implies greater occupational access for wives, does it concomitantly imply significantly greater familial involvement by husbands, particularly in the care of children? For reasons discussed elsewhere (Scanzoni, 1972; Blake, 1972) such increased participation by husbands in the home is not likely to occur either extensively or rapidly. Therefore, an apparent "structural adaptation" to the decrease in time for extensive child care due to both parents' choosing to be achievers (or perhaps even merely "workers") would be to produce fewer children for which the partners must care.

And that brings us precisely to the substantive core of this book. Is greater commitment to opportunity participation linked to reduced family size? One way to begin to grapple with such a question is to examine briefly the literature pertaining to working wives and family size.

WIFE EMPLOYMENT AND FERTILITY

As far back as the first *Growth of American Families* study, investigators have found an inverse relationship between wife employment and fertility (Freedman *et al.*, 1959). The second GAF study in 1960 produced similar relationships:

> The wives who had worked after their marriage had not only had fewer births by 1960 than those who had not worked, but also anticipated a significantly smaller total number of births. Furthermore . . . wives who had worked for longer periods of time had had fewer births by 1960 and expected to have fewer . . . than those who had worked for shorter periods. (Whelpton *et al.*, 1966:107)

These same investigators also found that the reason for employment given by wives who do work was related to fertility. For example, wives who worked because their families "really needed income" had more children and expected more than wives who worked because they "enjoyed" it or merely wanted "extras" for themselves. Likewise, November 1969 Census Bureau figures reveal that there were 2,886 children born to every 1,000 wives aged 35 to 44 (husband present) in the labor force, compared to 3,414 children for every 1,000 similar wives not in the labor force (*Current Population Reports*, P-20, No. 226). The same report revealed that 21% of employed wives had fewer than two children, compared with 14% of nonemployed wives, and that 24% of the latter category had five or more children, compared with only 16% among employed wives.

There are numerous other studies that indicate this same inverse association, not only for the United States but for other developed and developing societies as well (Haas, 1972). In some developing countries, however, where a woman's work is compatible with childbearing, fertility is not reduced (Stycos and Weller, 1967). For instance, in certain types of cottage industries and agricultural enterprises, having children does not interfere with the mother's working as would having to work outside the home. Therefore the structural incompatibility of work performed outside the home is an important factor related to depressed fertility in certain developing nations.

Nevertheless, to explain the recurrence of this inverse relationship within urban settings is much more difficult than to state it. For example, some wives work because they are subfecund, and being unable to have (more) children they work because they have few responsibilities for child care. Regarding fecund wives, several approaches are possible. Blake (1965), for instance, cites studies of unmarried high school and college students to argue that desire to work exists prior to marriage and results in a limitation of family size. Thus, from one viewpoint, size of family is "caused" in part at least by wife employment. On the other hand, Sweet (1970) contends that "an equally compelling case can be made . . . for the reverse causal sequence: that women who have smaller families for whatever reason [beyond subfecundity] have more time to work and fewer constraints on work." Ridley (1968), in citing census data which show that working wives had more children in 1960 (after the baby boom) than did working wives in 1950, points out that having children may some-times "cause" certain wives to go to work. Her notion is illustrated by other census data showing that the lower the husband's income, the more likely the wife is to work. Among husbands with incomes from $3,000 to $4,999, 56% of their wives had money earnings. When husband's earnings were $7,000 to $7,999, the figure for wives was 50%; it was 39% if husbands earned $10,000 to $14,000; and 25% if husband's earnings were $25,000 and over (*Current Population Reports,* P-60, No. 64). Therefore, in families with lesser incomes, an additional child may actually be a key factor propelling the wife into the labor force.

As Ryder and Westoff (1971:63) note, there is no easy answer, without a longitudinal study, to the question of why fertility and wife employment are inversely related. On the basis of her observations, Ridley suggests that wife employment may be less powerful as an indicator of future changes in women's roles and reduced fertility than is education (1968). On the other hand, Oppenheimer (1970), argues from her extensive de-mographic analyses for several decades past, that the high demand for and low supply of available women has been a major factor bringing them in increasing numbers into the labor force. She contends that as more and more women find themselves in the role of worker, their norms regarding occupational achievement and marital roles will begin to change. They will come, she says, to define work as more of a central life interest than a peripheral one as at present. Concomitantly, she predicts that traditional female domestic behaviors will be less the central life interest that they are now, including presumably the bearing of and caring for children.

Theoretical Perspective

Part of the task of this book is to help resolve these ambiguities and to contribute toward a coherent theoretical framework linking fertility with familiar variables such as education, wife employment, marital structure, religion, age at marriage, and the not-so-common notion of sex role. Yaukey (1969:100) remarks that theory development regarding fertility flourished in the fifties and early sixties, declined thereafter, and has only recently become a live issue once again. Fertility researchers have gath-ered an impressive array of empirical generalizations, but currently these generalizations appear to lack much systematic integration.

Yet several efforts have been made to try to work toward a "theory of fertility." Easterlin attempts to develop a framework based on "the eco-nomic theory of household choice," yet expanding it "to give explicit scope to the influence of [sociological] 'taste' factors." "Fertility behavior, then, becomes a matter of constrained choice, fertility variations . . . reflect variations in the relevant preferences and/or constraints" (1969:150).

By emphasizing the concept of taste, or social norm, Easterlin seeks to bridge the gap between economists such as Becker (1960) who describe children merely as "consumer durables," contending that parents make fertility decisions in the same way as for household purchases in general, and sociologists such as Dusenberry (1960) or Blake (1968) who contend that certain sociological factors operate in fertility behaviors that are equally as powerful as the alleged rational calculation by the couple of objective dollars and cents. Hawthorn elaborates on Easterlin by asserting that "fertility behavior, or associated methods of population regulation, can be understood and causally explained with a utility model" (1970:65). By "utility" he means that persons and groups (such as the marital pair) seek to maximize rewards and benefits and to minimize costs and punishments. Hawthorn is quick to point out that the definitions of reward and cost are not necessarily rational either in terms of objective criteria or to the detached outsider. Instead, he argues that social norms and the situations in which they operate serve to shape the definitions of rewards and costs, i.e., the range of available resources within his utility model.

To the objection that a utility framework presupposes a level of rationality in fertility control that simply does not exist, Hawthorn (p. 117) responds:

> All that the model demands is that the actor it is applied to will have at least one preference, and that he or she does not have unlimited resources to realize it. This demand probably defines, indeed, the necessary conditions for regarding someone as a human agent at all. A person with no preferences and aware of no resource constraint would only be a pathetic vegetable. . . . Nothing else in the model is assumed; everything else is a matter for empirical investigation.

Thus at the most general level, a utility approach presumes that fertility control is dependent upon perceptions of available resources, rewards, and costs. These processes may be quite unconscious, especially prior to marriage and at early parities, but they are nonetheless assumed to be operative. Some persons may have a child because it is defined as a benefit which outweighs attendant costs. They may desire this benefit more than, or else simply be indifferent to, other potential rewards. And they may be indifferent to potential costs as well.

Cain and Weininger are examples of economists who have recently used a utility framework in a way that is quite compatible with sociological perspectives (1973). Building on Becker's work, they suggest that "the theory of utility maximization . . . provides a general framework for postulating certain effects on family size of variables that measure 'costs' and 'benefits' of children." Using census data from urban centers they found "that fertility is negatively related to the potential earnings available to wives in the labor market." They then use their cost–reward framework as a vehicle to "provide causal interpretation and explanations for the observed relations. . . ." Certain working wives, in other words, apparently choose the benefits and costs of added income as over against the benefits and costs of additional children, and for other wives the converse should hold. Furthermore, in recent years, psychologists have also turned their attention towards reward–cost explanations of fertility control. Significantly, the interdisciplinary implications of this approach can be seen from two recently edited volumes by Fawcett (1972, 1973) that include contributions not only by psychologists but also by economists and sociologists.

CONTRACEPTION

At first glance, that which perhaps most complicates the notion that fertility behavior can be explained in motivational terms by a utility approach is the phenomenon of contraception. Given the predominance of pronatalist norms in American society, the literature on unintended births could give rise to the hypothesis that effective contraception is chiefly a matter of technology. That is, many children may be born who, instead of being accounted for by a reward–cost ratio, may be explained simply as the result of contraceptive failure. For instance, some persons may not define the child(ren) as a benefit at all but instead as a great cost and therefore seek to avoid conception. But a pregnancy may occur anyway in spite of perceived costs and rewards, allegedly because of a "failure" in the contraceptive process.

We cannot, of course, underestimate the significance of efficient technologies. Ryder and Westoff (1971:265) claim that "we are experiencing a contraceptive revolution . . . the pill is so substantially an improvement in efficiency over its predecessors that it represents a sharp disjuncture with the past." Nevertheless, a major conclusion from their study is the same as from many others, namely that contraceptive efficacy is fundamentally more a matter of motivation than of technology per se. Ryder remarks that "contraception is a difficult task, even for a sophisticated population" (1970). England in the late nineteenth century, the United States during the Great Depression, and Japan after 1945 are examples of societies that reduced birth rates substantially prior to the advent of widely disseminated and highly efficient contraceptives. Moreover, although many American couples tend to be contraceptively careless with respect to their first child(ren), most of them become quite efficient users when their desired family size is achieved (Ryder and Westoff, 1971:134; Whelpton et al., 1966). For such persons the state of technology has not changed; what is different is the level and intensity of motivation to control the number of children. As Ryder and Westoff note, "investigation of the voluntary component in childbearing is essential for rigorous analysis"

(p. 153). It is precisely that component examined within the context of utilities prescribed by sex role norms that this book is all about.

Controlling family size, argues Ryder (1970), rests on competence in handling efficient technologies and also on "the perceived gravity of the consequences of failure." To speak about "perceived gravity of failure" is to make the utilitarian assumption that a potential child emerging out of contraceptive failure poses certain perceived costs as well as rewards and that the balance of these cost–reward elements is a grave matter to be seriously weighed in deciding how rigorous to be in delaying or preventing that child. The fact that gravity attached to failure tends not to be foremost in the minds of many newlyweds, for example, does not obviate a utility model. Rather, it suggests that unconsciously perhaps they simply perceive few or no costs attached to a child but many benefits, or else are indifferent to the costs and behave accordingly insofar as the first child is concerned.

Sex Role Norms

This book is an attempt to elaborate a utility approach to fertility control with particular focus on sex or gender role norms for husbands and wives. Our choice of these kinds of variables as an elaboration of a utility model is not arbitrary. First, there is our long-standing interest in marital role structure discussed earlier. Second, the revival of neofeminism in America has as one of its prime foci changes in the structures of sex roles. Assessment of any such changes is an extremely important theoretical issue, as is the identification of any possible connection between such changes and fertility control. For example, it may very well be that declines in national birth rates observed during the early 1970s may in part be the result of changes in sex role norms operating within family structures.

Finally, in social policy terms, any alteration of marital roles and any impact on family size are important matters that have significant consequences for both public policy and private behavior.

As early as 1960, Hoffman and Wyatt speculated on a connection between the role of woman and family fertility in implicit utility terms:

> Having a child is highly creative both in the sense of producing it and in the social sense of molding it. . . . The case of the infant provides an area where the woman [in America] is not replaceable. . . . Bearing and mothering children are important as proofs of femininity . . . this is the traditional feminine role.

Kingsley Davis (1967) agrees but makes the utility component more explicit and suggests directions for population policy:

If it were admitted that the creation and care of new human beings is socially motivated, like other forms of behavior, by being part of the system of rewards and punishments that is built into human relationships, and thus is bound up with the individual's economic and personal interests, it would be apparent that the social structure and economy must be changed before a deliberate reduction in the birth rate can be achieved.

For Davis, "changes in social structure" include, among other things:

. . . modification of the complementarity of the roles of men and women. Men are now able to participate in the wider world, yet enjoy the satisfaction of having several children because the housework and childcare fall mainly on their wives. Women are impelled to seek this role by their idealized view of marriage and motherhood and by either the scarcity of alternative roles or the difficulty of combining them with family roles.

Concomitant with less differentiation of male–female roles within the family should come, Davis alleges, changes in the economic opportunity structure with respect to married female employment: "If . . . women were paid as well as men and given equal educational and occupational opportunities . . . many women would develop interests that would compete with family interests."

Probably more frequently than anyone else, Blake (1965) has iterated this type of utility theme in numerous places:

Children are high on the list of adult utilities. Offspring are not simple outlets (and inlets) for affection, they are the instrumentalities for achieving virtually prescribed social statuses ("mother" and "father"), and almost exclusive avenues for feminine creativity and achievement. . . . Until non-familial roles begin to offer significant competition to familial ones as avenues for adult satisfaction, the family will probably continue to amaze us with its procreative powers.

Furthermore, Goldberg has suggested that higher fertility observed among Catholics might be attributable to a more traditional definition of the female sex role held by them compared to Protestants (1960:144). As Catholic women may be more likely to see "motherhood" and related traditional behaviors in sacred terms, fulfillment of these kinds of behaviors may provide a sense of reward and satisfaction that they do not see as attainable in any other way. Evidence for the idea that Catholicism encourages higher fertility by strongly reinforcing traditional sex role ideals is found in the Westoff and Potvin (1967) study of college women.

Within the scope of a utility approach, children may be viewed as resources or rewards to parents, especially to the mother. Economists such as Cain and Becker have asked when this traditional type of reward is "affordable" in monetary terms and when it is too costly relative to other potential benefits. The sociologist might well ask the related questions of when do women (and men) seek these traditional kinds of rewards; when do they perceive *alternative* rewards that seem equally or more attractive than a child; and when would a child be too costly (beyond solely monetary factors) relative to these other potential benefits? The answers may hinge partially *on sex role norms which prescribe a priority of potentially available rewards* (Holter, 1970; Schiebe, 1970).

The sex role behaviors of the wife in her status as complement to her husband (nonemployed housewife), or even in her status as junior partner to her husband (employed full time), prescribe situations in which her prime rewards come from bearing children and caring for them, husband, and home (Scanzoni, 1972). The issue then becomes to what degree do certain groups of women seek rewards that are alternative to traditional rewards? According to many neofeminists (Mitchell, 1969; Harbeson, 1967), access to occupational achievement is a highly valued reward which increasing numbers of younger women may be coming to seek for themselves. The general consensus has been that most married women who work do not possess the same degree of work commitment as do men, nor has individualistic occupational achievement been central to their work behaviors. There is virtually unanimous agreement with Degler's observation (1964) that their concern has been with "jobs" rather than with "careers."

Poloma and Garland contend that even among married women professionals, it is the wife who virtually always gives way in the event of a clash of interests between the occupations of husband and wife (1971). For instance, rarely would the husband quit his job and follow a career-oriented wife to another city to allow her to take a "more challenging" position. Nevertheless, occupational achievement remains, in modern society, a prime vehicle for fulfillment, satisfactions, and rewards, both in prestige and materially. What if more and more younger women came to define individualistic occupational achievement as desirable, and as much desired by them as it is by men, i.e., in terms of career interests? Indeed, by using national samples of women over 21 who had ever been in the labor force, De Jong *et al.* (1971) found that every major generalization about occupational mobility that has been made for males applies with equal force to females.[2] (However, income differences by sex remain.) The authors suggest that we may need to modify our thinking that employed men and women view their occupations in very different terms.

Tomasson (1966), comparing America and Sweden prior to the revival of feminism in America, describes the differences between role definitions and fertility in the two societies. First he observes that Sweden's birth rate in 1960 was 14 per thousand population compared with America's 24. "Swedish wives born in the 1930's will probably have an average of 2.2 or 2.3 children by the time they complete childbearing years, compared with a minimum estimate of 3.3 children for their counterparts in America (and 3.0 children for those who are not Catholic) (p. 335). He also (p. 337) takes note of the increasingly large proportion of Swedish women who are located in traditionally male professions, compared to actually decreasing proportions of American women in such occupations:

> What is significantly different in the two societies is the increase in acceptable role possibilities for women that has occurred in Sweden over the past generation. The neo-traditional role for women has few spokesmen in the Swedish press and mass media compared to the United States. The feminism that became abortive in the United States about the time of World War II continued unabated in Sweden and has had far reaching effects in the society. Typical views of Swedish university students of women's roles are less differentiated and more egalitarian than those of [American college students]. The minimizing of sexual differentiation and the maximizing of sexual equality in education are guiding principles in the radical school reform in Sweden in the postwar years. . . . I think it is suggestive that more Swedish wives regard two children as "ideal" than any other number (48 percent compared with 19 percent of American views), whereas more American wives so regard four children than any other number (41 percent).

Clarkson *et al.* (1970), using a subsample of 60 Catholic women between ages 45 and 59, husband present, with at least two children, administered a series of 122 self-evaluative items measuring "sex role stereotypes." The range of items included those indicating "stereotypic male-valued" characteristics, i.e., items describing a "rational, competent, mature individual." The range also included "female-stereotypic" items indicating "warmth, expressiveness, sensitivity," and so on. The investigators found that "mothers with the high competency [high on the masculine stereotype] self-concept scores were found to have [statistically] significantly fewer children ($\overline{X} = 3.12$) than mothers who perceive themselves to be low on the competency cluster ($\overline{X} = 3.93$)." Moreover, women with "high competency" who had worked 7 years or less had a mean of 3.12 children, versus 3.13 when they worked 8 years or more, virtually identical. In contrast, among "low competency" women who worked 7 or fewer years, the mean was 4.43, compared with 3.30 for those working 8 years or more.

In sum, it would appear that women who possess an "instrumental" or "male" or "competency-oriented" perception of themselves, have fewer children than women with the more traditional female self-conception. Moreover, in view of the fact that almost every major fertility study shows an inverse relationship between duration of wife work experience and family size, it seems quite significant that among wives with more "modern" self-conceptions, this relationship is obliterated. Only among the more traditional females does work duration have the expected consequences. Although interpretation of these data is not without ambiguity, they do at least provide some empirical support for the hypothesis that the more traditional is a women's view of her role, the more children she is likely to have. They further suggest that sex role definitions may have at least as strong a correlation with completed family size as wife employment *per se.*

Rainwater, in a partial test of the Hoffman-Wyatt model, examined a subsample of middle-class wives in terms of "self-descriptions" and of desired family size (1965:191–92).

> There is a strong association between family size desires and how exclusively the wife sees herself as oriented to husband and outside interests as opposed to children. . . . 90 percent of those who want a small family mention outside or husband orientations, compared to . . . only 45 percent of the large family mothers. In contrast, over 80 percent of both medium and large-family mothers mention orientation to children compared to only 30 percent of small family mothers.

Stolka and Barnett used a series of three items to measure the "role of woman" both in the family and in connection with her career efforts (1969). They report that less traditional female role orientations were the single most important attitudinal factor in terms of depressing "motivations toward childbearing." Thus their work too provides some confirmation of the "feminist-fertility" linkage.

Rossi (1970), in a carefully designed longitudinal investigation of 15,000 women college graduates, found that those "with high career commitments tend to want fewer children . . . [and] to be willing to let others take . . . care of [their] children . . . [compared with] women who have no career goal for the future, but expect to be exclusively homemakers. . . ." Rosen and Simmons, in their study of family size in Brazil, also report a linkage between sex role orientations and family size intentions, as well as family size (1971). In a separate analysis of Brazilian data, Rosen and La Raia (1972) conclude that "an underlying dimension called modernity" is "positively related to a woman's education . . . and negatively related to her preferred and actual family size."

Haas (1972), also on the basis of investigations in Latin America, concludes that "of more crucial importance in [promoting] fertility decline" than "advocating the raising of female employment rate," may be "the woman's approval of any role alternative to motherhood. It is possible that social scientists have concentrated their research efforts on the woman's actual behavior and have underestimated the importance of her attitudes" (125). Finally, from a sample of American college senior women, Tangri (1972:196) found that:

> Role innovative women do not reject the core female roles of wife and mother though they expect to postpone marriage and have fewer children than more traditional women. . . .

In short, there does appear to be a small but expanding body of data which tend to support the notion of a linkage between sex role definitions and fertility control. Though in subsequent chapters we shall trace the link in detail, it might in broader terms be described in the following way. First, persons with more "modern" role conceptions may intend to have fewer children. Second, such persons, à la Ryder's "perceived gravity of failure" notion, may be more alert and rigorous, less sloppy, haphazard, and careless in their contraceptive efficacy than persons with more traditional role conceptions. Finally, these differing intentions and contraceptive patterns might result in differing completed family sizes within age cohorts (Scanzoni and McMurry, 1972).

Such linkages can be subsumed theoretically under a more general utility framework by bearing in mind Blake's suggestion that "the utilities gained by having children are not solely of the prestige [or economic] type" (1967:66). The range of childbearing utilities may also include significant intrinsic gratifications connected with traditional sex role norms.

Likewise the classic inverse relation between socioeconomic variables (education, occupation, income) and fertility, though it has become somewhat weaker, may also reflect the notion of alternative utilities. For example, Blau and Duncan argue that "on theoretical grounds . . . some differential fertility is an ingrained characteristic of industrialized society and will persist" (1967:427). They contend that the less successful (male) achiever (lower-status, blue-collar), in order to compensate for his lower material and status position, seeks alternative rewards in the form of a larger family: "the unsuccessful find a substitute in the authority they exercise in their role as fathers over a number of children." Their argument concludes on the contention that as in an industrial society some men will inevitably continue to fill less desirable occupations, they will therefore probably continue to have more children.

In terms of alternative rewards and female achievement, the literature suggests that it is the better-educated women who are currently pressing for greater individualistic opportunities, and it is they who are in the vanguard of any movement toward genuine sex role redefinitions that might be taking place (Holter, 1970). Better-educated women generally marry better-educated men who, according to Blau and Duncan, "seek" fewer children than less-educated men. If, in addition, such wives seek fewer children than less-educated women because of alternative rewards from occupational endeavors, this second factor may influence the classic inverse status–fertility linkage. Higher-status families may come to consist of husbands and wives both of whom, as a result of achievement rewards, possess less motivation for traditional rewards in the form of children.

Methodology

In the following pages of this chapter, we present the methodology of our study of 3,096 interviews on sex roles and fertility. In Chapter Two we examine in greater detail the literature on sex role *per se* and explain how we propose to measure sex role norms. We also investigate through analysis of our data five key correlates of sex role norms: race, gender, age, religion, and education. So far very little systematic work has been done to probe the normative structures of sex roles. Chapter Two seeks to make strides in that direction. The theme of Chapter Three is how sex role norms help to account for age at marriage, wife employment, and most importantly, birth intentions. In Chapter Four, the focus is on current family size, and how role norms and related "marital events" (including past timing failures) may have led to present parities. Chapter Five considers how sex role norms might influence current contraceptive behaviors, as well as expectations for future birth-planning success. The concluding Chapter Six is an attempt to tie together various strands from earlier chapters and to try to work systematically towards a theory of fertility control that takes account of the significance of sex role norms. The chapter also deals with the practical applications of our findings to policy-makers and to individuals.

The study analyzed in this book was sponsored by *The Center for Population Research,* of the National Institutes for Child Health and Human Development.[3] The data were collected from ten metropolitan areas within the five states defined by the Census Bureau as the East North Central region. *National Analysts* of Philadelphia was responsible for drawing of the sample and data collection. Tony Asman, *National Analysts'* sampling statistician, has prepared the following statement of sample designs:

The sample could be described as a probability selection of land areas with a quota selection of respondents within these areas.

The selection of the land areas was accomplished by a multistage process. The fifty-one metropolitan areas or parts of metropolitan areas in the states of Illinois, Ohio, Indiana, Michigan, and Wisconsin were defined as the universe for this study.

The fifty-one areas were stratified into ten strata. From each stratum one metropolitan area was selected at random, with probability proportional to the estimated size of the metropolitan area.

Within each selected metropolitan area, counts of housing units were cumulated over the nonpoverty portion of the metropolitan area. Area segments were selected systematically for these cumulated counts, by means of a random start and every n^{th} housing unit after that. The number of area segments selected into the sample from each metropolitan area was in proportion to the size of that metropolitan area's stratum.

The ten metropolitan areas selected into the sample and the number of area sample segments are:

Metropolitan Area	Number of Area Segments Selected
Chicago, Illinois	89
Detroit, Michigan	54
Springfield, Illinois	21
Cincinnati, Ohio	33
Cleveland, Ohio	27
Grand Rapids, Michigan	35
Muskegon, Michigan	31
Columbus, Ohio	31
Springfield, Ohio	36
Evansville, Indiana	18

The interviewing portion of the study was done in two waves, in order to provide the maximum adherence to quota requirements. In the first wave, the interviewers were instructed to obtain roughly 65% of the approximately 3,000 interviews desired. Quotas for age, sex, multihousehold interviews, and working and non-working wives were assigned to each interviewer.

The remainder of the 3,096 interviews were collected in a second wave, at which time the desired quotas were filled for the above variables and race.

In Chicago, Cleveland, Detroit, and Grand Rapids, the number of segments were expanded at the end of the second wave in order to insure the required quota of black respondents.

Special training for already-skilled *National Analyst* interviewers pertinent to the demands of our interview schedule was carried out at five regional centers within these states during May and June of 1971. Data collection began immediately after training and was completed by early October, 1971. The sample includes approximately equal numbers of women and men. Men were included on the theoretical grounds that it would be most ideal to compare male and female respondents to determine differences and similarities in the degree to which they reveal any sex role–fertility linkage. Few large-scale fertility surveys bother to include male respondents; hence, we know less about fertility control from the husband's perspective.[4] In 399 households both the husband and the wife were interviewed. Thus the total number of households sampled is 2,697; the total number of interviews 3,096.

Approximately 25% of the sample is composed of blacks. They were oversampled relative to their proportion in the population (12%) in order to provide sufficient cases for detailed analyses. Theoretically, their importance lies in comparison with whites relative to sex role definitions.

FIGURE 1-1. Number of Interviews in Sample, by Sex, Race, Age of Wife, and Employment Status of Wife

Age of Wife	White Husband		Black Husband		White Wife		Black Wife		Total by Age	Total Male	Total Female
	Work	Nonwork	Work	Nonwork	Work	Nonwork	Work	Nonwork			
18–24	183	145	21	31	167	213	28	43	831	380	451
25–29	90	135	39	28	88	132	38	21	571	292	279
30–34	87	132	41	28	66	114	50	59	577	288	289
35–39	87	95	54	18	68	91	60	93	566	254	312
40–44	105	99	51	35	92	104	29	36	551	290	261
Totals	552	606	206	140	481	654	205	252	3,096	1,504	1,592

Number of households where both husband and wife were interviewed   399
Total number of households interviewed   2,697
Total number of interviews   3,096

This illustration was prepared by Tony Asman of *National Analysts*.

There is data and theory indicating that some blacks may possess more modern sex role definitions than do some whites (Scanzoni, 1971). Substantively, although knowledge about black fertility is expanding, it remains less complete than knowledge about white fertility. This is especially so for black men and especially for blacks living in "stable" or husband-wife households. Some 45% of our households contain a wife who works full time (35 hours per week or more). In March, 1968, 39% of all wives from husband-wife households were classed as year-round full-time workers (*Current Population Reports,* P-60, No. 64). In 1970 in the north and the West of the United States, 36% of white wives from such households worked full time, as did 52% of black wives (*Current Population Reports,* P-23, No. 39).

Some oversampling of employed wives in our study was justified on the basis of cases sufficient for detailed analysis. Theoretically, it seemed important to have a large pool of employed-wife households to examine some of the central concerns of our problem.

The sample was also stratified into age cohorts by age of wife. Approximately 27% of the households in the sample contain wives aged 18 to 24; 18% have wives aged 25 to 29; 19% have wives aged 30 to 34; 18% have wives aged 35 to 39; 18% have wives aged 40 to 44. Oversampling within the youngest cohort is based theoretically on the contention by some observers that it is among the young that changes in gender role norms are occurring. Bits and pieces of data exist to shore up these speculations. For example, Katona *et al.* (1971:143), in comparative surveys carried out in the United States, United Kingdom, France, Germany, Spain and the Netherlands, found that younger persons (under 35) were much more likely to report favorable attitudes toward the employment of working mothers than were older persons.

The U.S. Census Bureau supplies data which are merely suggestive of changes among the young because insufficient time has lapsed to observe clear trends or patterns. For example, younger women (ages 14 to 24) expect fewer children than older women, and this finding holds when controls for race, metropolitan residence, and education are introduced (*Current Population Reports,* P-20, No. 211; P-20, No. 232; P-20, No. 240). These figures may be evaluated in the light of Ryder and Westoff's warning that persons who are married longer may simply elevate their birth expectations as a function of contraceptive failures and the number of children that are actually present (1971). In spite of this caution, however, we find that younger cohorts of women are actually bearing significantly fewer children than did older cohorts when they previously were at the same life-cycle stage (*Current Population Reports,* P-20, No. 205).

Interviewers screened respondents at the door of the household to obtain information (on age and so forth) to fill their quotas of eligible respondents. Additional eligibility requirements were that husband and wife be currently living together in that household, that neither spouse had ever been married before, that each spouse had been born in one of the 50 states or in Washington, D.C., and that the husband of the household was not overseas for any reason.

In summary, our sample consists of men and women from husband–wife households (persons who have been married only to each other) drawn from generally nonpoverty areas. Wives' ages span the childbearing period from 18 to 44. Blacks, younger couples, and working wives are somewhat overrepresented. What are the possibilities of generalizing beyond the sample to the East North Central region or to the nation as a whole? One procedure would be to restrict generalizations to the scope of the sample and go no further. A second procedure would be to treat conclusions from the sample as hypotheses which might apply to populations beyond it. Part of the second approach would involve comparison of our sample data with findings from other sources as a check on the reliability of our findings. As this second procedure increases the validity and potential significance of the study and better serves the interests of theory building as well as policy applications, it is the approach we shall follow throughout. In current-day sociology, virtually every study, no matter how carefully the sample is drawn, is a prologue to the next investigation. Given the paucity of our theory and the primitive nature of our measuring instruments, this type of sequence is inevitable. Therefore, it is in this sense of ongoing interrelated contributions to a growing body of knowledge about fertility control that this book should be read.

A missing element in this report is one that characterizes fertility research and social science research in general. As shall become apparent when we move into data analysis, the ideal study design would be a longitudinal one in which we would question our respondents over several points in time. As Ryder and Westoff argue (1971:226, 265), until we possess more longitudinal studies of fertility behavior, we shall inevitably lack considerable accuracy in explaining that behavior. Thus, we are using a cross-sectional design in what is essentially an exploratory fertility study insofar as gender role variables are concerned. The hope is that, as relevant variables and their measures are identified, the kinds of notions explored here might eventually be utilized in a longitudinal design.

Besides the household sample just described, we shall give some brief attention to data from a sample of university students. In April and May of 1971, a sample of white, single, male and female undergraduates was randomly drawn from the student directory of a large midwestern university. Interviews were conducted with 368 students, and many of the questions used are identical to items found in the household survey. Therefore, though limited in scope, these student data provide an additional basis of comparison with the household sample. This student sample is very much a part of that younger college generation about which there has been so much speculation in terms of their orientations toward social change. Comparisons will be made in Chapters Two and Three to see how much if at all the students differ from married persons in the household sample.

Conclusion

The central focus of this study is the relationship between the role structures of modern marriage and fertility control. The issue goes far deeper than the well-known inverse link between wife employment and family size. Indeed we would hope to explain that relationship by sex role norms and to try to arrive at additional paths of influence among key fertility-related variables. These conclusions must be treated as hypotheses to be tested on a panel of couples followed over time. Sex role structures and other key variables are conceptualized under a utility framework, in which costs and rewards are assumed to influence motivations toward family size intentions, marital events, and contraceptive behavior. A major theoretical objective will be to increase our grasp of the validity of utility-type notions to determine how useful they may or may not be in explaining fertility behavior.

The potential policy implications of the study lie with how well sex roles actually explain fertility control. For if meaningful relationships emerge, we shall be sensitized to a fundamental tool which would significantly aid in the control of population, for both developed and developing societies.

Notes

1. As my office janitor put it in reaction to hearing the theme of this book ("to figure out why people have babies"): "That's simple—they slip up!"
2. For criticisms of that report, see Havens and Tully, 1972.
3. Contract Number 70–2192.
4. Westoff et al., 1961 and 1963, include limited data for men. See also Rainwater, 1965.

Chapter 2. The Structure of Sex Roles

We begin this chapter with a brief review of what is known about sex or gender roles from both psychological and sociological perspectives. We then try to show how sex roles and cost–reward notions of a utility framework are linked together. Next, we raise the general problem of the relations between norms and behaviors, with the specific concern being connections between sex role norms and fertility behaviors. The focus then shifts to the learning of sex roles preceding the behavioral events which are part of marriage. Next, in order to broaden our grasp and deepen our understanding of sex roles we introduce five factors (race, sex, religion, education, and age) related to the degree of sex role traditionalism. We suggest hypotheses about how each of these factors might affect the ranking of persons on a continuum of sex role traditionalism-modernity.

A substantial portion of the chapter is devoted to the derivations of our measures of sex roles. We emerge with two role dimensions which are part of the wife position within the family, three dimensions that belong to the husband position, and two that are part of the mother position. In addition, we develop measures of two dimensions of self-concept, plus an index based on the evaluation of wife skills and capabilities. Throughout we compare differences in mean scores of our subjects for these ten role and self-perception indices in terms of the five factors related to sex role traditionalism. We close the chapter by summarizing how these five factors may have helped to account for differing degrees of role traditionalism and modernity within our sample.

Sex Differentiation

Because the field is still relatively unexplored, there is a paucity of empirical evidence concerning many of the hypotheses about sex differentiation as an integrated part of the social system. (Holter, 1970:11)

19

In Chapter One we reviewed the available literature describing possible linkages between sex roles and family fertility. However we did not explore in any great depth the notion of sex role itself. As Holter's statement indicates, there has not been much systematic research into the area of sex role, although there has been considerable modern-day theorizing (as distinct from theory building) about social differentiation based on gender differences at least as far back as Marx, Engels, and Durkheim (Holter, 1970:10). Our objective here is not to review in depth the existing literature on sex role, but only to draw on elements pertinent to our theoretical and empirical objectives regarding fertility control. Sources are readily available to the reader interested in exploring the area more fully.[1]

To try to define sex role we begin at the most general level and refer to differences among persons and groups that are the result of gender, i.e., differences based on ascribed characteristics. Holter contends that sex differentiation contains at least "two facets, one normative and the other behavioral and attitudinal" (p. 17). Sociologists have been mostly concerned with the former—the norms, ideologies, values, and beliefs that are used to label, apply to, or define the two sexes. In this and the following chapters our use of sex role will be largely in this structural sense of "sex role norms" or "gender norms." Psychologists have been concerned mostly with the behavioral facet, defined broadly to "include character and personality traits, attitudes, and overt actions and interactions" (Holter, 1970:17). We have not neglected personality characteristics for in addition to efforts to measure gender norms we also attempt to apprehend aspects of self-concept.

To pinpoint potential differences between the normative and behavioral aspects of sex role is part of a larger fundamental issue in social theory, namely, the connection between norms and behaviors in general. Basic questions are involved in seeking (1) to establish the degree to which norms may actually predict behavior; (2) to determine the extent to which behavior deviates from norms and why; and (3) to establish the conditions under which behavior may actually alter existing norms or give rise to new norms. Sociologists by and large, however, have not delved systematically into the processes that connect norms and behavior in most substantive areas of sociology, including sex roles. A second criticism of existing research into sex roles is that little attempt has been made to link it to other aspects of social structure (Holter, 1970; Millman, 1971). By attempting to link sex role to fertility control we are, in effect, seeking to draw connections between norms and behavior and also trying to tie together two significant aspects of the larger social structure. Furthermore, we shall go a step further to show how their linkages are in turn related to still other dimensions of social structure, especially to the economic-opportunity systems of modern societies.

As suggested in Chapter One, we also wish to focus on these problems in more general terms by expanding on what is amorphously known as a "utility" approach to fertility control. As Holter (1970) notes, "sex differentiation is one of society's distributive systems. It contains a set of norms requiring individuals with given attributes to perform certain tasks. . ." (p. 18) and in exchange for task-performance allocates certain types of degrees of utility or rewards. The most obvious consequence of gender differentiation is the way in which it distributes household work and occupational participation (p. 33). Connected with each gender sphere are sets of costs and rewards—costs necessary to perform the requisite tasks, rewards that flow from performing those tasks.

It is not a simple matter to subsume the costs and rewards of gender differentiation under a utility model. First, the kinds of outcomes involved vary so much in comparability. They may range "from measurable economic gains to subtle psychological reinforcements. Men may profit the most economically. . . from a given form of gender differentiation, yet it may also be advantageous to women by protecting them from occupational strains" (Holter, 1970:34). Second, what some persons consider a reward others might consider a cost and vice versa—for example, participation in an occupation or certain varieties of occupations or participation in household tasks. In order to arrive at such evaluations, comparisons have to be made. Wives who are satisfied or dissatisfied with their present cost-reward ratio must compare their situations with other women, and with men.

"Third, standards of equality, justice, or reasonableness have to be applied to such comparisons. It is relative rather than absolute gains and burdens that lead to either satisfaction or frustration. . ." with these gains and burdens (p. 34). Finally, reactions toward what is perceived as an unfavorable reward–cost ratio are elusive to measure. The nagging problem of rationality (conscious or unconscious) alluded to in Chapter One enters here. To what degree, if at all, do husbands or wives, for instance, actually perceive present and future rewards and costs as emanating from current behaviors and act accordingly to maximize gain and reduce costs (Beshers, 1967)?

None of these problems, however, is insurmountable in seeking to connect gender differentiation to fertility control under the rubric of a utility framework. Once the basic premise is granted, namely, that gender differentiation is a distributive system of costs and benefits, then the task of research becomes one of identifying and measuring the most significant sex role and fertility control variables. Theoretically, the task is to show how these variables actually do indicate particular sets of rewards and costs in such a way as to speak to the four types of problems raised by Holter. This type of theory development and research is difficult to execute, particularly in the early stages of identifying key variables and significant relationships. Therefore, the work reported in the following pages must be considered initial and path-finding insofar as it deals with the sex role–fertility linkage.

To be sure, our work builds squarely on the fertility literature of the past 30 years, and we have a vast and rich tradition on which to draw.[2] There are numerous established relationships, many excellent measures, and a large number of reliable and valid empirical generalizations. One of our objectives is to expand this rich literature theoretically by linking it to the as yet relatively unexplored realm of gender differentiation.

This objective is, of course, subsumed under the larger issue we have referred to, the connection between norms and behavior. That is, to what extent can we expect norms describing gender differentiation to be related to and perhaps even to predict fertility behavior? Evidence from Scandinavia (where sex role investigations have been pursued much more systematically than in America) speaks to the general question of the link between sex roles and behavior. There is, for example, a study by Haavio-Mannila of Finnish adults which "concludes that expectations derived from sex roles correspond with actual behavior in eight different spheres" (Holter, 1970: 175).

From Norwegian data, Holter (pp. 179–81) reports the following findings among employed women:

1. The more egalitarian women are, the more ambitious they are on two behavioral indexes: "willingness to assume a supervisory position, and preference for an independent job." "It may be expected," claims Holter, "that more ambitious women want more male rights and responsibilities than the less ambitious. Or, possibly, more egalitarian women feel more obligated than traditional ones to claim responsible work."

2. "More egalitarian women report significantly less often than the traditional ones that they lose emotional control" of themselves.

3. "Egalitarian women are less affectively-oriented than the traditional women, indicating a more masculine value orientation on the egalitarians' part."

4. "Egalitarian women tend to lean on authority less often than traditionally-oriented women."

5. "Compared to traditional women, the egalitarian ones report less quarreling in the work groups," behavior which is "consistent with the notion that women who are egalitarian behave more like men than do the traditionally oriented women."

6. Another characteristic of egalitarian women which indicates their behavior to be more similar to "masculine work behavior" than to traditional female behavior is their strong identification with the company.

These data thus permit the general proposition that gender differentiation or sex role does discriminate in terms of actual behavior. The question as to how wide a range of behaviors are effectively discriminated by gender definitions is open to research. A basic hypothesis which guides this investigation is that one set of behaviors within this range are those connected with fertility and its control.

Sources of Sex Role Norms

Perhaps even more complex than positing the association of gender differentiation and fertility control is to talk about direction of influence, or priority in time, or causality. To deal with this issue we need to consider the literature on the acquisition of sex role. A thorough review of that literature is neither possible nor appropriate for our purposes. However, we can draw on Holter's careful review and summarize the conclusions at which she arrives, conclusions which are shared by most behavioral scientists (classical Freudians excepted) who otherwise hold differences about more specific issues involved in sex role learning.

First, sex roles are learned. "Sex role norms and sex typed behavior are acquired by contact with sociocultural agents" (parents mostly, but other figures as well) "and not primarily influenced by biological factors" (Holter: 193). Second, "the learning begins in the early stages of childhood." How early varies with particular schools of thought, but all agree that by the preadolescent period sex roles are very firmly embedded in the psychological and sociological make-up of the individual. Hartley's work (1959) shows that by age 5 boys and girls reveal the prevailing and accepted sex role orientation. More recent work has documented sex role stereotyping in prize-winning picture books for preschool children and indicated its impact on socialization into traditional gender role spheres (Weitzman *et al.*, 1972). Third, "children's early exposure to gender differentiation leads to sex roles that are highly resistant to change" (Holter: 193–94). Though conditions in the social milieu of which persons are a part may change as they move through maturity and adulthood in such a way as to render a "fit" between their learned sex role definitions and their milieu difficult, it is evidently not a simple matter for those definitions to accommodate themselves to the changed milieu.

Fourth, the outcomes of this learning are "male sex roles" and "female sex roles," the former generally associated with concepts of masculinity appropriate to a particular milieu, the other with "appropriate" concepts of femininity (Holter: 196). Masculinity usually "involves some degree of dominance, aggressiveness, and instrumentality"; "feminity is frequently defined in terms of submissiveness, modesty, and nurturance" (p. 196). These concepts will be discussed in terms of instrumental and expressive dimensions later in this chapter. Concomitant with these personality characteristics is a certain structuring of society in which men hold greater access than women to occupational achievement, economic resources, and political power (p. 196).

Finally, once learned, gender differentiation is reinforced and maintained through pervasive mechanisms of social control. "Social control mechanisms help to keep the individual in line with sex role norms, partly reinforcing his internalized norms and motivations, and partly checking his desires to violate the systems of norms" (pp. 197–98). Holter suggests that activist feminist or "women's liberation" groups may be thought of as emerging (in Merton's terminology) from blocked access to direct attainment of commonly held success goals (p. 199). At any rate, it is possible that men or women who do not conform to sex role norms defined as appropriate by their significant reference groups face the risk of being labeled as "deviant" with all the negative sanctions that labeling implies. Conversely, conformity is rewarded by positive sanctions.

For our purposes, the major implication of this brief literature summary is that sex roles exist prior to the time of heterosexual dating, possible sexual involvement (including premarital pregnancy), and marriage. Bumpass, for instance, has suggested that women who possess more traditional sex role conceptions may be more willing to forego additional education and to marry younger (1969). He provides evidence that females who marry younger tend to have the first child sooner and eventually to have more children than those who marry later. This series of influences is one possible means whereby gender differentiation influences family size. There are others, of course, and we shall explore many such elements in later chapters.

To posit such influence is not to assert that most persons entering marriage are self-consciously aware of the full implications of gender differentiation. However, regardless of the degree of conscious rationality, certain "material-event" behaviors such as those just described may nonetheless flow from particular sex role orientations (Scheibe, 1970). At the same time, to posit such a flow is not to imply that certain marital events, in addition to other larger social forces, could not alter the sex roles of married persons, particularly in a period of revived emphasis on feminism. For example, many female high school graduates have entered marriage with rather traditional sex role definitions. A subsequent change in these orientations toward greater modernity might indeed have some influence in propelling some toward additional education and/or a "fulfilling" occupation. But if the change does not occur until age 30 and if there are 3, 4, or more children already present, the consequences of modernity for family size will be small unless, of course, one or more additional children are avoided because of her aspirations. In all but the most highly motivated wives, we could expect the presence of that many children at that relatively young age to inhibit many "modern" behaviors. It would seem, in short, that if role modernity is to have some important influence on family size, in most instances its force has to be felt prior to marriage and during the earlier years of childbearing. We shall, of course, return to this temporal issue repeatedly in later chapters.

Correlates of Sex Role Norms

As this is not a study of socialization into sex roles, we are limited in what we can say about factors that influence the learning of modernity and traditionalism. Nonetheless, we can call attention to five key socio-logical variables which the literature indicates should be associated with sex roles and which we already know to be associated with fertility variables. Understanding these kinds of relationships should not only enhance our grasp of what sex roles are all about, it should also help us begin to grasp whatever links exist between sex roles and fertility control.

Sex

Holter suggests that men can be expected to be more traditional and women more modern in their sex role orientations (1970:79–80). Because women are the subordinate group vis-à-vis the dominant male group, women experience fewer privileges, rights, and benefits. It is, therefore, in their interests not to maintain the status quo in terms of gender differentiation but instead to seek for change. On the other hand, men presumably perceive that it is in their own best interests to maintain gender differentiation as it is now constituted, i.e., to maintain traditional role structures.

Age

A second hypothesis is that we might expect younger persons to be more oriented to the modern than older persons. Feminism as an historical movement dates back at least to the early nineteenth century, and the intervening decades have witnessed a gradual eroding of male dominance both in and out of the home.[3] Each new generation has accepted slightly greater degrees of female autonomy and independence. There is every reason to expect this long-range trend to be observable today, and given the recent revival of neofeminism, there is reason to suspect that it may have become accelerated. This is not to say that trends toward gender egalitarianism could not in the future be reversed among certain segments of the population (see Chapter Six).

RACE

There is also literature which suggests that black persons and black marriages may be more egalitarian (and therefore less traditional) than white persons and white marriages at the same status levels.[4] These differences are probably not the result of rationally planned events or of greater feminism among blacks but may, in large measure, be an unintended consequence of long-standing economic discrimination against black men. Since Emancipation, black women have been forced into the labor market in order to survive because black men were given little or no opportunity to become educated and to attain meaningful occupations. One (unconscious) result of greater female access to economic resources and to the power it provides may have been to institutionalize a greater degree of husband–wife egalitarianism among blacks than among whites. Such processes have nothing to do with myths and stereotypes about "the black matriarchy" but rather are the result of large social forces impinging differently on white and black family systems.

RELIGION

Westoff and Potvin found that the "family ideology" of Catholics is "basically traditional" (1967:220). "Marriage is considered a career in itself, one only to be entered if the goal is to have a family. This 'family career', moreover, is apparently believed to be so all-embracing in its demands on the woman and in its intrinsic importance that a career role in the occupational world is regarded as incompatible" (p. 222). In short, owing to a wide array of theological and socioreligious reasons we might expect processes of egalitarianism to be proceeding more slowly among Catholics than among non-Catholics. Therefore, we would hypothesize that, compared to Catholics, non-Catholics would possess more modern conceptions of gender differentiation.

It is for these kinds of theoretical and empirical considerations that in this and in succeeding chapters we separate Catholics from non-Catholics. Whatever sociological differences exist among varieties of non-Catholics, none appear so significant as those which distinguish Catholics from all others. An additional and related reason for the Catholic–non-Catholic distinction is the literature showing Catholic fertility behavior to be substantially different from that of other whites (Ryder and Westoff, 1971). Although there is evidence that the fertility behavior of Jews may differ somewhat from that of other non-Catholics, we do not possess enough cases to treat them separately. As it appears they are considerably more like Protestants than like Catholics, we include them with the former.

EDUCATION

Since its inception feminism has been identified with those who are better educated (Holter, 1970). There is every reason to expect that currently those with more years of schooling would be less role-traditional than those who are less educated. Education tends to have a "liberalizing" or "modernizing" effect in many spheres of beliefs and behavior, and gender differentiation should be no exception. Although orientations toward egalitarianism are probably spreading to all educational levels, those who are the best educated are the ones best able to perceive most clearly the most rewarding alternatives to traditionalism (Bumpass, 1969). For example, the more education a woman has, the more likely she is to have actual access to those occupations that are most rewarding in both tangible and intangible ways.

Reference was made earlier to the unsettled nature of the sex role and fertility control casual sequence. Education is known to be associated with both parts of that relationship. In the absence of a panel design, we may assume the following type of pattern, which later in this chapter shall receive some verification. Children from higher-status homes are socialized to expect to attain higher levels of education. Simultaneously, over the years, they are socialized into gender role differentiation which is comparatively less rigid than that learned by children in lesser-status homes. In the case of girls from higher-status homes, both their internalized expectations for education and their less-traditional sex role definitions operate to keep them in high school, to graduate, and to motivate ever more of them to gain additional schooling. (Among black and deprived white households these processes are especially important in keeping females from going to work prematurely in order to help support the family.)

This training in turn should contribute towards further modernizing of their sex roles. Thus, we may posit that background status and adolescent sex role orientations influence academic attainment but that each higher rung of attainment functions to increase young adult role modernity. Hence, for those married persons in our sample we cannot say that education is the sole cause of gender differentiation; but we can say that it is an exceedingly meaningful correlate and that both are traceable to background situations and experiences.

At this point, there should be sufficient preparation to permit us to turn to an examination of the ways in which we attempted to measure gender differentiation and the ways in which our measures are related to these five key variables.

From that body of literature known as "role theory" there is considerable support for the technique of measuring roles in terms of norms that structure them (Bertrand, 1972; Turner, 1974). Therefore, drawing on the work of Alice Rossi (1970), a series of items was developed to measure three family statuses, in the Linton–Merton sense, or positions, in the Bates sense (Bertrand, 1972).[5] These were the positions of wife, husband, and mother. Figures 2–1, 2–2, and 2–3 display the several dimensions that emerged upon factor analysis of the items within each position. We shall assume that these dimensions are sex roles intrinsic to the three major structural positions before us.

FIGURE 2-1. Social Position of *Wife,* with Norms Organized in Terms of Two Role Dimensions, with Factor Loadings (after Varimax Rotation)

Traditional Wife Role (TW)	Men	Women
a. A married woman's most important task in life should be taking care of her husband and children.	.60	.56
b. She should realize that a woman's greatest reward and satisfaction come through her children.	.53	.59
d. If she works, she sould *not* try to get ahead in the same way that a man does.	.38	.45
f. A wife should *not* have equal authority with her husband in making decisions.	.27	.26
g. If she has the same job as a man who has to support his family, she should not expect the same pay.	.32	.28
j. A wife should realize that, just as a woman is not suited for heavy physical work, there are also other kinds of jobs she is not suited for, because of her mental and emotional nature.	.38	.45
k. A wife should give up her job whenever it inconveniences her husband and children.	.58	.60
l. If a mother of young children works, it should be only while the family needs the money.	.53	.53

Wife Self-Actualization (SA)		
c. Having a job herself should be just as important as encouraging her husband in his job.	.55	.55
e. She should be able to make long-range plans for her occupation, in the same way that her husband does for his.	.45	.51
h. If being a wife and mother isn't satisfying enough, she should take a job.	.48	.34
i. There should be more day-care centers and nursery schools so that more young mothers could work.	.49	.56

The Social Position of Wife

Some of the items in the figures may follow the identical wording of the sources from which they were drawn, but in most instances, an idea was borrowed and items revised and altered—sometimes considerably, sometimes only in minor fashion. In yet other cases, a fresh idea may have emerged and a whole new item been created to apprehend it. This kind of process illustrates a pressing problem in the present state of research into sex roles: the lack of a set of indexes or scales that have been widely used, standardized, and shown to be reliable and valid. It is hoped that the indices described in this chapter will contribute toward the goal of achieving some consensus over appropriate structural measures of sex role norms.

Figure 2–1 shows the two sex roles or gender roles, along with factor loadings, that emerged from factor analyses of these items separately for men and women.[6] The first factor or dimension that emerged might be labeled the "traditional wife role" (TW). It can be defined as representing an emphasis in which the interests of husband and children are placed ahead of those of the wife. It is described in terms of the convictions that a women's central mission in life is to care for husband and children (item a) and that the mission is believed to provide her with her chief source of satisfactions. Although working is not totally proscribed, individualistic achievement is (d), and so is the right to the same pay given a man who has a family to support (g). It is further believed that certain tasks are ill suited for the feminine body and psyche (j), that inconvenience to family demands caused by her job indicates that she should terminate her work (k), and that working while the children are young should occur only during severe economic necessity (l). Equal authority with husbands is not felt to be desirable (f). Respondents were asked if they strongly agreed, agreed, had mixed feelings about, disagreed, or strongly disagreed with each of the items. The responses are coded and summed; the highest possible score is 32.[7] A high score indicates a "modern" emphasis in which there is reduced commitment to the notion of the subordination of wife interests. A lower score, on the other hand, indicates a "traditional" emphasis or greater commitment to superordination of husband and child interests. Degree of commitment to or acceptance of subordination of wife interests is a continuum ranging from traditional (greater acceptance) to modern (greater rejection). Subsequently, when we refer to degree of traditionalism or degree of modernity in connection with this role, we will have in mind the extent to which interests are considered to be legitimately subordinated.

The second factor (Figure 2–1) that emerged might be labeled "wife self-actualization" (SA). That role is defined as one in which wife interests are equal to those of husband and children. Specifically, it can be described as a dimension in which the wife's job is equal in significance with encouragement of her husband in his job (item c), the wife is able to make long-term plans for her job that are not automatically upset by changes in the husband's job situation (e), domestic satisfactions are not considered absolutely sufficient for every wife and mother (h) and organized child-care facilities are seen as a boon for the employment aspirations of mothers (i).

The same response categories were used for these items, and 16 is the highest possible score on the SA dimension. However, a high score on SA means a traditional orientation or greater rejection of equality of interests. A low score indicates what we shall subsequently refer to as orientation towards or greater acceptance of equality of interests.

These two dimensions or continua of traditionalism–modernity appear to have considerable face validity as well as conceptual and theoretical validity. Items c, e, h, and i (SA) are the ones which do in fact stress individualistic occupational achievement for the wife and concomitant changes in traditional conceptions of her domestic behaviors. This structural dimension of wives' roles could provide part of the impetus to move the wife along the route toward what has been termed the status of equal partner with the husband (Scanzoni, 1972). In that sense the SA role may be construed as the more extreme or radical of these two dimensions. Its thrust toward genuine husband–wife equality marks it off as distinct from its more moderate counterpart, the TW role.

The TW dimension is based actually on the status quo and allows merely for flexibility in attainment of wife interests within traditional parameters in which these interests remain primarily subordinate to those of husbands. The eight TW items describe the aspect of wives' roles that has been the predominant one for decades. It was the first factor extracted, and it explains more variance than the SA dimension.[8] The TW dimension is part of the wife's status as complement or junior partner vis-à-vis her husband (Scanzoni, 1972). In either of these two latter statuses, her *raison d'etre* is centered in husband and children. Many working wives, for example, may be characterized as junior partners in the limiting senses that items d, g, j, k, l impose.

The wife in the status of complement is the nonworking wife. In many instances, wives move in and out of the labor force rather irregularly in response to elements tapped by items such as k or l (Ridley, 1969). This lack of continuous long-term involvement with work means that many wives move between the statuses of junior partner and complement often during their lifetimes; hence the line between these statuses is fine indeed. The great gulf is between the statuses of junior partner and equal partner, the latter status being one the wife can occupy only to the degree that she functions as co-provider in the same senses as her husband, i.e., in a context of role interchangeability rather than traditional role specialization (Scanzoni, 1972).

Recalling the five hypotheses regarding the relationships between role modernity and the factors of sex, age, race, religion, and education, let us test them in terms of these two dimensions of the wife's position.

SEX

The first hypothesis is that women because of their subordinate status are more modern-oriented (oriented toward change or toward greater pursuit of their own interests) than are men, who might be expected to prefer the status quo. Comparing the first two columns of Table 2–1, we find that this hypothesis is not generally supported with respect to the "traditional wife" role.[9] In all but two instances there are no significant differences between men and women. Among young Catholics and non-Catholics alike, men actually score significantly more modern than women. Therefore when it comes to this more moderate dimension of wife role behaviors, the sexes appear to be in general concurrence over their relative modernity or the extent to which wife interests should be subordinated. And there is some indication that young married men may actually be more amenable to these kinds of "low-key" changes than are young married women.

The top two rows of Table 2–1 represent responses from the university sample of single white undergraduates described in Chapter One.[10] The bottom rows represent those households where both spouses were interviewed, and thus these latter comparisons are between husbands and wives married to each other.[11] The identical items which appear in Figures 2–1 through 2–4 were also administered to these university students. To achieve exact comparability student dimensions were limited to the same items as those that made up the adult dimensions.[12]

Quite the opposite pattern from the TW dimension appears in connection with the more extreme or radical dimension of "self-actualization" or equality of wife interests (columns 3 and 4 of Table 2–1). There the stated hypothesis is supported, for in every comparison women do score more modern than men, and in all but four instances the differences are significant. On this fundamental indicator of preference for traditionalism over modernity (equality of interests) in the wife's role behaviors, it appears that women are more oriented toward change than are men. The kinds of benefits and rights that are subsumed by the SA dimension are far-reaching indeed. Precisely because the SA dimension is so rewarding to wives, it is quite costly to husbands; because of the cost to them, in terms of traditional rights and benefits within the family, men are likely to resist the implications inherent in the SA dimension. Therefore, in terms of the issue as to whether or not gender discriminates in terms of wife role modernity, the answers appears to be "apparently not," when what is in view is a more moderate and widely-accepted conception of wife role behaviors in which rewards and costs to husbands and wives would not be substantially altered from what they are now in most marriages. On the other hand, the answer to the question seems to be "yes" when what is in view is a more extreme redefinition of the wife role in which costs and rewards would be substantially altered from dominant patterns.

AGE

What of the second of the five hypotheses? Does age make any difference in wife role definitions? Looking again at Table 2–1, we can examine age differences by comparing rows. For example, we see that young (spouse age = 18–29) non-Catholic men show a TW score of 15.08, which is significantly more modern than the figure of 13.65 for older non-Catholic men (spouse age = 30–44). Similarly, in the three remaining TW comparisons for men, those who are younger continue to report greater TW modernity than do those who are older, although between older and younger black men the difference is not significant. Younger women (18–29) too rank more TW modern than older women (30–44) in each of the four comparisons, though differences in only two rankings (non-Catholics, blacks) are significant.

Thus on the TW aspect of wives' role behaviors, the hypothesis that youth is associated with greater modernity (or less interest-subordination) appears to be verified. The overall trend for the eight comparisons is clearly in the predicted direction.

The same age trend also holds with regard to the SA dimension. There five of the eight comparisons show significant differences by age. Younger persons—Catholic and non-Catholic, black and white, persons from the same marriages—all reveal that they are more oriented toward greater self-actualization for women than are older persons. Youth does seem to make a difference in terms of this more extreme (equality of interests) as well as the more moderate aspect of the structure of wives' roles.[13]

RACE

Besides sex and age, does race discriminate over these particular role dimensions? If we compare, for instance, the 15.08 score for young non-Catholic men with the 13.00 TW score for young black men, we find that non-Catholics are significantly more modern than are blacks.[14] The same strong difference emerges between young black and young Catholic men (TW = 14.88), with the latter again scoring more modern.[15] Among older men, both non-Catholics and Catholics score more TW-modern than blacks, but for Catholics the differences are not significant. Among men, therefore, our expectation regarding color differences is reversed. At least on the more moderate TW dimension, whites appear to be less traditional than blacks. The same conclusion emerges among women, but is much less convincing. That is, in each of the four comparisons (of younger blacks compared to both young non-Catholics and young Catholics and of older blacks compared to both older non-Catholics and older Catholics), although white women tend to be more modern-oriented than black women, the differences are not great nor statistically significant. Hence the original hypothesis of greater black TW modernity is not supported among women either, but at least there is no reversal as there was for men. Race simply does not discriminate among women on this particular role dimension.

Turning back to men we find that race also discriminates among them on the SA dimension, but now in the expected directions. Comparing the mean scores in the SA column of Table 2–1 between young black men and young non-Catholics and Catholics, and older black men with older Catholics and non-Catholics, we discover strongly significant differences, showing in each instance greater modernity for black men when it comes to wife self-actualization.[16]

Precisely the same result occurs when we compare black women—younger and older—with similar-age Catholics and non-Catholics. In each of the four comparisons blacks are significantly less traditional than whites.[17] Thus on the more extreme aspects of wives' roles, the hypothesis regarding greater black modernity is confirmed. Why it should not be confirmed on the TW dimension is not totally clear, but we recall that sex was a less consistent discriminator on that dimension also.

RELIGION

The fourth hypothesis had to do with religion. Are Catholics more traditional than non-Catholics? Restricting ourselves to whites we learn from Table 2–1 that young Catholic men are slightly more TW traditional than young non-Catholics but not significantly so. Older non-Catholics, however, are significantly more TW modern than older Catholic men;[18] and at the other end of the age spectrum, male Catholic college students are significantly more traditional than their non-Catholic counterparts.

Interestingly, among married women, it is the younger non-Catholics who are significantly more TW modern than younger Catholics;[19] whereas among older women TW scores from the two religious groupings are virtually identical. However, among white college students, Catholic women, like men, are more traditional than non-Catholic women. In short, apart from college students, the results are mixed as far as assessing the impact of religion on the TW dimension is concerned.

In terms of the SA dimension, Catholic men (young and old) are slightly but not significantly more traditional than non-Catholic men. Exactly the same findings emerge for married women. Regarding students, as was true for them on the TW role, greater SA modernity is found for both sexes among non-Catholics than among Catholics.

Religion, therefore, apparently shows little consistent or patterned relationship with either aspect of wives' role, except among well-educated students. This fourth hypothesis, therefore, must apparently be discarded insofar as it applies to wives' roles as assessed by married persons. However, as well-educated single Catholic students reveal such strong TW and SA traditionalism, we should turn to our fifth hypothesis to see what differences exist in the role orientations of married persons (especially Catholics) when we distinguish between levels of academic achievement.

Education

Table 2–2 shows (comparing rows) that among younger and older non-Catholics and among younger Catholics our expectations are confirmed regarding the consequences of education for the TW and SA roles.[20] For both dimensions and for both men and women those with high education (13 years or more) are significantly more modern-oriented than those with low education (12 years or less). Thus within these religious and age categories education does have a "liberalizing" or modernizing influence on wives' roles. Education, however, makes no significant difference among older Catholics (neither men nor women on either role). This contrast between older and younger Catholics, and the similarity of the latter to non-Catholics, suggests that younger educated Catholics are becoming more like non-Catholics on these particular orientations, thus indicating a break with patterns of older Catholics. To the degree that this change is actually occurring and to the extent that sex role norms may actually be linked to fertility control, such change may help to account for recently increasing convergences observed between younger Catholics and non-Catholics in terms of their fertility behaviors (Ryder and Westoff, 1971). Further support for the convergence notion comes from the earlier findings in Table 2–1 showing that religion did not consistently distinguish differences in wife role orientations between married Catholics and non-Catholics.

Nevertheless, any such convergence is not always found, for as Table 2–1 indicates, currently single Catholic college students are more SA and TW traditional than non-Catholic students. Moreover, Catholic college students are very similar to young, similarly educated married Catholics in their role orientations. There are no significant differences between the TW and SA mean scores of students and of young highly educated Catholics, both men and women. Thus whatever trends toward modernity exist among well-educated Catholics, the group that is still single (and younger) does not differ in these norms in any meaningful sense from those who are somewhat older and married. (It is possible, of course, that these findings could be affected by the comparatively low number of cases of Catholic students.)

By way of contrast, both men and women non-Catholic college students are significantly more TW-modern than young, well-educated married non-Catholic men and women.[21] Thus there is some indication that young, single highly-trained non-Catholics may be pushing trends, in at least one aspect of role modernity, beyond the point to which young educated married persons have now moved. Recall, of course, that the latter group has already moved significantly beyond older married persons.

Among blacks, differences in the TW dimension by education are consistent and strong. Highly educated blacks—men and women—are more TW modern than are blacks with less education. However, on the more extreme and perhaps more important SA dimension, significant differences by education do not appear for either sex. The finding that education does not discriminate on this dimension among blacks may reflect the greater and more pervasive institutionalization of wife role rights throughout all levels of black society. Because of the historical circumstances noted earlier, wife self-actualization may be a more meaningful phenomenon in more levels of black than of white society.

In brief, our hypothesis regarding the positive relationship between greater education and greater role modernity is confirmed for wives' roles among younger whites—men and women, Catholic and non-Catholic. The same holds for older non-Catholics. Among younger and older blacks it is partly confirmed, and in remaining instances education does not appear to have a significant effect.

RECAP

Before turning to the position of husband, we may say that four of the five stated hypotheses (allowing for exceptions) appear to be quite useful insofar as our two dimensions of the wife-position are concerned. Age, sex (especially on the SA dimension), race, education (and to a much lesser extent, religion) are the variables that enable us to begin to identify those persons who are least traditional and most modern on the "traditional-wife" (wife-interests subordinate) and "self-actualization" (equality of wife interests) dimensions.

The Social Position of Husband

Although the literature reveals some systematic effort to analyze the content of the position of the wife, there has been considerably less focus on the husband's position. It is true, of course, that the positions and roles of women have undergone extensive change during the last 200 years, while those of men have changed much less. While wives were, over this period of history, moving through the statuses of mere property to complement to junior partner, concomitant alterations in husbands' statuses were from owner to head to senior partner. These changes consisted mostly of relinquishing certain powers, privileges, and rights. However, husbands have been able in general to maintain marital role specialization and the prime right to provider-type behaviors. A major consequence has been to keep the wife in a position where she is principally responsible for the domestic scene. Few husbands share the same degree of responsibility as do wives for domestic demands, just as few wives share the same degree of responsibility as husbands for occupational demands. But it is precisely this drawing of husbands into greater domestic involvement, thereby permitting greater wife occupational involvement, that some women are beginning to seek (Blake, 1972).

Respondents were asked to indicate their reactions to the items in Figure 2–2. We may label the first role dimension that emerged as "problematic husband alterations" (PHA).[22] The rationale for the label emerges

FIGURE 2–2. Social Position of *Husband*, with Norms Organized in Terms of Three Role Dimensions, with Factor Loadings (after Varimax Rotation)

Problematic Husband Alterations (PHA)	Men	Women
d. If *her* job sometimes requires her to be away from home overnight, this should not bother him.	.57	.51
e. If a child gets sick and his wife works, he should be just as willing as she to stay home from work and take care of the child.	.38	.50
f. If his wife makes more money than he does, this should not bother him.	.50	.58
h. On the job, men should be willing to work for women supervisors.	.38	.46
i. A married man should be willing to have a smaller family, so that his wife can work if she wants to.	.42	.49
Institutionalized Equality (IE)		
b. If his wife works, he should share equally in household chores such as cooking, cleaning, and washing.	.55	.72
c. If his wife works, he should share equally in the responsibilities of child care.	.76	.72
Traditional Husband Role (TH)		
a. A married man's chief responsibility should be his job.	.45	.45
g. The husband should be the head of the family.	.32	.34

from the notion that each of the items represents a tentative, a temporary, or a problematic element in the husband's job and family priorities. None of them necessarily implies any permanent, significant, or far-reaching alterations in his behavioral patterns. They are problematic in that they may or may not even occur to particular husbands; even if they did, their consequences for actual behavior, rights, power, and privileges are not at all certain. In short, we may define this role as one in which husband's interests remain basically superior to or more significant than those of the wife, but yet there exists the live option of temporary incursion into the husband's interests for the sake of wife interests.

Item *d*, for example, specifies that a wife might be away overnight only occasionally, if at all. Likewise in *e*, the assumption is that when and if a healthy child becomes ill the situation requires only temporary behavioral adjustments by the husband-father. The proportion of American working wives who actually earn more money than their husbands (*f*) is small, but any couple's situation may change. Salaries can go up or down for either sex. The same reasoning would hold for *h*—there is nothing certain nor fixed about the sex of supervisors. Item *i* is problematic in the sense that a wife may or may not wish to work. Even if she does, she may or may not want a smaller family on that account: Her children, for example, may all be in high school or beyond.

To be sure, even to allow the possibility of these problematic alterations represents a considerable change in the normative content of husbands' roles from, say, 100 or even 50 years ago. They very likely describe the major emerging content of the roles of most husbands since World War II. But the very fact of their problematic nature mutes their significance for basically altering the structure of marriage. The wife remains chiefly responsible for the domestic scene. Nevertheless, to the degree these norms are assented to and/or are actually fulfilled they do represent husbands being drawn to a certain extent into greater involvement in conjugal matters. They thus indicate a change in the direction of more modern (lesser overriding significance of husband interests) and way from more traditional husband-role orientations. The highest possible score on the PHA dimension is 20, with a high score indicating a traditional orientation and a low score a modern orientation.

The two items that emerged on the second factor (Figure 2–2) give rise to a role dimension which can be labeled as "institutionalized equality" (IE). In both items, the emphasis is on sharing equality—if the wife works —in both household chores and children. Note the very strong factor loading in Figure 2–2 for women on each item. Although for men the child-care item is very strong, the household-chore item is considerably less strong. Men are apparently less enthusiastic about institutionalizing equality over household routine than about doing so in regard to child care.

In any case, the theoretical implications of this dimension are clearly quite different from those of the PHA dimension. Whereas the changes in that role were tentative and situational, here they are certain and definite, i.e., institutionalized as part of the normative structure of the marriage. Hence we may define this role as one in which the husband's interests are not superior to nor more significant than the interests of his working wife. Past literature tends to indicate that working wives often perform just as many household tasks as nonworking wives. Instead of their husbands taking on significantly more chores, working wives simply add occupational duties to their household tasks.

The IE dimension suggests the possibility of a different pattern in which responsibility for households would unequivocally fall equally on husbands as well as wives, if the latter work. One outcome of such a pattern would be that wives would be substantially freer than at present to pursue occupational endeavors along the lines suggested by the SA dimension. Another could be that husbands might want fewer children if they thought they might have to participate equally in their care, thus potentially limiting flexibility in terms of their own occupational pursuits. A score of 18 is the highest possible on the IE dimension, with a high score being traditional (husband's interests more significant) and a low score being modern (wife's interests not being less significant).

The final husband role dimension, the one that accounts for the least amount of variance and is probably therefore the least important of these three dimensions, is the "traditional husband" role (TH). Both items (Figure 2–2) are general in their wording as compared with the more specific behavioral prescriptions detailed in the PHA and IE dimensions. For instance, if a man's chief responsibility is his job, then by definition any family behaviors must be subordinate to it in terms of significance and priority in the event of a clash. This of course has long been an integral part of the notion that the male should be the unique provider for the family. Precisely because he has been placed in this unique situation, he has also traditionally been defined as the head of the family. Therefore this role may be defined as a form of the "patriarchal ideology" (Scanzoni, 1970:151) in which the greater significance of the husband's interests and authority are legitimated in statuses ascribed to him by sex.

Taken together, these two items spell out the traditional prerogatives of the husband: as head, considerable power in ultimate decision-making rests with him; and as unique provider, he has the freedom to organize his life and the lives of other family members around his occupation. But significantly, the fact that the TH dimension is statistically the least powerful of the three suggests that most Americans are probably moving away from these traditional orientations. At the same time, the movement has not been so intensive nor extensive as to make the most modern orientation

—the IE dimension—the most significant of these husband roles. Just as the SA—the most modern wife-role dimension—ranked in importance behind the more moderate TW dimension, the more moderate PHA dimension is the most significant of the husband roles. Social change with respect to husband and wife roles clearly exists, but as with most changes that ultimately have profound consequences for the larger social structure, it is evolutionary, gradual, and most often very difficult to observe. Moreover, most persons tend at any point in time to be found within the moderate ranges of such change. A score of 8 is the highest possible on the TH dimension. Here, however, a high score reflects modernity, a low score traditionalism or greater acceptance of the "patriarchal ideology."

SEX

Let us now determine how the five hypotheses apply to these three aspects of the husband position. First, are women more modern-oriented here than men? Going back to Table 2–1 and comparing columns 5 and 6 (men and women on the PHA dimension), we find that among college students (Catholic and non-Catholic), among young and older non-Catholics, and among young couples, that men score significantly more modern than women. And among Catholic married persons the men are also more modern, though the differences are not significant. This is a surprising pattern, given our theoretical rationale, which suggests that women's interests are best served and men's interests least served by alterations in marital sex role structure. Apparently our conceptual schema must be refined to indicate that (white) women are more concerned with changes in the wife position than in the husband position, especially changes with regard to the SA dimension (Steinmann, *et al.,* 1968). Perhaps the strategy (unconscious or otherwise) of conflict and change held by most women is to press for rights and benefits where these are most clearly justifiable and more attainable, i.e., in terms of their own role behaviors. Concomitantly, they may be less willing to press for changes in role structures that are not their own and over which they have far less control—changes which relatively may be harder to justify and which are much more difficult for women to bring about.

At the same time (white) men are evidently quite willing to modify temporarily certain of their own behaviors when and if wives work. Indeed, they appear to be more willing to change than wives are to press for these particular changes. We must recall, of course, that in terms of "radicalness" PHA is the most mild of the three husband roles we have extracted, and it is far more moderate in terms of meaningful changes in marital structure than the SA role. Thus there is simply less reason for women to press for change along the PHA than the SA dimension. In terms of trends in changes over the PHA aspect of the husband position, it would appear that men will continue to be less traditional than women, at least for a while.

When it comes to the dimension pertaining to "institutionalized equality" (IE), significant differences emerge only for young and older non-Catholics and for older blacks. Among the non-Catholics it is men who are once again more "modern" than women, but for blacks the opposite holds. Over all, however, as most of the IE comparisons do not reveal significant differences, we may conclude that sex is not a powerful distinguishing element in terms of this most extreme aspect of husband role behavior.

The pattern that emerges for the "traditional husband" (TH) role is somewhat closer to that for the PHA dimension than for the IE dimension. Non-Catholic men (young and old) are significantly more TH-modern than non-Catholic women, and the same difference holds among Young Catholics. Among the remaining white and couples' categories men show more modern (but not significantly) mean scores than do women.

Blacks at all three types of husband role categories show patterns opposite to that of whites—women more modern than men. Why this should be is not certain but it may be related to the generally greater marital egalitarianism within black society discussed earlier. As a result, while white women are more willing to press for changes in the wife role than in the husband role, black women, who already possess greater rights in terms of the more "extreme" SA dimension, want in addition greater changes in the husband position as well. As in other instances of group subordination, the more the benefits of the subordinate group are increased the greater their aspirations become. As black wives already have greater privileges and rights, they may believe they are entitled to still more of the same. To the degree this process occurs, it suggests that as white wives gain increasing marital benefits they too may come to raise their aspirations for even higher levels of such gratifications with respect to husband position behaviors.

AGE

When we compare rows in Table 2–1 we see that age makes no significant differences for men or women, black or white, on either the PHA or the IE dimension of the husband position. Only younger men from our couples' subsample are more meaningfully modern than older men from that subsample. By and large, therefore, compared to the differences in wives' roles associated with age, it would appear that change is occurring at a much slower pace with respect to the husband roles than for wives' roles. Add this conclusion to our finding that white women are less likely to press vigorously for changes in the husband position, and it appears that the elements of sex and age taken together reinforce the notion that the husband position is quite likely to remain fairly stable in structure over the next few years compared to alterations that may occur in the wife position.

Nonetheless, it is important to note that in terms of what is considered the most anachronistic of the three husband role dimensions, the TH dimension, young non-Catholic men and women and young Catholic men score significantly less traditional than their elders. What is more, in each of the remaining TH comparisons differences lie in the expected direction of greater youth modernity. Therefore, it does appear that younger persons (non-Catholics especially) are clearly easing away from the dimension that is most extreme in its delineation of traditional male prerogatives. Although as yet there is not the acceptance of PHA or IE orientations that is accorded to the SA and TW dimensions, it seems evident that at least some changes have occurred among younger persons with regard to this particular aspect of the husband position. Family headship based on ascribed characteristics and priorities that place job above family seem to be increasingly less viable to younger women and men.

RACE

When we compare young non-Catholic white men with young black men over the three role dimensions within the husband position, we find significant differences only in the TH dimension. Contrary to our expectations regarding the effects of race (similar to the comparison for the TW role) white non-Catholics are significantly more TH-modern than blacks.[23] Young Catholic men are also more TH-modern than young black men, but the latter emerge as significantly less traditional on the PHA dimension.[24]

Young black women are significantly more modern-oriented than young non-Catholic women on both the PHA and the IE dimensions, and more modern than Catholic women on the PHA role only.[25] Thus among young women in particular our expectation is confirmed that blacks are generally less traditional than whites, this time in terms of the husband position.

Among older men, blacks are significantly more PHA-modern than non-Catholics, but the latter are more modern on the TH dimension.[26] At the same time, identical patterns emerge for both dimensions when older black men are compared to older Catholic men.[27] Older women, however, resemble younger persons in that blacks are more PHA-modern and IE-modern than non-Catholics and also than Catholics.[28] In short, older as well as younger black women clearly reveal greater modernity than whites on the two more salient and extreme aspects of husband role behaviors. As suggested, their having already gained greater role benefits than white women probably influences them to desire and press for still more.

At the same time, it is interesting to speculate why black men should be more modern than white men on the PHA dimension but less so on the much more moderate (in terms of behavioral changes) TH orientations. It may simply be that although blacks have outdistanced whites in their acceptance of specific behavioral alterations intrinsic in wife-employment, their own formal legitimation of these alterations has not changed correspondingly. White men, on the other side, may currently be more amenable to change at the ideological rather than at the behavioral level. It seems likely that over the next several years we might expect greater convergence between white and black men in that whites will gradually come to accept the greater legitimacy of actual changes in their own behaviors, while blacks will probably come to accept more formally (and verbally) what they already appear to accept in reality.

RELIGION

We saw above that the link between religion and wife role differences was minimal among the married persons. But here we discover, when we compare their mean scores in Table 2–1, that among younger white men, non-Catholics are significantly more modern on the PHA dimension (but not the IE or the TH) than are Catholics.[29] However, among young women, the one role measure that shows a significant difference is IE, but it is Catholics who rank more modern than non-Catholics.[30] Older women show no significant differences over the three dimensions by religion, but among older men we find a situation identical to that for younger men: Catholics are more PHA traditional than non-Catholics.[31]

Likewise, among male college students, Table 2–1 reveals that non-Catholics are significantly more modern in terms of the PHA role only, though differences on the remaining husband roles are in the same expected direction. Non-Catholic college women, as we see, are significantly less traditional on both the PHA and the IE dimensions. Religion, therefore, seems to emerge for married men in our sample as a more consistently meaningful discriminator of husbands' roles than it did for either sex in terms of wives' roles. Among single college students its discriminatory power is approximately the same.

The conclusion seems to be that Catholic men are less amenable to changes in the husband position (even the moderate PHA dimension) than are non-Catholics. Although we saw that men in general may be more willing to accept alterations in the husband position than wives are to press for them, male willingness varies by religion. Even among highly educated single students as well as those representing all education levels, there is a tendency for non-Catholics to be less traditional in this respect —to be more willing to make certain alterations rather favorable to their wives and somewhat costly to themselves.

EDUCATION

Except for Catholic men (younger and older) and for blacks, Table 2–2 shows that the relationship between greater PHA modernity and higher education is not based on chance. This relationship holds for younger and older non-Catholics (men and women), and younger and older Catholic women. Moreover, when we compare non-Catholic male students with younger non-Catholic highly educated married men, we find the students significantly more modern on the PHA dimension.[32] An identical relationship emerges between non-Catholic women students and younger non-Catholic highly trained married women.[33] Conversely, neither Catholic male nor female students rank as meaningfully different from their married counterparts. Over all, therefore, among white persons, education clearly has the expected effect of helping to modernize PHA orientations. Moreover, among non-Catholics the trend is even stronger than among Catholics, because students who are younger have exceeded comparably educated young marrieds in their rejection of PHA traditionalism.

Much the same conclusions apply to the discussion of the TH role. As Table 2–2 shows, education discriminates in the expected direction among young marrieds (Catholic and non-Catholic, men and women). Moreover, non-Catholic students (men and women) score significantly more modern than young educated marrieds, whereas Catholic students do not.[34] Here too education modernizes, and non-Catholics who are the best-educated and single are the most modern.

However, on the most extreme of the husband role dimensions, the IE, Table 2–2 reveals only two scattered significant differences, and neither religious category of students ranks as more modern than young marrieds. Thus although the more moderate aspects of the husband position seem to be influenced by education, the notion of institutionalized equality does not. Evidently few even of the young and the most educated seem able to bring themselves to accept the virtual elimination of major role differentiation within the conjugal family in the event of wife employment. This observation elaborates the notion that change is occurring much more slowly with regard to the husband position than to the wife position. Not only is that true in general, but within the total range of husband role behaviors those pertaining specifically to institutionalized role interchangeability are proceeding hardly at all. Even in spite of increased numbers of persons becoming highly educated we may expect, among whites, much slower movement toward egalitarianism in the IE sense, than, say, movement toward acceptance of PHA behaviors.

Among blacks, Table 2–2 suggests that education makes hardly any difference at all for either sex at any of the three role dimensions of the husband position. Reasons for these nondifferences may be related to the finding that blacks in general are more role-modern than whites and that role modernity is more pervasive and more greatly institutionalized throughout all levels of black society.

RECAP

With regard to these five hypotheses as they apply to the three dimensions of the husband position, we may say that overall, though with exceptions, each of them has at least some relevance. Men, as it turns out, are generally more modern than women, the opposite of what was expected. Youth has not moved much beyond older persons except in the most anachronistic dimension (TH) of the husband role. Blacks are, as expected, less traditional than whites; and Catholics generally are less modern than non-Catholics, also as expected. Finally, education has had its predictable modernizing influence on the two more moderate role dimensions.

The Social Position of Mother

Turning from the positions of wife and husband, we focus next on the dimensions of the maternal position. Respondents were asked to reply either "yes" or "no" to the items appearing in Figure 2–3. The first factor that emerged we have labeled as "religious legitimation of the mother" role (RLM).[35] There were several theoretical reasons for including items a and b in our interview schedule. Religion and religious devoutness have been shown to be related to fertility control in important ways in numerous surveys. Among Catholics, Ryder and Westoff (1971) found that frequency of receiving communion was the single best measure of religious devoutness in terms of its consequences for fertility. It has been difficult to obtain some comparable measure of devoutness for non-Catholics as mere denominational label or even church attendance are generally unreliable predictors of fertility variables.

DeJong devised an index of "religious fundamentalism" which he found was related to fertility control among rural non-Catholic Appalachian whites (1965). Although his particular items were not deemed suitable for our heterogeneous urban sample, we did think the basic

FIGURE 2–3. Social Position of *Mother*, with Norms Organized in Terms of Two Role Dimensions, with Factor Loadings (after Varimax Rotation)

Religious Legitimation of Mother Role (RLM)	Men	Women
a. Do you believe that the institution of marriage and family was established by God?	.68	.57
b. Do you feel that being a mother is a special calling from God?	.80	.80
Traditional Mother Role (TM)		
c. Do you think that a working mother can establish just as warm and secure relationship with her children as a mother who does *not* work?	−.59	−.58
d. Do you feel that a parent gets more satisfaction when a son gets ahead in his occupation than when a daughter gets ahead in hers?	.19	.15
e. Do you feel that a marriage is *in*complete without children?	.17	.21
f. Do you think that young girls should be permitted as much independence as boys?	−.18	−.13
g. Do you feel a preschool child is likely to suffer if the mother works?	.70	.66

idea was useful for developing some sort of index to measure religious orientations that might indicate fertility control among non-Catholics as well as Catholics. As part of the theory underlying this research links performance of the traditional maternal position to fertility, it was decided to develop items that would pinpoint the religious or sacred significance of the mother role. Item a (Figure 2–3), for example, affirms the divine origin of marriage and family patterns, while item b specifically indicates that motherhood is a unique divine calling. Taken together, these two items would seem to suggest a certain important legitimation or justification for performance of traditional kinds of female behaviors, especially in terms of the bearing of and caring for children. Hence this particular role dimension may be defined as the degree of sacredness attached to marital and familial patterns. The highest possible score on the dimension is 2, a high score indicating a secular (less sacred) or modern orientation.

The second factor that emerged may be labeled the "traditional mother" role (TM). This role may be described in the following terms: because a marriage requires a child, the wife must become a mother to render the marriage whole (e); small children are likely to be harmed if the mother is not with them because she works (g); a nonworking mother can get closer to her children than a mother who works (c); sons are sought because of the unique satisfactions they bring parents through occupational achievement (d); daughters have to be treated differently (i.e., protected more) than boys because of their alleged greater vulnerability (f).

Taken as a whole, these items appear to represent the basic elements of the traditional mother role—necessity of children (alternative satisfactions will not suffice), necessity to be with them, and child socialization that points the next generation into sex-typed patterns. This role can be defined as one in which the interests of children are placed ahead of those of the woman. Mother-centered considerations are placed ahead of person-centered or individualistic considerations. The highest possible score for the TM dimension is 5, with a high score indicating a more modern orientation, or one in which the mother's individualistic interests are relatively more significant.

Sex

If we look at Table 2–3 we find an instructive contrast between patterns for the RLM and the TM dimensions. Men are consistently (though not always significantly) more secular or modern than women when it comes to "religious legitimation" of the mother role. On the other hand, in terms of the "traditional mother" dimension, the evident tendency is for women to emerge as more modern than men.

The differential impact of sex may be due to the nature of these two dimensions. The RLM index, for example, is essentially a measure of the sacred-secular character of the mother role. There is some literature to indicate that men in general tend to be more secular than women with regard to religious orientations (Moberg, 1962). Therefore, on this particular measure of the secularity of the maternal role the men are perhaps simply reflecting this prevailing tendency among males in our society. Thus the hypothesis that women would be more modern than men because it is in their interest to be so must be modified in connection with the RLM dimension. Apparently the element of current male secularity tends to outweigh the effects of female self-interest.

Although costs and rewards to husbands and wives are implicit in the RLM dimension, they tend to be more explicit in the TM role, which may be the prime reason that women tend to be less traditional here than men. Women are perhaps very likely to perceive that the more traditional they are on the items that make up this dimension, the more limited they are in seeking alternative rewards outside the family. Thus this dimension, somewhat as the SA role, does fit the hypothesis regarding greater female modernity and for much the same kinds of reasons. Although not as extreme as the SA role, it does nonetheless stand as an important indicator of alternative sets of rewards open to wives. Up to this point in time at least, most men would evidently lean toward the more traditional end of this maternal dimension and would prefer their wives to seek familistic kinds of rewards, a course simultaneously less costly to the husbands. On the other side, women tend to lean toward the modern or more individualistic end and would evidently prefer greater access to rewards other than those inherent in maternal behaviors.

AGE

At the same time, as Table 2-3 shows, young men are substantially more modern than older men on both the RLM and the TM dimensions. In seven of the eight RLM and TM comparisons for men (non-Catholics, Catholics, blacks, couples) youth is significantly associated with modernity. Thus although men are less modern than women on the TM role, younger men are more modern in general than older men and more closely approximate women. The long-range trend would therefore seem to be in the convergence of male–female orientations over the TM dimension and, as women probably will become more secular, over the RLM dimension as well.

Age makes for fewer significant differences among women than among men. Evidently these two particular aspects of role modernity had begun to be relatively accepted among women for some years. (Or perhaps older women too have recently become less TM-traditional.) Those significant differences that do emerge between older and younger women suggest, however, that the future should reveal even more widespread acceptance by younger women of a more modern position on both the RLM and the TM orientations.

RACE

Racial categories seem to discriminate minimally as far as men are concerned. When we compare young blacks with young non-Catholics and with young Catholics over both roles (Table 2-3) we discover the only significant difference to be between blacks and non-Catholics on the RLM dimension, with the latter scoring more modern.[36] Among the four comparisons for older men over both roles, we find once more that the only significant difference is between blacks and non-Catholics on the RLM role, with the latter again more modern.[37] Clearly, therefore, the hypothesis that black men would be less traditional than white men on the TM and RLM roles is not substantiated. Except for non-Catholics, and that only on one role, men of both racial groups appear to be rather homogeneous with respect to these two orientations.

Among younger women, blacks are significantly more modern on the TM dimension than both Catholics and non-Catholics.[38] These instances however are the only places where our hypothesis of greater black modernity is upheld, for among older women we discover for the third time that non-Catholics rank significantly more RLM modern than blacks.[39] On the religious ideology dimension therefore, black men and older black women are much more sacred-oriented than whites.

Recall that earlier we found a similar pattern for blacks in regard to the TH dimension and indicated there that blacks may be traditional at more generalized and formal level of the husband position, yet modern at more specific and behavioral levels. In this instance, too, some black males may indeed be more traditional at the more generalized and formal level of maternal roles, yet over time we would expect younger black men to move to a position similar to that now occupied by young black women (who are RLM-similar to whites). But at the same time that they are changing, we would expect whites to be changing too in the direction of greater TM modernity, so that we would expect whites eventually to rank similarly with blacks over both dimensions. The projections here and earlier in this chapter assume that black spokesmen who advocate traditional patterns of male authority will not be able to influence significant numbers of black persons.

Religion

Among white men we would expect, given the basic religious thrust of the RLM orientation, that non-Catholics would emerge as significantly less traditional than Catholics. This finding holds for both older and younger men.[40] No significant differences occur, however, over the TM dimension, which contains no intrinsic religious overtones. An identical situation over both dimensions occurs between Catholic and non-Catholic older women,[41] but there are no differences on either dimension between younger women. It would thus appear that young married Catholic women (as we might expect) have moved furthest away from traditional Catholic views regarding the sacred nature of motherhood and are closer than older Catholics and young male Catholics to a more secular position.

Nonetheless, we note from Table 2–3 that Catholic students, both men *and* women, are more RLM traditional than non-Catholic students. As we shall see when we discuss education, these differences may be due not so much to the traditionalism of Catholic students as to the relatively great modernity of their non-Catholic counterparts. Thus although Catholic students may have become less traditional than young married Catholics, the pace of change toward RLM secularity maintained by non-Catholics has evidently been even more rapid.

Over the TM dimension, Catholic women students do not differ significantly from non-Catholics, whereas Catholic males remain more traditional. Thus at least on this particular aspect of maternal behavior, single Catholic women (like young married Catholic women) appear to be closer to non-Catholic secularity than do Catholic men.

EDUCATION

Table 2–4 allows us to conclude that education is a consistently more powerful discriminator of maternal role differences than were any of the earlier four demographic characteristics. Comparing rows, we find that for men and women separately on both RLM and TM dimensions, in 20 out of 24 comparisons, those with high education are significantly more modern than those with less education. In short, education is positively related to the greatest levels of secularity as far as maternal religious legitimation is concerned, and education is also linked with the highest levels of modernity with regard to mother–child relationships. Moreover, the finding that this pattern holds across color, sex, age, and religious lines underscores the strength and pervasiveness of the "liberalizing influences" of higher education.

In addition, when we compare single, and younger, non-Catholic students with highly educated young non-Catholic marrieds (men and women), we find that the students emerge as significantly more modern on both dimensions than the marrieds.[42] Thus, among non-Catholics at least it appears that the trend in the future will be towards still greater levels of maternal role modernity. In contrast, however, significant differences between single Catholic female students and well-educated Catholic married women are nonexistent, while Catholic male students are more modern than well-educated married Catholic men only on the RLM dimension.[43] Movement toward maternal role modernity does not appear to be quite so rapid among the youngest, best-educated Catholic adults as it does among comparable non-Catholics.

Overall, education emerges as a sensitive and highly important means of identifying and predicting differences in maternal role orientations. More even than in its relationship to the wife or the husband position, education beyond high school is distinctively linked with reduced maternal traditionalism. Earlier we suggested that we may expect to see greater changes in the wife position than in the husband position in the near future. It may be that maternal roles, particularly among the well-educated, may become altered at a pace similar to that of the wife roles and beyond that of the husband roles. For one reason, more persons (especially women) are becoming better educated, and we can observe from Table 2–4 the consequences of additional training.

Second, there is inherent in most Western families, as they are now structured, a more intimate connection between traditional behaviors of wife and maternal roles than there is between the behaviors of maternal and husband roles. Thus those same forces that may be accounting for apparently differential rates of change between wife and husband roles may also account for similarly different rates of change between husband and maternal roles. One of these forces, for example, is concern on the part of married women for greater individualism. And as they are generally more likely than men to desire greater benefits in terms of wives' "self-actualization" (SA), they are also more likely to desire the same with regard to the TM role. For if married women are to have greater privileges in their behaviors as wives, it follows that they must have the same in their behaviors as mothers, as traditionally and currently the two positions are so closely intertwined.

RECAP

The five hypotheses apply in mixed fashion to these two aspects of the maternal position. In terms of sex, men are modern on the RLM dimension, and women are more modern on the TM dimension. With regard to age, young men are clearly more secular and egalitarian than older men. However, older and younger women are not so different over either RLM or TM. Race is only minimally able to discriminate over these role orientations, less so for men than for women. With regard to religion, Catholics are generally more traditional on the RLM but not the TM dimension. Finally, education discriminates powerfully on both roles for both sexes, racial groups, and religious categories. Education would appear to be the single best indicator of trends toward increasingly liberalizing traditional views toward maternal role structures and behaviors.

Dimensions of Self-Concept

At this point we shift the level of analysis from the normative or structural components of wife, husband, and mother roles to social-psychological elements of self-perception.[44] The items used to measure these elements are borrowed from Rossi's work (1970), though they are also found in the varied adjective-checklist methods of self-concept measurement. Items of this type were reported by Clarkson et al. (1970) to be related to actual family size. As detailed in Chapter One, they found that items fulfilling the stereotype of masculinity were linked to lower family size than were feminine-stereotype items.

For example, the first dimension described in Figure 2–4, labeled as "instrumental self-concept" (ISC), contains items that have in the past been thought to be chiefly "masculine" (ambitious, aggressive, hard-driving, competitive), whereas items in the "expressive self-concept" (ESC) dimension have been thought to be chiefly "feminine" (emotional, gentle, patient, warm).[45] The ISC dimension may therefore be defined as indicating the degree to which persons perceive themselves as active,

FIGURE 2–4. Dimensions of Self-Concept, with Factor Loadings (after Varimax Rotation)

Instrumental Self-Concept (ISC)	Men	Women
A. Ambitious	.46	.45
E. Aggressive	.53	.53
F. Strong	.35	.40
G. Self-Confident	.34	.45
M. Creative	.30	.31
N. Hard-Driving	.47	.44
O. Easily Influenced	−.24	−.30
P. Energetic	.45	.39
Q. Intellectual	.36	.42
R. Competitive	.33	.41
T. Dominant	.31	.33
U. Outgoing	.34	.42
Expressive Self-Concept (ESC)		
B. Moody	−.33	−.31
D. Quiet	.21	.34
H. Emotional	−.25	−.28
J. Logical	.24	.26
K. Gentle	.34	.39
L. Rebellious	−.41	−.42
S. Patient	.53	.53
T. Dominant	−.38	−.34
W. Realistic	.23	.25
X. Warm	.30	.24

aggressive, competitive, and the like. The ESC dimension is defined as indicating perceived degree of nurturance, support, and so on. Respondents were asked to respond "yes" or "no" to each item.

Critics of this kind of approach have rightly contended that neither set of characteristics should be exclusively or stereotypically attached to either sex, but that rather a male personality may contain both instrumental and expressive components, as may a female personality (Tangri, 1972). The finding in Figure 2–4 that both dimensions emerged for both sexes lends credence to the position that these items should not be viewed in stereotypic masculine–feminine fashion. Most men do view themselves as having certain instrumental characteristics, but so do most women. Most women view themselves as having certain expressive characteristics, but so do most men.

Although the items in the ISC index are self-explanatory, several in the ESC dimension require comment. Apparently expressiveness does not imply ·moodiness (b) nor emotionality (h). The negative signs on both these items suggest that these two characteristics, which are often viewed suspiciously, are not necessarily the companions of quietness (d) or of patience (s). The fact that being "logical" (j) loaded on ESC rather than ISC suggests that for most persons of both sexes there is a certain tempering of their expressiveness; it is not necessarily illogical nor nonrational. The same applies to "realistic" (w): Expressiveness does not imply lack of awareness of the genuine realities of given situations. Likewise, expressiveness is tempered in that it does not imply being rebellious (1). A person can be expressive and still be reasonable and cooperative. Because the strengths of the factor loadings on "dominant" (t) were about the same for both dimensions, it was decided to include "dominant" in both of them. Note, however that the negative signs for dominance on ESC imply that while being instrumental suggests dominance, being expressive suggests its absence. Finally, the following three items do not appear in Figure 2–4 because, although they were put to respondents, their factor loadings were far too low (.01) for both sexes to be meaningful: submissive, dependent, sentimental.

The highest possible score on the ISC dimension is 12, with a high score meaning low instrumentality and a low score the opposite. For the ESC dimension, the highest score possible was 10, with a low score meaning high expressiveness and a high score the opposite. Because the level of analysis has shifted from structural components of roles to components of self-perception, the question arises as to how the five hypotheses used in connection with role orientations might apply to the self-concept dimensions. In the case of the gender variable, for instance, past literature would lead us to expect that men would rank higher than women on ISC but lower than women on ESC. As far as the remaining four variables are concerned, the literature is less clear and thus theoretical expectations are harder to formulate. Therefore, we shall not try to state any predictions regarding them, but simply observe what patterns emerge.

SEX

As Table 2–3 reveals, men at every comparison except one (college students), rank as more instrumental (ISC) than women. Although that part of our expectation regarding the effects of sex are confirmed, the other is not. That is, if we examine the ESC columns, we find no significant differences (except for young couples) between men and women in their levels of expressiveness. Apparently, therefore, married men and women maintain approximately the same levels of expressiveness or nurturance, but married men add to these characteristics a greater level of instrumentality than do married women. It is not that the latter are not instrumental, but rather that, as a whole, they seem to be less oriented in that direction than men. Whether the lack of meaningful differences between male and female college students on either orientation portends movement toward greater convergence between the sexes in these self-concepts is as yet impossible to tell.

AGE

There are no significant differences at all between younger and older married persons over the ISC dimension. Hence, perceived instrumentality appears not to change with age for either men or women, blacks or whites, Catholics or non-Catholics. On the other side, Table 2–3 presents clear evidence that expressiveness increases with age for each of these categories (except for Catholic men). We cannot be certain whether older persons were simply more expressive all their lives or have "mellowed" and become more nurturant with time. Likewise, only a longitudinal study could determine whether those who are currently young will, over time, continue to perceive themselves at their present levels of expressiveness or will move in the direction of more positive nurturance. All we may now conclude are current differences by age.

RACE

In comparisons between the mean scores of young black men and both young non-Catholic men and young Catholic men (Table 2–3), we find that in both instances black men perceive themselves as significantly more instrumental than white men.[46] The same finding emerges for both comparisons among older men: Blacks are more strongly instrumental than whites.[47] No differences appear, however, on the ESC dimension. Among women, blacks continue to score more strongly instrumental at all four comparisons,[48] and what is more, they rank as more positively expressive in three of the four comparisons.[49]

It is not completely clear why blacks should consistently perceive themselves as so much more instrumental than whites. It may be that black persons are responding more strongly than whites to the demands of an achievement-oriented society and its occupational system. As blacks have been deprived so long by educational and economic discrimination and because there are relatively more opportunities open to them now than before, they may have learned or be adopting personality patterns that stress high levels of ambition, aggressiveness, creativity, and energy. Because they have been forced to be "number two" for so long, they may now in effect be "trying harder." It should be clear that there is nothing intrinsically "white" about the ISC pattern, anymore than it is inherently "masculine." These orientations possess neither gender nor race—they are simply the kinds of personality orientations requisite to achievement for any person in modern society, irrespective of sex or race.

The almost equally pervasive evidence for greater black female expressiveness is more difficult to explain. Perhaps there is a kind of unconscious tendency toward balance of the two types of personality dimensions among black women. If their socialization and life-situations as blacks has influenced them to become strongly instrumental—or task and goal-oriented—their basic socialization as women may also have instilled a greater sense of "need" than white women have to balance out these characteristics with a high degree of expressiveness, nurturance, person-orientation, and so on.

RELIGION

A possible hypothesis that one might bring to an examination of personality differences between non-Catholics and Catholics is that the latter might be less instrumental. There was some literature to suggest that Catholics may be less "keyed in" to certain implications of the "Protestant ethic," especially as they might pertain to familial and occupational behaviors (Lenski, 1961). However, when we compare Catholics with non-Catholics—young and older, men and women—we find no significant differences in terms of the ISC dimension. With respect to expressiveness, the only one of the four comparisons that is significant is for young men: Catholic men show a more positive ESC score than non-Catholics.[50] It would thus appear that religion makes virtually no difference over these self-concept orientations. The Protestant ethic or other similar notions notwithstanding, Catholics and non-Catholics seem very much alike in their levels of instrumentality and expressiveness.

EDUCATION

One could predict that better educated persons might show higher ISC scores, first because it takes greater instrumentality to complete high school and go on to the rigors of college and second because the advanced training itself should in turn stimulate greater levels of instrumentality, i.e., increase the strength of those characteristics that make up the ISC dimension. Table 2–4 shows that better-educated husbands and wives do consistently possess stronger ISC scores than those with less training. However, among men, only for non-Catholics (young and older) are the differences significant. Among women the differences are significant only for blacks (young and old).

Therefore, we must modify our expectation somewhat and conclude that education and instrumentality are positively related to some degree, but not consistently for all color, sex, and age groups. Further modification comes from the additional finding (alluded to previously) that male students (both Catholics and non-Catholics) rank as considerably less instrumental than comparably educated married men.[51] (No such differences emerge between well-educated single and married women.) It may be that once these young men leave college and enter the "real (occupational) world" their levels of instrumentality will increase. For now, they represent an important exception to the education-ISC link.

As far as the ESC dimension is concerned, Table 2–4 indicates that education seems to make no consistent or patterned difference; and the same is true when we make comparisons with college students. Moreover, there is no apparent theoretical reason why we should expect such differences; and thus we may conclude that although education does discriminate to a degree in terms of ISC, it does not do so with respect to ESC.

RECAP

These five variables seem to apply to perceptions of self-concept in the following ways: Men have more instrumental self-perceptions than women, but both sexes appear to be equally expressive. Older persons are more expressive than younger persons, but both age groups are similar in their instrumentality. Blacks are consistently more instrumental than whites, and black women give some indication of more positive expressiveness than white women. Religion does not seem to discriminate at all over either self-concept orientation. Finally, those with more education appear somewhat more instrumental than those with less, but expressiveness does not vary significantly by educational attainment.

In the following chapters, these two personality variables will be used along with the previously discussed role dimensions to see what they might add to our understanding of fertility control. Given the past history of fertility research in which personality variables have in general produced only slight payoff (Westoff *et al.*, 1961, 1963), it will be interesting and important to see what significance, if any, these kinds of personality variables will have.

Evaluation of Wife Abilities

The final set of items used in the interview schedule to try to apprehend orientations toward the behaviors of married women were also borrowed from the work of Alice Rossi (1970). This index appears in Figure 2–5, labeled "ability evaluation" (AE) of wives. Women were asked to evaluate themselves on each item as "very good," "average," or "poor." Men were asked to do the same for their own wives. The underlying rationale for these kinds of items is to assess the perceptions that wives have (and that husbands have of their wives) of abilities and skills in a variety of specific areas. Items a, b, and c are capabilities linked to the home; items d, e, f, g, and h are broader and could apply either outside or inside the home but are perhaps less pertinent to the latter sphere. Hence these items differ from the three sets of wife, husband, and mother role items in that they are not norms that structure role behavior. Instead, they are closer (but not identical) to the self-concept items just discussed in that they represent self-evaluations (or perceptions)—in this instance, not of personality characteristics but of abilities to execute specific types of tasks or skills. This dimension is defined as the degree of perceived skill-competence of wives.

These eight items were factor-analyzed separately for men and women to determine if any distinct dimensions might emerge. It had been thought beforehand that the first three or four items might cluster together separately from the last four or five, which might also cluster together. However, in spite of using several different factor analytic techniques, the items continued to cluster for both sexes in one single dimension. Because of this apparent unidimensionality, rotation of items was not possible, and the factor loadings reported in Figure 2–5 represent an unrotated factor matrix.[52]

The finding that these eight items are so persistently unidimensional leads us to conclude that wives do not see themselves, nor do husbands see their wives, as having distinct sets of competencies. Instead, it would appear that most women have certain levels of capabilities in strictly

FIGURE 2-5. Ability Evaluation of Wives, (AE) with Factor Loadings (Unrotated)

AE Dimension	Men	Women
a. Cooking, budgeting, home management	.55	.46
b. Entertaining, being a good hostess	.47	.46
c. Taking care of and understanding children	.39	.37
d. Knowledge and appreciation of literature, music, and art	.44	.47
e. Knowledge and experience necessary to hold a job now or later	.42	.43
f. Ability to organize things	.60	.58
g. Intellectual ability	.64	.60
h. Ability to handle a number of responsibilities	.67	.58

domestic activities at the same time that they possess comparable levels of skills in areas that could enable them to interact beyond domestic confines.

Thus, women appear to see themselves (and to be seen by husbands) as relatively capable over a broad unidimensional range of task performance. There does not seem to exist a dimension of expertise which applies to domestic skills and a distinct dimension applicable to extra-domestic skills. To the extent, therefore, that some wives may be more modern-oriented and some wives more traditional than others in their role orientations, this divergence does not appear to be reflected by distinct spheres of task performance in which the more modern are more capable in extra-domestic concerns and the more traditional excel in domestic behaviors. Obviously, unidimensionality does not imply that some women might not score higher on certain AE items and lower on others. Nor does it imply that for women role modernity and skill capabilities might not be positively associated. The highest possible score on the AE dimension is 16, with a high score implying a poor evaluation and a low score a more positive evaluation.

The Five Demographic Characteristics

Tables 2–3 and 2–4 present in straightforward fashion the impacts of sex, age, race, religion, and education on the AE dimension. It is therefore sufficient merely to summarize these findings. Women rank themselves lower on the AE dimension than husbands tend to rank their own wives. Too, age and religion appear to have no consistently meaningful impact on these kinds of evaluations. Third, black women rank themselves higher on this dimension than do white women, but race does not distinguish male evaluations of their wives. Finally, education is positively related to AE scores: Wives and husbands possess more positive evaluations the more years of training they have had.

The Social Context of Sex Role Learning

Reference was made earlier to literature that indicates that sex role orientations are formed quite early in the life of the child, some years prior to heterosexual involvement and marriage. Lipman-Blumen's report (1972) is one of the few efforts that seeks to link childhood experiences to normative aspects of sex role, the aspect which is our central concern. (See also Kammeyer, 1964, 1966.) Lipman-Blumen found that the usual measures of social status—parents' income, education, or occupation—had no noticeable effect on the sex role ideologies of the women in her sample.

However, it is likely that her sample was skewed upward in terms of social class background, as it consisted exclusively of wives of graduate students in the Boston area. Nonetheless, in spite of status variables having no effect on sex role, she did discover that patterns of parent–child interaction within their families of orientation did affect the wives' sex-role orientations.

Unfortunately, though we had originally planned to do so, constraints of interview schedule length made it impossible to retain items designed to measure parent–child interaction. Nevertheless, if we take the five variables (sex, age, religion, race, and education) we have just examined and try to summarize their effects, we may be able to emerge with a better grasp of the structural context that influences sex role learning. Future research would then need to examine parent–child interaction within this structural context.

First off, then, let us summarize differences by sex. When we defined role modernity as preference for greater individualism for wives, we found that women were more modern on the more extreme SA (self-actualization) dimension than were men, but differences on the TW (traditional wife) dimension were minimal. Turning from wife role to husband role dimensions, we found that husbands were actually more modern than were wives. When it came to maternal role dimensions, women emerged as more modern or individualistic on the TM (traditional mother) dimension, but husbands were more modern or secular on the RLM dimension (religious legitimation of motherhood). Turning from normative role structures to self-concept, it appears that men are more instrumental than women and that both are equally expressive. With respect, finally, to the AE dimension (wives' abilities), husbands tend to rank their wives higher than wives rank themselves.

Second, younger persons are more modern than older persons on both aspects of the wife position; age seems to make little difference when it comes to husband roles; but younger men do tend to be less traditional than older men with regard to maternal roles. Expressiveness seems to increase with age, but instrumentality does not; and age has no relationship to AE rankings.

Third, whites are somewhat less traditional than blacks on the TW dimension, but blacks are strongly more modern on the SA aspect of the wife position. Blacks are generally less traditional on the husband roles, but not much different than whites in terms of the maternal roles. Instrumentality is much more strongly in evidence among blacks than whites, and black women generally seem more expressive than white women. Black women also evaluate themselves in much more positive AE terms than do white women.

Fourth, religion has only minimal effect when it comes to wife role orientations, but when it comes to husband roles, Catholics are more traditional than non-Catholics. Catholics are also more traditional or less secular on the RLM dimension, but religion has no consequence on the self-concept or AE orientations.

Finally, persons who had at least some college education tended to be more modern on both aspects of the wife position, on the PHA (problematic husband alterations)and the TH (traditional husband) role dimensions, and on both aspects of maternal position behaviors. Greater education was also linked with stronger instrumentality and more positive AE rankings.

This discussion gives us some sense of the relative importance of sex, age, race, religion, and education in shaping sex role orientations and self-perceptions. Moreover, Tables 2–5, and 2–6 show for men and for women the intercorrelations among the several variables in question.[53] In subsequent chapters we shall divide the sample more finely by age, religion, race, and wife employment, as well as sex; and at that point we shall elaborate more fully on the various relationships among these sets of variables. One point worthy of mention here, however, is that the several role and perception variables are interconnected. Women, for example, who rank themselves in more positive AE terms are also more SA-modern. SA modernity is linked with PHA modernity, which is linked with TM modernity, and so forth. While we shall explore the matter more fully as we go on, it is possible to conceive of marital role modernity as a kind of general construct measured by these less abstract and more specific role and perception dimensions. Thus when we refer to sex role modernity in general, we have in mind an overall syndrome which contains numerous and related segments such as these ten dimensions, and very likely additional elements as well. We would expect that, in the "real world," persons who are more or less modern on one role dimension would rank comparably in terms of their relative modernity over certain other dimensions as well. (Kammeyer, 1964).

Conclusion

This chapter has reviewed those parts of the sex role literature pertinent to the investigation of linkages between gender roles and fertility control. Also described are the theoretical rationales and empirical bases for our measures of sex roles, self-concept, and perceptions of wives' task-capabilities that shall be employed in subsequent chapters. We also introduced the approach we shall follow in attempting to link sex role norms and fertility control within a cost-reward framework. Utilization of the five factors of age, sex, race, religion, and education in connection with the ten role and self-perception dimensions provided leverage in understanding the conditions under which orientations toward modernity (or greater individualism) develop.

The major point to keep in mind is the assumption that these ten orientations were largely formed prior to marriage and family formation. Nevertheless the possibility was raised that subsequent marital events could alter the content of these orientations, and we shall discuss that matter fully in succeeding chapters.

Notes

1. See for example, Holter 1970; Rossi 1970; Scanzoni 1972; Steinmann, et al., 1968.
2. For a detailed description of the GAF and Princeton Studies, see Ryder and Westoff, 1971, pp. 3–6. A broad survey of the fertility literature is in Pohlman, 1969.
3. This literature is reviewed in Scanzoni, 1972.
4. This literature is reviewed in Scanzoni, 1971.
5. Martha McMurry and Ellen Liff participated fully in the construction of items in Figures 2–1 through 2–5. Professor Rossi generously provided instruments used in her earlier studies.
6. The type of factor analysis used in all five instances is what Nie *et al.* (1970:220) label as "the most universally accepted factoring method" or "principal factoring with iteration." The number of factors extracted is determined by the number of factors with an eigenvalue greater than or equal to 1.0; the diagonals of the correlation matrix are initially replaced by squared multiple correlations; the iteration is stopped if the convergence reaches the .001 criterion; the maximum number of iterations is 25. The method of rotation used was an orthogonal-varimax technique which simplifies the columns of the factor matrix. This is the rotation method which is evidently also most widely used by social scientists. (Nie *et al.*, 1970:224). Oblique rotational methods were also employed to determine whether they would produce any meaningfully different clusterings of items but they did not. Instead the results were virtually identical to what appears in Figures 2–1 to 2–5.
7. For each set of items that clustered together the values of each item were added to form an additive or sum scale. (Nie *et al.*, 1970:68–69).
8. For women, TW accounted for 19% of explained variance; SA for 7%. For men, TW = 18%; SA = 7%.
9. n's: Young non-Catholic men = 383; young non-Catholic women = 373; older non-Catholic men = 397; older non-Catholic women = 344. Young Catholic men = 161; young Catholic women = 217; older Catholic men = 206; older Catholic women = 189. Young black men = 126; young black women = 138. Older black men = 233; older black women = 329.

10. n's: non-Catholic males = 130; non-Catholic females = 160; Catholic males = 37; Catholic females = 39.

11. n's: Young couples: men = 243; women = 243. Older couples: men = 156; women = 156.

12. Separate factor analyses for students produced dimensions very similar to those that emerged for married adults.

13. Mason and Bumpass (1973), however, did not find evidence of change by age in sex role "attitudes" among their sample.

14. $p < .001$

15. $p < .001$

16. $p < .001; p < .001; p < .001; p < .001$

17. $p < .001; p < .001; p < .001; p < .001$

18. $p < .05$

19. $p < .05$

20. n's: Young non-Catholic men: high education = 180, low = 203; women: high = 88, low = 285. Older non-Catholic men: high education = 130, low = 267; women: high = 76, low = 268. Young Catholic men: high education = 65, low = 96; women: high = 50, low = 167. Older Catholic men: high education = 69, low = 137; women: high = 46, low = 143. Young black men: high education = 35, low = 91; women: high = 27, low = 111. Older black men: high education = 43, low = 190; women: high = 45, low = 284.

21. $p < .05; p < .05$

22. As above, response categories were "strongly agree," etc. Variance explained for women: PHA = 18%; IE = 7%; TH = 4%. Men: PHA = 18%; IE = 6%; TH = 4%.

23. $p < .001$

24. $p < .05; p < .05$; no differences on the IE dimension.

25. $p < .001; p < .05; p < .05$

26. $p < .05; p < .05$

27. $p < .05; p < .05$

28. $p < .05; p < .05; p < .01; p < .01$

29. $p < .05$

30. $p < .01$

31. $p < .05$

32. $p < .001$

33. $p < .001$

34. $p < .05; p < .05$

35. Variance explained for women: RLM = 18%; TM = 10%. For men: RLM = 19%; TM = 12%.

36. $p < .05$

37. $p < .01$

38. $p < .01$; $p < .001$
39. $p < .001$
40. $p < .01$; $p < .01$
41. $p < .01$
42. $p < .01$; $p < .01$; $p < .01$; $p < .01$
43. $p < .05$
44. Some "role theorists" might prefer to think of role norms as "social psychological" as well, but the perspective here is based on that tradition which prefers to view norms as elements of social organization or social structure (see Bertrand, 1972).
45. Variance explained for women: ISC = 10%; ESC = 6%. For men: ISC = 8%; ESC = 5%.
46. $p < .01$; $p < .01$
47. $p < .01$; $p < .01$
48. $p < .05$; $p < .01$; $p < .05$; $p < .01$
49. $p < .01$; $p < .05$; $p < .05$
50. $p < .01$
51. $p < .05$; $p < .05$
52. Variance explained for women = 26%; for men = 29%.
53. In Tables 2–5 and 2–6 and in subsequent tables in Chapters Three, Four, and Five, the signs of the role modernity dimensions are always interpreted in positive fashion, for consistency and clarity of understanding. So in spite of the coding described earlier in which modernity was sometimes reflected in low scores and other times in high scores, the signs shall henceforth be read consistently as reflecting a "positive" characteristic.

Chapter 3. Sex Roles and Birth Intentions

THE PURPOSE OF THIS CHAPTER is to seek to establish connections between the sex role norms and self-perceptions identified in Chapter Two and the number of children persons intend to have. The full-time employment of wives and related factors will also be examined for their influence on the intended number of children. The consequences of sex role norms will be examined separately for non-Catholics, Catholics, and blacks. In addition each category of women will be further subdivided by employment and education in an effort to test the effects of sex role norms in a variety of situational contexts. Finally, a flow-chart model is developed to show presumed paths of influence among a number of variables, most central of which are sex role norms and birth intentions.

Measuring Orientations Toward Childbearing

A useful discussion of the conceptual and empirical distinctions and similarities among various measures of birth orientations appears in Ryder and Westoff (1971:19–35). Their analyses show that when comparisons are made between the number of children intended and the number expected, "the absolute differences are very small . . . the number expected and the number intended are very much alike on both an individual and an aggregate basis." This "empirical redundancy" along with indications that number intended possesses "greater conceptual purity" than number expected led them to place the major focus of the analysis of their 1965 data on the former variable.

In the interview schedule designed for their 1970 National Fertility Survey, questions pertaining to birth expectations were dropped entirely, and items pertaining to intentions were retained. Through the kindness of Professor Ryder, we were given access to the 1970 instrument, and we followed their practice of measuring intentions, not expectations. Ryder and Westoff define birth intentions (or total number of children intended) "as the sum of the respondent's current parity and the additional children she said she intended to have. 'Current parity' is defined . . . as the total number of previous live births to the respondent, plus one if the respondent was currently pregnant."

National census data from June 1971 (the same month that our sample survey commenced), showed that white wives 18 to 24 years old expected 2.4 children (*Current Population Reports*, P-20, No. 232). Black wives in this age cohort expected 2.6 children, which difference could have been due, the investigators say, to "sampling variability." Assuming as do Ryder and Westoff that "expectations" and "intentions" are conceptually indistinguishable, those figures may be compared with birth intentions for 18- to 24-year-old persons in our sample.

Table 3–1 shows that white wives 18 to 24 in our sample intend to have somewhat more children (2.6) than those from the national sample. The slight difference between young wives in our region compared to the national sample may be due to the fact that our sample includes only wives with husbands present. Wives whose husbands are not present (included in the national sample) have been shown to have fewer children and may also intend to have fewer children than wives from intact marriages (Lauriat, 1969). The table also reveals that white non-Catholics intend to have fewer children than white Catholics and that this finding holds for both sexes. Therefore, in spite of trends showing increasing convergence between Catholics and non-Catholics with regard to fertility control, these data indicate the persistence of some differences in the traditional direction.

Interestingly, 18- to 24-year-old black women in our sample intend to have slightly fewer children than white wives, but younger black husbands intend to have slightly more than younger white husbands. The 2.6 figure for young black wives in our sample puts them on a par with birth expectations for young black wives nationally. Finally, while actual differences are not great, there is a consistent pattern of younger (18 to 24) husbands (blacks and whites; Catholics and non-Catholics) intending to have slightly more children than younger wives.

Overall, therefore, it would appear that younger wives in our sample share the same level of birth intentions held by wives nationally. The census report from which the national figures were drawn makes the important point that birth expectations of 18- to 24-year-old females have steadily declined from a figure of 3.2 in 1955 to what they are now (*Current Population Reports*, P-20, No. 232). Several kinds of explanations have been offered for this long-term decline in expectations and in actual births (*Current Population Reports*, P-20, No. 263). However, no one explanation is sufficient to account for the phenomenon. A complementary explanation may be advanced, based on the discussion of Chapters One and Two. Certain of the literature cited there suggested that the great American baby-boom of the fifties may in part have been a function of revived traditionalism in womens' roles. The bearing of and caring for children may have become an especially sought-for and highly prized objective. Alternative rewards such as individualistic gratifications may for many women have become by comparison much less significant.

The sixties saw a renewal of emphasis on the individualism of women. This emphasis became more explicit in the latter part of the decade when many wives who were 18 to 24 in 1971 had commenced their marriages. It is not that most wives consciously embrace "women's liberation" or even support many of the movement's objectives, much less participate actively in efforts to attain them. Whether or not most women are in sympathy with the Movement, however, there may well be seeping into the normative structure of increasing numbers of American women (and some men) the notion that besides the gratifications intrinsic to being a wife and mother, there are other kinds of gratifications open to women (Gardner, 1974). These rewards are not encompassed solely by the dollars that an occupation offers, but equally and perhaps more importantly by achievement orientations inherent in the opportunity structure. That is, occupational endeavor remains, in our society, the most highly valued and rewarded form of behavior—more so even than motherhood. Just as blacks as a minority group have been excluded from these rewards, so have women been excluded as another type of minority group. Increasingly, women just as blacks may be gravitating towards these individualistic rewards, and one consequence of this movement may be relatively less emphasis on familial rewards or children. (See Bumpass, 1973, for a more extended discussion of these issues.)

Recall from the data of Chapter Two that younger persons were generally more modern-oriented than older persons. As a result of earlier socialization as well as other forces in the larger social structure, American society, therefore, may be undergoing a very gradual change in the structures of sex roles. Concomitant with this is a change in the level of birth expectations and intentions. Our suggestion is that these two changes—so highly significant for the larger society—are linked together and that indeed the latter may in part be an outcome of the former.

Table 3–1 also presents the figures for number of children wanted. The latter measure is based on a technique devised by Bumpass and Westoff (1970), in which any children described by the respondent as "unwanted" are subtracted from the total number of children they intend to have. When Ryder and Westoff applied this technique to their data on birth intentions, they found consistent evidence that wives wanted fewer children than they intended to have or desired (1971:92–95). Table 3–1 shows that our data reveal the same pattern for both wives and husbands, and that the pattern becomes more evident with age.

Finally, Table 3–1 presents a third measure of birth orientations—birth desires. As Ryder and Westoff note (1971:26–27), there is an unfortunate lack of comparability among studies which use varying measures of this particular dimension of birth orientations, but the measure we used has appeared often in various KAP (knowledge, attitudes, practice of birth control) studies around the world (Population Council, 1970): "If you and your (husband-wife) were starting married life all over again and could have any number of children you wanted, how many would you like to have in all?"

Comparing desires with intentions we find that women are more consistent than men in desiring more children than they actually intend to have. The measure of birth desires utilized here may reflect a tendency toward wistfulness and wish-orientation rather than reality. It may reflect a situation in which the cost factors (all varieties) of children are taken into account only minimally. If costs have only minimal significance, then it is possible to seek more children. But if costs have greater significance, as they probably do in the intentions measure (as intentions are built on the experience of actual parity and its attendant costs), then the number of children sought is likely to be lower.

Of these three measures of birth orientations, we shall focus on *intentions*. One reason for this choice is its comparability with data collected from national samples, both by the Census Bureau and with data collected in earlier sample surveys such as the GAF and Princeton studies (Ryder and Westoff, 1971). A second related and highly important reason is the demonstrated reliability of this kind of measure to predict completed family size. In particular, the Princeton studies involved a panel design in which many of the same respondents who had been interviewed at one point in time were again interviewed several years later. The investigators report that "the strongest predictor of fertility at second interview is the number of children desired at first interview . . ." (Westoff *et al.*, 1963:67). The wording of the item used in the Princeton studies was how many children were wanted altogether, counting the number existing at the time (Bumpass and Westoff, 1970:42). Thus, although the Princeton item is not exactly comparable with the Ryder-Westoff measure of *intentions*, it is reasonably close.

Besides problems in wording comparability of various items used over the years to measure birth orientations (Ryder and Westoff, 1971:38–49), there is the additional issue of how stable these verbal orientations are in predicting completed family size. Orientations have tended to shift over the course of the life cycle, especially in response to unwanted pregnancies (Bumpass and Westoff, 1970). Nevertheless, as cited before, birth orientations have been shown to be extremely useful in indicating what later parity will be. A more recent study which arrived at the same conclusion was carried out by Wilson and Bumpass (1973). One of the great benefits of a longitudinal study would be to show how role modernity affects constancy of these orientations over time. We would expect, for instance, that persons who commence marriage with greater modernity and lower birth orientations are more likely to retain lower orientations than those who begin with greater role traditionalism. In any case, given the limitations of a cross-sectional approach to explaining intentions the analyses of this chapter are based on the notion that birth intentions do have some degree of influence on eventual completed family size. Ryder indicates that "there is no prima facie case that people have any reproductive target at all, in the sense of a number they intend to end up with" (1973:504). A panel study focused on ongoing processes would tell us a great deal about the ways in which birth intentions interact with numerous situational factors to account for actual parity.

It may very well be that in the past women were more lax or fuzzy about reproductive targets than today's younger women who are currently in the early childbearing period. In prior years the costs of an additional child or children were linked to individualistic aspirations by relatively few women. Today the number of women who are aware of such costs, while still comparatively small, may be increasing. In the past an additional child or two had little significant impact on the life styles of wives, as their lives remained centered around husband and children. To the degree that more individualistic life styles are sought for by greater numbers of younger wives, to that extent will the issue of number of intended children take on increased significance and salience.

Veevers, for example, in a study of couples who are voluntarily childless, reports that "their marriages are characterized by very egalitarian sex roles, with an orientation in which the husband and wife are considered to be of equal value to the relationship, with equal levels of authority and equal levels of competence" (1974). Nationally only about 4% to 5% of young white and black wives in 1973 expected to have no children (*Current Population Reports*, P-20, No. 254). Similar proportions appeared in our sample for both sexes of both races. A 1967 census survey showed that at that time the proportion of women expecting no births was around 1% or less. In spite of this shift upward between 1967 and 1973, it is abundantly clear that the vast majority of wives continue to opt for one or two (and sometimes more) children. However, the phenomenon of increased preferences for voluntary childlessness tied to preferences for wife autonomy serves to underscore the point that the notion of a reproductive target may not be outmoded. Indeed, among younger women it may hold greater significance for eventual family size than was perhaps true in the past. Therefore, family size intentions remains an important variable to explain, and that is the task of this chapter.

Norms of White Non-Catholic Wives

DIFFERENCES BY FULL-TIME EMPLOYMENT

The left-hand panel of Table 3–2 compares white non-Catholic wives aged 18 to 29 who do work full time with those who do not, in terms of sex roles, self-perceptions, status, and fertility control variables. By way of reminder, the two roles that are part of the position of wife are labeled "traditional wife" (TW) and "self-actualization" (SA). The three roles that are included under the position of husband are labeled "problematic husband alterations" (PHA), "traditional husband" (TH), and "institutionalized equality" (IE). The position of mother contains two role dimensions: "religious legitimation of motherhood" (RLM) and "traditional mother" (TM). ISC refers to instrumental self-concept, ESC to expressive self-concept, and AE to evaluation of the wife's task and skill capabilities. The data show that working wives are significantly better educated. Furthermore, their husbands also have more education and higher job status than husbands whose wives do not work. In addition working wives are significantly more modern on the TW, SA, IE, RLM, and TM dimensions. They also possess stronger instrumental self-concepts (ISC) and higher AE (ability-evaluation) rankings. Both they and their husbands married later than couples where wives do not work, and they also experienced a longer interval between marriage and the first child. And as much earlier literature has shown, working wives intend, want, desire, and have fewer children. Did currently working wives become less role-traditional after marriage, say, as their having fewer children "permitted" them to work and subsequently become more individualistic? Only a longitudinal study can ascertain these kinds of issues definitively, but as these women are currently fecund the question arises as to why they initially had fewer children. Even more fundamentally, if we take into account the discussion in Chapter Two regarding the formation of sex role norms prior to marriage, plus these data showing differences in marriage age and first-child spacing, certain conclusions at least become strong possibilities.

FACTORS RELATED TO FULL-TIME EMPLOYMENT

Specifically, it is possible to argue that role modernity precedes both employment and fertility decisions. Thus persons who are more individualistically oriented would tend to seek the gratifications of an occupation, as well as to minimize excessive costs related to the bearing of and caring for children. To pursue this further, if we examine all 18- to 29-year-old non-Catholic white women, we find that the strongest correlate (out of the ten role and self-perception dimensions, plus education of both spouses, husband's income, and parity) of full-time employment is parity ($-.39$). But SA modernity is also positively related to employment ($+.26$), as is an instrumental self-concept ($+.20$), AE ranking ($+.24$), and wife education ($+.24$). Did parity "cause" employment, or employment parity? One could argue that SA modernity, education, and AE and ISC perceptions influenced both employment and parity.

Moreover, if we sort on parity and ask among all wives with one child or less ($n = 197$) what is the strongest positive correlate of employment, the answer is SA modernity at .25, followed by education (.24) and AE rank (.23). Thus among wives who have the same number of children, their individualistic orientations, educational attainment, and task abilities are the strongest indicators of the decision to work. If we examine wives with 2 or more children ($n = 174$) the relationships with a positive work decision are more modest (ISC $= .15$, SA modernity $= .14$, TM modernity $= .13$) but in the same direction.

The literature also indicates that besides number of children (parity) being related to employment decisions, the age of the youngest child is also a crucial factor (Cohen, 1969). A young child—especially of pre-school age—is known to impede female entrance into the labor force. In our sample among all younger non-Catholic wives with at least one child, the age of the youngest is indeed correlated with female enjoyment. The younger the child the less likely the wife is to be working ($r = .21$; $n = 131$). Nonetheless, within this very same subset of wives an even stronger correlate of wife employment is IE modernity ($r = .25$). The more strongly that wives prefer an arrangement of "institutionalized equality" between themselves and their husbands, the more likely they are to be working. Conversely, the more IE-traditional they are, the less likely they are to work. And when we put IE and age of youngest child in a regular regression equation along with the socioeconomic and remaining role dimensions, we find that IE modernity shows a beta of .24 in influencing wife employment. By comparison the age variable reveals a beta of .11.[1] Thus it could be argued that among mothers with children, greater modernity on the IE dimension has a more substantial influence on their work decision than does the age of their youngest child. Preferences for egalitarianism on this rather radical role dimension appear to make them more strongly motivated to seek the rewards (and bear the costs) of a full-time job.

By way of balance, however, it could be that employment has contributed towards their becoming more egalitarian. As these wives were not followed over time we cannot be certain that IE modernity preceded instead of followed the work decision. The costs of working plus household and child-care responsibilities may have made them seek for greater benefits from their husbands in the form of concessions to participate more equitably in those responsibilities.

In sum, our cross-sectional data, as well as other similar designs (Holter, 1970), reveal that role norms are at least related to wife employment and may often precede and influence it. To the degree that employment behavior results in lowered fertility (Table 3–2), these norms may have had some impact on family size through employment behavior. Moreover, a recent longitudinal design provides additional support for the impact that norms and attitudes may have on employment. From a national sample of women, "respondents were asked in 1967 how they felt about work outside the home for mothers of children between 6 and 12 years of age . . ." (Dual Careers, p. 39). Respondents were classified as "permissive," "ambivalent," or "opposed" to that behavior. On the basis of a 1969 reinterview of these same women the investigators conclude that "in general the predictive validity of the attitude scale is confirmed" (p. 41). Among those who were in the labor force in 1967, those who were "opposed" were less likely still to be employed in 1969 than those who were "ambivalent." And the latter were less likely to be working than those who were "permissive."

STRUCTURAL CONTEXTS AND BIRTH INTENTIONS

Awareness of the potential effects of situations on role orientations is reflected in Table 3–3. There we find four different situational contexts which could possibly influence the operation of sex role modernity. That is, to the prior discussion that role orientations influence work decisions and that individualism and employment incrementally affect each other, we must add the balancing notions that once in a situation of employment–non-employment, or once education is completed, the particular situation might function to make role orientations more or less salient. In certain contexts role and self-concept may have greater or lesser impact on birth intentions.

In Table 3–3 (and following) the range of variables that was examined for possible correlations with birth intentions included the 10 role and self-concept dimensions, plus husbands' income, education, and job status, age at marriage of husbands and of wives, number of months between marriage age and first child, wife's education, her employment before and after marriage, marital satisfactions, economic satisfactions, and a measure of husband–wife authority. When wives are employed, possible correlations are examined in terms of their own SES, income, husband's perceived reaction to their working, and stated reasons for working. However, in the interests of parsimony and clarity, we shall in each instance present a regular regression equation which contains only the strongest available correlates of birth intentions. This will mean that independent variables may not be the same from table to table and among panels within tables. This of course complicates efforts to utilize what is commonly known as "path analysis." Besides this problem there is a very serious question as to whether a cross-sectional design such as ours could legitimately utilize strict modeling procedures to explain the processes of fertility control. Family size and fertility control are not simple events that are constant over time. Instead they are complex processes in which, for instance, sex role modernity might affect the birth of the first child and the child affect sex role modernity (Ryder, 1973). Nevertheless, we shall as much as possible reason in terms of causal paths of influence (as we already have done in this chapter and in Chapter Two) with the hope that subsequently a valid "path analysis" could be utilized to test our conclusions within the context of a longitudinal study. As we shall see, Figure 3–1 is an attempt to subsume the wide range of numerous possible correlates of birth intentions under a set of concepts arranged in flow-chart fashion. Thus variables that are not important or relatively less important do not appear in the tables. The reader may concentrate on those elements and on the patterns they form which seem best able to account for birth intentions in each situation, and in summary form in Figure 3–1.

Employed Wives

Looking at the upper left panel of Table 3–3, we find that four of the role dimensions are correlated with birth intentions in the expected direction. The more modern or egalitarian or individualistic the wives are, the fewer children they intend to have.[2] All these correlations are stronger than the one with education, and two of them exceed the figure for age at marriage. As marriage age and education increase, birth intentions decrease. These latter relationships are well documented by earlier investigations, and they continue to persist at the national level (*Current Population Reports*, P-20, No. 263). As measured by betas, the relative predictive power of marriage age is strongest, followed closely by that of TM modernity. The SA and PHA dimensions follow more modestly behind. Moreover, TM and SA together account for 12% of the total explained variance, as against 7% for marriage age.

It would thus appear that wives in this particular situational context do provide evidence that preferences for individualistic rewards and egalitarian role structures depress orientations toward children or familistic rewards. The more they seek the former kinds of gratifications, the less they seek the latter. Furthermore, the total set of influences affecting birth intentions are all highly interrelated. For example, education is strongly related positively to TW ($r = .41$) and also correlated with PHA (.21) and TM (.17).

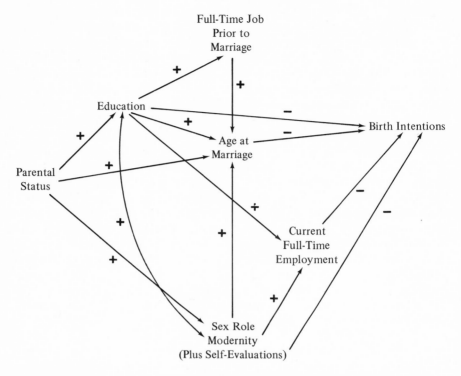

FIGURE 3-1. Flow Chart Showing Factors That Influence Birth Intentions for Wives Aged 18–29

Influences on Age at Marriage

In addition, education is for these wives by far the single strongest predictor of age at marriage as Table 3–4 reveals. Next in 'importance is having had a full-time job prior to marriage. And while AE rankings, role dimensions, and status background factors reveal only modest betas, they are all correlated with marriage age. In short, higher status background, more years of education, working prior to marriage, rating higher in terms of task performance, and being more sex role modern—all tend to delay the age at marriage. The latter variable can be conceptualized as describing the commencement of the experience of marital rewards or gratifications. Thus we may say that the rewards of education and preferences for correlated individualistic rewards (sex role dimensions) tend to delay the onset of marital-type rewards. Furthermore there are links between the mother's education and the wife's own education (r = .54), their AE rankings (r = .37), and their RLM and TW modernity (r's = .35 and .31). In short, working wives from higher status homes are better educated, more task-capable and more role modern.

Figure 3–1 ties together in flow chart fashion the major variables we have discussed so far. We begin with parental socioeconomic status and trace its positive effects on education, on sex roles, and on task-performance evaluation. Education and sex role norms are mutually reinforcing, and both of them presumably influence delay of marriage, as does parental status. (Wives who receive greater status benefits from parents are more likely to defer marital rewards.) Interestingly, premarital full-time employment, which also delays marriage age, is linked with no other variables among these particular wives (though among nonworking wives it is related to education). Approximately two thirds of all households in the sample report that the wife worked full time prior to marriage. This behavior is evidently quite common, and its predictors difficult to isolate. Nevertheless its consequences for deferring marriage are quite apparent. One could hypothesize that those women least likely to work before marriage are those who become pregnant while still in school or very shortly thereafter and marry relatively quickly, thus allowing little time ,energy, motivation, or opportunity to work while still single (Kantner and Zelnik, 1972, 1973).

Next in Figure 3–1 we conclude that sex role modernity (along with education) affects current work decisions which probably depress birth intentions. Education, marriage age, and sex role norms (plus AE all tend to depress birth intentions as well.

In sum, preferences for the gratification of having children are inverse to a variety of socioeconomic variables, variables that measure willingness to defer marital gratifications, and variables that assess preference for the individualistic gratifications inherent in more egalitarian sex roles. The least explored of these factors—sex role norms—tends to have substantial direct impact on birth intentions, as well as being highly interrelated with these other, more well-known influences. The next question then becomes, to what degree does the model of Figure 3–1 apply to wives in a situational context of nonemployment?

Nonemployed Wives

The upper right panel of Table 3–3 reveals that the strongest correlates of fewer children intended are more education and later age at marriage, followed by ISC and TW. As with working wives, we find interconnections between education and role modernity (r's: TW = .28; RLM = .34). And if we glance at the comparable panel in Table 3–4 we can see how both these role dimensions are linked with a later age at marriage.

However, in predicting the lower birth intentions of nonworking wives, the betas suggest it is the wife's instrumental self-concept (ISC) that carries the strongest direct influence. Clarkson *et al.* (1970) report that a similar measure is related to actual lowered parity. In any case it appears that even though these wives are not working, their degree of instrumentality has implications for future behaviors. That is, wives who define themselves as more "active," "competitive," "energetic," and the like may be anticipating future entry (or reentry) into the labor force. Or they may have other kinds of individualistic pursuits in mind for which a larger number of children would pose unacceptable costs. Conversely, wives who are less "hard-driving," "self-confident," "aggressive," and the like may perceive fewer current or future alternatives to the gratifications of childbearing and caring.

Among wives in this context the ISC dimension does not correlate with sex role norms or with education, but it does relate strongly to AE ($r = .52$). Wives who possess more of an instrumental self-image in general also evaluate themselves as more capable in both household and occupational tasks. To rank as more task-capable by itself does not seem to stimulate reduced birth intentions. But among those wives for whom it exists in combination with an instrumental self-concept, task-capability may have some effect. Perceptions that they actually can do things well may operate through ISC to depress the potential costs of enlarged families. After ISC, later marriage age and RLM modernity are next in their effects on birth intentions.

Age at Marriage

Table 3–4 reveals that education is once more the most potent influence by far on deferred marriage. As we have seen, education is related to the two sex role dimensions in the table (also to TH and AE, r's = .22, .29), and of course to mother's education ($r = .37$). Finally mother's education has evidently influenced more egalitarian sex role norms (r's: RLM = .25, TW = .23) as has father's SES (TW = .25, TM = .24). Working before marriage again delays marriage age, only this time we find it to be linked positively to more years of schooling ($r = .26$).

Thus in Figure 3–1 we would need to add an arrow from education to "premarital job" for wives in this situation. In addition we would need to display the effects of ISC on birth intentions. (We include it under "sex role modernity.") The left-hand segments of the model seem to apply equally well to both working and nonworking wives, except that for the latter the parental status carries no direct impact on marriage age. Moreover, the direct effects of sex role norms on birth intentions seems to be comparatively less for wives in this second context. It may be that because they are not currently employed sex role norms are less salient and significant in affecting birth orientations. Conversely, for employed wives, issues of relative rewards and costs in the home and on the job "cause" marital role egalitarianism to be that much more significant and salient. A panel study would probably show both that both kinds of causal processes occur within the same marriages at sequential points during the early years of childbearing. However, as Table 3–2 revealed, these nonworking wives have lower status, are more role traditional, and were married earlier than their working counterparts. For these reasons, therefore, most of the currently nonworking wives will probably end up with more children than those now employed.

Low-to-Average Education

The lower left panel of Table 3–3 also reveals a very modest link between sex role norms and birth intentions. The correlation of TM with intentions is below that for sex roles in any of the remaining panels. The strongest influences on depressed intentions are age at marriage and a longer spacing interval between marriage and the first child. Delaying discussion of the latter variable until Chapter Four, we note from Table 3–4 that among wives in this context premarital employment is the strongest determinant of a later marriage age. As with currently employed wives we found no correlates of that premarital behavior. Greater education on the part of their husbands is also related to later marriage, as is higher self-evaluation on the AE dimension.

Within the context of low-to-average education, therefore, the model of Figure 3–1 applies with perhaps less force than it did in the nonemployment context, and certainly much less than for working wives. Table 2–2 revealed that less-educated wives are substantially more sex role traditional than those who are better trained. Questions of individualistic gratifications, egalitarian sex roles in marriage, and the enhancements of those gratifications and behaviors through depressed childbearing are much more muted than, say, in the lower right panels of Tables 3–3 and 3–4. Although the data reveal that in this situation such linkages are not totally absent, they appear to be relatively weak. Wives who find themselves in a social context of "low to average" education are less likely to seek very strongly for individualistic rewards or more modern sex roles either before or after marriage. Consequently, there is somewhat less motivation to restrict the relatively accessible and satisfying alternative benefits of children.

High Education

In decisive contrast, the lower right panel of Table 3–3 reveals that five of the seven sex role dimensions are strongly correlated with reduced birth intentions. One of them (TW) reveals a substantial beta weight in influencing the number of children intended by these highly educated women. TW by itself accounts for 22% of the explained variance. A second variable—marriage age—continues to predict lower birth intentions in this context as it has in the former ones, but Table 3–4 reveals that the strongest predictor of marriage age is TM modernity.

Two related conclusions stand out regarding women who have high education. First, the effects of sex role norms are more evident in this context than in any of the others. In terms of the consequences for marriage age and birth intentions, the evidence here is quite strong that wives who are modern, individualistic, and egalitarian are more willing to defer the gratifications of marriage and also to limit the quantity of familistic gratifications. Second, although these well-educated wives in general are less sex role traditional than those with less schooling, there does exist some role variation among them. Those who are less individualistic will marry relatively sooner and have comparatively more children. A recent census report projects "that women under 30 with a college education may fall short of replacing themselves" (*Current Population Reports*, P-20, No. 254, page 2). Correspondingly, our data suggest that college women who are most egalitarian in terms of sex role norms may be the ones most likely to fail to reproduce themselves, whereas those who are more traditional will probably have somewhat larger numbers of children.

Table 3–3 also reveals variation among educated wives in terms of their husbands' education and whether or not they are currently employed: more spouse education and present employment result in lower birth intentions. Two additional factors that have not appeared before are also correlated with depressed birth orientations. The first of these is labeled primary relations (PR), or an index of wives' perceived satisfaction with husband–wife companionship and with sexual gratifications.[3] The table shows that the more satisfaction wives report with their primary relations, the more children they intend to have. Earlier research indicates that actual number of children has a negative effect on measures such as primary relations, and we shall deal with that issue in the next chapter. Why these younger well-educated women should show a positive link between PR and birth intentions is not clear. Perhaps it has something to do with the fact that these young wives have few children and are thus not aware of the actual intangible costs of child care. Or it may somehow be linked to repeated past findings that highly educated wives experience more satisfactory primary relations (Scanzoni, 1971). In any case were we to follow these wives over time we would expect to find that over the years as actual numbers of children increase, the positive PR–intentions correlation reported in Table 3–3 would either disappear, or else become negative as the number of children intended moves closer to the actual number they have.

The second variable appearing in the table and not hitherto discussed is the phenomenon of social mobility. A long-standing issue in population studies has been investigation of possible links between fertility and social mobility (Blau and Duncan, 1967:427–431). In a rigorous analysis of national data from the Princeton surveys, Featherman (1970) found no support for the hypothetical linkage between these two variables. However, he did leave the door open for the possibility that fertility and mobility might be related for what he calls "selected subgroups" (p. 125). We were able to locate several "selected subgroups" within which at least some evidence for such a connection exists. One of the subgroups is the category of 18- to 29-year-old highly educated white non-Catholic women; the others are discussed in Chapter Four.[4]

Intergenerational social mobility is defined as the difference between the wife's father's job status when she was 16 years old and her husband's current job status. (Job status here and throughout the book is measured by Census SES scores, *Working Paper No. 15.*) Among these well-educated women Table 3–3 reveals the correlation and relatively modest beta weight between birth intentions and intergenerational mobility: the more mobile the fewer intended. Women who are mobile are also more instrumental (r = .20), and they report a higher score on our index of perceived economic satisfaction (r = .29).[5] Do women who intend to have fewer children subsequently become mobile, or do persons who want to be mobile subsequently intend and have fewer children? We would need to include measures of life-style aspirations to sort out adequately this causal problem (Easterlin, 1973), but undoubtedly over time both paths of influence operate on each other. Mobility aspirations may decrease fertility; and decreased fertility may make greater mobility possible, thus reinforcing the aspirations.

Theoretically, in terms of a reward-alternative model, the argument can be made that within this very select subgroup of the population those women who aspire most strongly to higher status and consumption gratifications will intend and have fewer familial gratifications. Less familism will be "required" because of compensatory status benefits; they will "want" less familism because it will be a cost undercutting the use of resources that could go into consumption symbols other than children.

In sum, white non-Catholic wives with high education fit well the model portrayed in Figure 3–1. Parental status does not seem to affect their age at marriage directly, and in the figure we have not included the effects of intergenerational mobility or primary relations. Nevertheless, the chart apprehends the flow of events for better educated wives as well as it does for those who are currently working full time. (There is of course some respondent overlap between the categories.) Preferences for individualistic rewards, as measured by norms favoring sex role egalitarianism, are apparently learned prior to marriage and presumably influence wives to be more willing to defer the gratifications of marriage. The gratifications of education and plus a full-time job have the same consequence. Subsequently, marrying later, or having deferred marital rewards, has the effect of minimizing intentions for children or familistic gratifications. Likewise more modern sex role norms have the same effect. Wives who seek individualistic gratifications for themselves tend to seek fewer rewards that come from children. The situations in which sex role norms are most salient and significant are those in which wives are highly educated or work. And yet those situations themselves are in part accounted for by sex role modernity.

A point that needs to be elaborated in connection with this type of framework is the question of how early in life birth orientations are formed. Gustavus and Nam (1970) found that pre-teen children and adolescents have fairly clearly defined notions of "ideal" family size. During adolescence do these ideals influence sex (or gender) role norms or vice-versa, or are there yet other possibilities? If family size ideals exert major influences on gender norms we are still left with the question of where birth orientations arise. On the other hand, the literature on sex role socialization (reviewed in Chapter Two) suggests that parent–child interaction is a basic determinant of gender norms. In support of that conclusion, this chapter has already revealed positive correlations between parental status and more egalitarian sex role norms, as reflected in Figure 3–1. These influences may be analyzed in the following terms: parental socialization affects gender norms and through those sex role norms affects birth orientations. Important decisions regarding staying in school and for how long are partly affected by gender norms—especially for women. And of course increased education positively influences sex role norms.

Gender differentiation thus influences events up to and including the time of marriage, when issues of birth orientations actually become salient. They have never been salient to the same degree before. Consequently, during the period when the potential for sexual activity commences, gender norms presumably begin to exert particular influence on birth orientations because now more than ever before the situation is no longer abstract, but real. If rewards other than children are indeed valued and are to be attained, then the number of children must be controlled (Kantner and Zelnik, 1972, 1973). Nevertheless, as Ryder (1973) suggests, events subsequent to marriage may have significant impact in altering that target number of children.

UNIVERSITY STUDENTS

Some additional light can be shed on the matter through examination of Table 3–5. Recall that in Chapters One and Two reference was made to a random sample of white never-married university undergraduates. Those single persons responded to items worded identically to those used for married persons, as displayed in Figures 2–1 through 2–4. In Table 3–5 the seven sex role dimensions plus ISC and ESC are constructed in the same fashion as they are for the married sample.[6] The birth intentions of these students was measured by the following item:

"If you marry, how many natural born children do you intend to have?"

First, column one of the table reveals that for women all seven of the sex role dimensions are clearly related to births intended. TW and TH are especially strong, but all seven indicate that the more modern, egalitarian, or individualistic these female students are the fewer children they intend to have. Catholic women intend to have more children than non-Catholics; but age, year in school, and father's job status seem to have little effect on intentions of the college women. The same holds for both dimensions of self-concept. In column two males reveal weaker correlations than women over every one of the seven sex role dimensions. Over two of the husband dimensions (IE and TH) relationships are especially weak. However, the signs are in the same direction as for females: the more egalitarian or role-modern they are, the fewer children they intend to have; and Catholic men intend to have more than non-Catholics. Similar kinds of findings are reported by Kelley (1973). In a sample of college students from a large west-coast university, he found significant relationships between measures of less traditional sex role orientations and lowered birth orientations.

Columns three and four report findings from a sample of comparable undergraduates drawn from that same midwestern university three years later. The items to which they responded are identical to those used earlier. Two conclusions stand out in these additional data. First, the inverse relationship between gender role norms and birth intentions appears once more, underscoring its reliability and thus contributing further to its validity. Second, the correlations are generally stronger in 1974 than in 1971, especially for women and particularly in terms of PHA, RLM, and TM.

Both sets of data in Table 3–5 make plain that prior to marriage sex role norms and birth intentions are inversely related in the same way that they are subsequent to marriage. As these respondents are educationally most similar to our well-educated married subsamples, we can once more conclude that even among the best educated there is variation in birth intentions that can be explained in part at least by sex role norms. Nonetheless, the inverse sex role–intentions link is considerably weaker among men than women—a conclusion similar to the one arrived at for married persons and discussed more fully at the chapter's end. Here we may simply note that women remain, and will probably remain for some time to come, ultimately responsible for child care even if it be nothing more mundane than transportation to and from a day-care center. Thus the "perceived gravity" of the consequences of fertility control is apparently greater to women, even those who are currently single college students. The trade-off of reward alternatives is still much more salient to them than it yet is to men. Finally, the data reveal that whatever the ongoing convergences between Catholic and non-Catholic fertility control patterns, these younger "elite" persons continue to demonstrate some differences in the familiar direction. Nevertheless the finding in Table 3–5 that religion is less strongly related to birth intentions than are sex role norms lends support to literature that suggests the possible decline of religion as an extremely significant discriminator of fertility differences and the likely increasing importance of role orientations. For if among students, religious preference is secondary in explaining birth intentions, then clearly what will likely emerge with greater significance for fertility control in Catholic (as well as non-Catholic) marriages will be role structures. This is not to say, however, that religious differences in fertility control will disappear entirely in the foreseeable future—only that they will likely decline relative to the significance of trends toward increased role modernity.

However, the major value of these data is that they shed at least some additional light on the causal problems previously discussed. Both sex role norms and birth orientations can be identified and measured among single persons before their marriages, and the direction of the relationship turns out to be inverse as was theoretically predicted. To determine whether single persons, if they marry, actually attain or exceed that target number of children would require a follow-up study. The same is true regarding links between role norms and the age at which persons may finally marry. However, based on earlier observations in this chapter we may be quite certain that compared to their high-school classmates who did not go to college, these college persons are much more sex role modern and will almost surely have married at a median age greater than that for their noncollege cohorts. Moreover, observations in this chapter lead us to predict that those among these college persons who are more role modern will defer marriage for a longer period of time.

In sum, it would seem that we can fit these single persons into those parts of the model in Figure 3–1 that are appropriate to them. Whether they are conscious of the tradeoffs or not it appears that single women (especially) who prefer and seek individualistic rewards and are thereby willing to assume the concomitant costs also tend to seek fewer familial rewards—to forego them—and to avoid related costs. Although subsequent events could very well significantly alter both their norms and their intentions, earlier observations among well-educated married wives make it reasonable to expect that their current sex role norms will exert at least some causal influence on behaviors that are central to the process of family fertility control.

Norms of White Catholic Wives

For some time it has been known that Catholics want and have more children and use less efficient contraceptive techniques with less rigor than non-Catholics. Ryder and Westoff (1971), however, provide evidence that over time this divergence has been narrowing. Nevertheless, Chapter Two revealed that certain differences exist between Catholics and non-Catholics with regard to certain sex role structures. Westoff and Potvin produced evidence which suggests that Catholics possess a conception of themselves, their church, and their marital roles that is very different from that of non-Catholics in its implications for fertility (1967). Furthermore, Tables 3–1, 3–5, and 4–1 indicate that differences by religion continue to exist in those particular indicators of fertility control. Given these perspectives, we now turn to Catholic women aged 18 to 29 to examine the extent to which they might be fitted under the conceptual framework displayed in Figure 3–1.

DIFFERENCES BY FULL-TIME EMPLOYMENT

First off, the center panel of Table 3–2 shows there are fewer significant differences in role modernity between Catholic working and non-working wives than exist among non-Catholics. Indeed, over the IE dimension nonworking Catholics are actually more egalitarian than Catholic wives who are currently employed. Furthermore, working and nonworking Catholics reveal no significant differences in education, husband's job status, marriage age, first child spacing, or birth desires. Non-Catholics show differences in all these areas. Catholics also reveal a significant difference not indicated for non-Catholics: husbands of nonworking wives have substantially higher incomes than husbands of employed women. However, on birth intentions, number wanted, and parity (plus SA, RLM, and AE) Catholics reveal the same kinds of results as do non-Catholics. In short, while full-time employment makes some differences over key variables, the breadth and scope of divergence among Catholic wives is not so great as that observed among non-Catholics.

FACTORS RELATED TO FULL-TIME EMPLOYMENT

As reported in the text for non-Catholics, lower parity is the strongest correlate ($r = -.43$) of employment among this entire cohort of younger wives ($n = 217$). However, unlike non-Catholics none of the role dimensions correlates meaningfully with employment, whereas husband's income does ($r = -.21$): The more dollars their husbands make the less likely these wives are to work. And again in contrast to non-Catholics, when we examine wives with comparable parity ($0–1$; $n = 117$), we find only a modest link between RLM modernity ($r = +.16$) and employment. A similarly modest correlation emerges between devoutness (frequency of receiving communion) and not working ($r = -.15$).[7] Incidentally, as we might expect, wives in this cohort who are more secular on RLM (a measure of religious ideology) are also less devout ($r = -.38$).

When we shift to Catholic wives with 2 or more children ($n = 100$), the effects of husbands' status become most apparent. The higher his education, job status, and income, the less likely are wives to be working (r's $= -.24, -.20, -.31$). Thus where income is low but parity is high, young Catholic wives go to work. Where parity is equally high but dollars are more available, they do not. This pattern may be linked to findings from earlier literature that higher-status Catholic couples complete their childbearing with larger families than Catholics of lesser status (Whelpton *et al.*, 1966). In any case what is clear is that compared to non-Catholics socioeconomic factors maintain a much greater function, and sex role norms a lesser function, in decisions that younger Catholic wives make regarding employment.

Another contrast with non-Catholics occurs when we examine that subset of Catholic wives ($n = 74$) with children to determine the impact of age of youngest child on employment. Here there is only a .10 correlation between the age of the youngest child and a negative work decision; for non-Catholics it was .21. More importantly, among non-Catholics, husband's social position was not related to their working. Here the greater their husbands' education the less likely they are to work ($r = -.27$). In a regression equation, husbands' education reveals a beta of $-.46$ in predicting a negative decision in comparison to .22 for age of youngest child.[8] Hence, although for non-Catholics role modernity was more significant than child's age in influencing employment, and socioeconomic factors were unimportant, for Catholics the pattern is somewhat different. Here the status factor of husband's education is considerably more potent than any other factor, including age of youngest child. Therefore, these data further support the earlier conclusion that while sex role norms may contribute toward moving younger non-Catholic wives into the labor force, among Catholics it is husband's social position that has most impact in this regard. Nonetheless, among this particular subset of Catholics, sex role dimensions are at least somewhat operative. Wives who are more modern or secular on the RLM dimension are more likely to be employed ($r = .22$). But curiously enough wives who are more egalitarian on the "extreme" IE dimension tend not to be currently employed ($r = -.20$).

STRUCTURAL CONTEXTS AND BIRTH INTENTIONS

EMPLOYED WIVES

Turning to the upper left panel of Table 3–6 we discover that just as among working non-Catholics TM modernity is a strong predictor of birth intentions: Wives who are more modern or individualistic on this sex role dimension seek fewer familistic gratifications. Moreover, RLM secularity and SA modernity are also correlated with depressed birth intentions, and TM is highly intercorrelated with both (SA, r = .39; RLM, r = .29; RLM and SA, r = .31). These three dimensions together account for 11% of the total variance. Thus even though we could not find much evidence that sex role norms influence Catholics to seek employment, it seems apparent that once in that situation, such norms are stronger than any other single force we examined in influencing birth intentions. In that important respect younger Catholic and non-Catholic working wives resemble each other quite closely.

However, there are three variables in the panel that appeared only for Catholics. One is a measure of work-motivation: working wives were asked the standard question on whether they worked mainly because "your family needs the money" or because "you enjoy working." [9] The table substantiates what earlier studies have revealed: Those who say they work for enjoyment intend to have fewer children than those who say they work for money. But what influences wives to go to work primarily for enjoyment? The data indicate that an enjoyment-motivation is prompted among wives who possess an instrumental self-concept, who are more AE capable, more egalitarian on the TW role, whose husbands have higher job status, who perceive that their husbands react positively towards or support their working,[10] and who attribute more marital authority to themselves[11] (r's = .21, .19, .18, .22, .24, and .20).

Thus instrumentality, task-capability, and egalitarianism along with having higher-status husbands are factors prompting Catholic wives to work for other than financial reasons. At the same time husbands' reactions and authority are of particular interest. Earlier research shows that husbands' support is an important factor keeping wives in the labor force (Kreps, 1971). Among these Catholic women, a positive perception of husband support is related to a stronger ISC, a more positive AE, and a greater role modernity (r's = .31, .29, TW = .27, SA = .21, TM = .22). In past literature on family and fertility control, female authority has not been discussed much except to indicate that it is greater in households where wives work.

These data regarding husband support and marital authority underscore a vital consideration that must be introduced into any future longitudinal study of family fertility. That is that husbands and wives are continually engaging in processes of bargaining, negotiation, exchange, and decision-making that affect the whole range of family behaviors including fertility behaviors and outcomes. These outcomes themselves very likely influence subsequent decision processes. Sex role norms provide a context in which these processes occur, and the outcomes may indeed affect those norms. The model in Figure 3–1 is basically a structural model and is valid as far as it goes. But what is lacking are the feedback loops between such factors as sex role norms, shifts in authority, husband approval, work motivations, work decisions, fertility decisions and outcomes, and so forth.

AGE AT MARRIAGE

A second factor that appears in the upper left panel of Table 3–6 and did not emerge for non-Catholics is husband's age at marriage. Why this variable instead of wife's marriage age should correlate with birth intentions is not certain, but the two marriage ages correlate strongly at .51. Wives who defer their marriages tend to choose partners from a pool of eligibles who have also put off marital gratifications. In that sense the variable of wife's marriage age is the close equivalent of that of husband's marriage age. For that reason and also to be comparable to Table 3–4, in Table 3–7 we explain wife's marriage age. The pattern that emerges there for working wives is similar to that which we found for non-Catholics. When we look specifically at husband's age at marriage, we find that wives who are more PHA-modern and also RLM-modern married men who were older (r's = .26, .24). Thus in viewing Figure 3–1 we may say that the benefits of education, alongside preferences for individualistic rewards, delayed the point at which these wives began to experience marital gratifications. But marriage deferral has much less effect than among non-Catholics in depressing familism.

Husband's income also has a negative effect on intentions, at least for wives in this context. There is some uncertainty in the literature as to whether dollars make children more "affordable" or whether as alternative rewards they function to depress birth orientations (Hill and Klein, 1973). As suggested earlier, this issue may be more salient among Catholics than non-Catholics. The contrasting effects of income in the two upper panels of Table 3–6 indicate that, depending on the situational context, income may sometimes function as alternative and other times as stimulus to children. For these working wives it is currently an alternative reward. Furthermore, we should certainly add income to the list of "process-factors" just discussed. That is at certain points within husband–wife decision-making processes, dollars may sometimes motivate one or both partners to argue that the addition of a child may be too costly, or not sufficiently rewarding, or else affordable.

Finally, the upper left panel of Table 3–6 shows that deferring the gratification of a first child also depresses birth intentions, a finding similar to the lower left panel of Table 3–3. As indicated there we shall treat that spacing variable more fully in Chapter Four.

NONEMPLOYED WIVES

Shifting to the situation where wives do not work, the upper right panel of Table 3–6 reveals that the single strongest predictor of birth intentions is income. The more dollars their husbands make, the more children they plan to have. Recall from Table 3–2 that these husbands make significantly more money than husbands whose wives work. Thus where there are more dollars and wives are not involved in the responsibilities and rewards of a job, the result among Catholics is to stimulate the feeling that the financial costs of additional children can be borne and are outweighed by the intrinsic gratifications they provide. Related to dollars per se is the sense of economic satisfaction perceived by these wives. Table 3–6 shows that it too has a positive impact on birth intentions, and furthermore it correlates positively with actual income (.29). As we might expect, wives who possess more actual resources tend to feel more satisfied with their socioeconomic circumstances. Both the objective situation and corresponding subjective definitions influence orientations towards more or towards fewer children.

Rainwater has identified what he calls a central pronatalist sentiment: "One shouldn't have more children than one can support, *but one should have as many children as one can afford*" (1965:150; italics in original). He claims that there are moral connotations attached to the second part of the statement. A "good" or "unselfish" person is not "afraid" to use his money for children. Although we have no direct measure of this sentiment, it would seem that Catholics hold to it more strongly than do non-Catholics. Perhaps because of religious ideals, the notion of "goodness" and "morality" attached to utilizing money to have and rear children seems much more important among Catholics than it is among non-Catholics.

Nevertheless, even within this context of nonworking Catholic wives, Table 3–6 reveals that there are three sets of sex role norms that are correlated with reduced birth intentions. PHA indicates that wives who seek for alterations in husband's sex role behavior also seek fewer children. RLM and TM suggest that Catholic wives who are more sacred and traditional regarding the maternal position seek more children than wives who are more secular and modern.

Age at Marriage

Lengthening the first-child spacing interval also tends to depress birth intentions, as does a later age at marriage for their husbands. As before, the two marriage ages correlate at .64; assuming the two to be equivalent in importance, Table 3–7 reveals influences on wife's age at marriage. The pattern is very similar to that for employed Catholic wives, except that here if their mothers worked they tended to marry earlier than if their mothers did not. In both situations in Table 3–7 (top row) education is the most potent predictor of marriage age, followed by premarital employment. The latter element correlates meaningfully with little else, but education and task-evaluation (AE) are positively related in both settings, as are education and more egalitarian or modern sex role norms (working wives' education correlation (r) with AE = .29, with TW = .26; non-working wives' education correlation (r) with AE = .30, with TW = .26, with RLM = .22). Father's education has some positive link with marriage age in both contexts, and in both it is also a positive influence on TW modernity (working wives' r = .22; nonworking wives' r = .24).

Overall, therefore, we may conclude that, although there are basic similarities, working Catholics can be fitted somewhat better than nonworking Catholics into the model of Figure 3–1. This is partly because of the more powerful effects of sex role norms on birth intentions in the former. And partly it is because in the latter the model would have to allow for the inclusion of economic factors as well.

Low to Average Education

The lower left panel of Table 3–6 reveals two sex role dimensions that have stronger correlations and betas than appeared for comparable non-Catholics in Table 3–3. RLM secularity and TM modernity do seem to depress desires for familial gratifications on the part of these less-educated Catholics. Nevertheless, as in Table 3–3, the impact of sex role norms on birth intentions is relatively less in this context, and in the preceding one, than it is in the remaining two. Among the less educated in Table 3–6, first-child spacing has slightly more impact than does RLM; and Table 3–7 suggests a pattern comparable to Table 3–4 (lower left panel) regarding factors that influence deferral of wife's age at marriage. Both here and there husband's education can be considered the "functional equivalent" of wife's education in terms of impact on marriage. Because the education of husband and wife are highly intercorrelated it may be said that the rewards of educational attainment by both partners contribute jointly towards deferral of their mutual marital gratifications. Moreover, wives who hold more egalitarian sex role norms are married to men with more years of schooling. Thus degree of female modernity may contribute towards deferred marriage age through male education, as well as through their own education. Here, for example, SA and TW modernity of wives are positively related to husband's academic attainments (r's = .21, .20).

High Education

However, as with non-Catholics, it is when we move to the lower right panels of Tables 3–6 and 3–7 that we observe most strongly the consequences of sex role norms. (Beta weights are not shown because fewer cases restrict us to correlations.) First off, we see that in Table 3–6 four sets of sex role norms correlate in the expected inverse direction with birth intentions: the more egalitarian, modern, individualistic, secular, and so on these wives are, the fewer children they want. Although a later age at marriage for wives is also associated with lowered intentions, Table 3–7 shows that PHA and RLM along with instrumental self-concept are the strongest correlates of that later marriage age. Thus in terms of a fit with Figure 3–1, it appears that here too sex roles directly influence both marriage age and birth intentions and that they also affect intentions indirectly through age at marriage. As before, this pattern holds not solely for wives but partly involves husbands too. Table 3–6 shows that the older their husbands were when they married the fewer children these wives want. Wives who are more PHA-modern and RLM-modern—and more instrumental—married men who were older (r's = .38, .21, .41).

An additional variable that appears to depress birth intentions strongly is the wife's evaluation of her own task-performance (AE). Though not shown in the table, AE is related positively to a strong instrumental self-concept (.46), and also to greater egalitarianism on SA, PHA, and RLM (.27, .21, .29). Also of interest is the finding that wives who have a higher AE also see themselves as having greater marital authority (.29). So that operating through AE to lower intended family size are the effects of sex role norms, self-concept, and greater participation in family decision-making. As it did for comparable non-Catholics, full-time employment depresses birth intentions, and wives who work are more SA modern (.32). Of the several we have examined, this seems to be the subset of Catholic wives where sex role norms are most directly related to employment decisions.

On the other side, Table 3–6 shows three dimensions that stimulate familism. (Familism is defined as orientations and behaviors that lead to larger family size.) Husband's education and economic satisfaction are linked at .32, and their joint positive effects on intentions can be interpreted similarly to those of income and satisfaction in the upper right-hand panel. For the first time in the tables devoutness appears and also stimulates increased birth intentions. Earlier studies have indicated similar connections between frequency of receiving communion and fertility control (Ryder and Westoff, 1971). What is of particular significance among this subset of Catholics is that in six of the seven possible instances, sex role traditionalism is positively associated with greater devoutness (RLM, TW, PHA, SA, TH, TM: r's = .54, .31, .37, .34, .25, .22). As with other variables in our overall conceptual framework, it is likely that over the years devoutness and role traditionalism have contributed to each other in mutually supportive fashion. Wives who have been more traditional have been more devout, which in turn reinforces and perhaps increases traditionalism, and so forth. Acting together, both elements have evidently resulted in larger families.

In summary, we may conclude that younger Catholic wives can be fitted under the rubric of Figure 3–1 with some modifications. As with non-Catholics it is from working or highly educated wives that we have the strongest and most pervasive evidence for an inverse link between individualistic sex role norms and familial rewards. Among Catholics the husband's rather than the wife's marriage age is a more frequent indicator of birth intentions; but given the equivalency of age at marriage for both spouses, that does not alter the basic model very much. That is, in both religious categories background status seems to influence female education, sex roles, and age at marriage. Women who are better trained and more individualistic and marry later choose men who are better trained and who also have deferred marriage for a longer period of time.

The most significant modifications in the model surround the function of economic resources for Catholics. Although for non-Catholics such resources depress familism, for certain Catholics they result in less likelihood of labor force participation and sometimes increased birth intentions. For instance, within the subset of working wives, husband's income and birth intentions are inversely linked. If wives do not work or are highly educated, pronatalist norms of "good people having as many children as they can afford" seem to operate. Thus among younger Catholics (as contrasted with non-Catholics) there are countervailing forces operating on familial orientations. On the one hand deferral of marital gratifications, along with preferences for individualistic benefits do seem to depress the number of children intended. But concurrently material resources supplied by husbands tend to increase that number. Therefore, in spite of the effects of individualism as seen in Tables 3–6 and 3–7, as long as the flow of material factors functions in the opposite direction, we may expect continued fertility differentials between Catholics and non-Catholics.

One additional important element that surfaced, beginning with our discussion of working wives, is the issue of husband–wife negotiation, bargaining, and decision-making insofar as these elements affect changes in sex role norms, labor force participation, and fertility control. Underscored was the conclusion that fertility control is an ongoing process embedded in the larger structure of husband–wife sex roles and decision-making processes.

Norms of Black Wives

We shift now to a third set of respondents, black women aged 18 to 29, to determine further the scope and validity of the model displayed in Figure 3–1. As several accounts are available, it is not necessary to review in detail literature covering the fertility of black Americans (Westoff and Westoff, 1971). Like white Catholics, blacks have tended to have more children than white non-Catholics. Nevertheless, there is no known theoretical nor empirical reason to suspect that fertility control among husband–wife black households would not fit under the rubric of reward-alternatives elaborated to this point. For at least 50 years black fertility patterns (demographic increases and declines) have tended to parallel those within white society (Westoff and Westoff, 1971:261). And these same authors conclude that the major reason for black–white fertility differences lies in "the control of fertility rather than in the number of children desired" (p. 269). Postponing our discussion of contraceptive behaviors for the next two chapters, we turn now to a consideration of the determinants of black birth orientations.

DIFFERENCES BY FULL-TIME EMPLOYMENT

Table 3–2 indicates that black working wives are significantly more modern than nonemployed wives only on the SA and RLM dimensions. This represents considerably fewer sex role differences than emerged for white non-Catholics and in this regard makes blacks more similar to white Catholics. Another divergence in that table from white patterns is that although there is some difference in the expected direction between those two groups of black wives in terms of mean parity, the differences are not significant. Nonetheless, working wives do intend to have and desire significantly fewer children. In terms of three objective status indicators (husband's job status, education of each spouse) none shows significant differences, another pattern similar to white Catholics. But unlike the latter and comparable to non-Catholics there are no significant differences in husband's income. Conversely, like Catholics, marriage ages and spacing length do not differ meaningfully, whereas they do among non-Catholics. Hence, while there are some expected divergences among these two categories of black wives, there are substantially fewer than there are for white non-Catholics, and slightly fewer than for Catholics. With regard to an overall summary of Table 3–2 it seems apparent that among younger households, a greater range of differences occur over sex role, socio-economic, and fertility control variables by wife employment among non-Catholics than is true for either Catholics or blacks.

FACTORS RELATED TO FULL-TIME EMPLOYMENT

Among younger white women we found that parity was the single strongest correlate of employment. Among these black wives, however, SA modernity is considerably more strongly associated with a positive work decision ($r = +.25$) than is parity ($r = -.11$). RLM modernity is also associated with the decision to work (+.18), as is higher husband SES (+.15). Recalling the problems of assessing causality between parity and employment, it seems clear that the number of children is far less a factor in the work decisions of young black wives than of young white wives. Evidently of far greater significance to young black women is their own orientation toward self-actualization. Related to this conclusion is the point made in Chapter Two regarding white economic discrimination against black males. Black women have often been "forced" to work regardless of the number and ages of their children, and this long-standing pattern has likely influenced gender role norms throughout black society (Scanzoni, 1971).

These arguments are further supported when we sort first by low parity (0 or 1; n = 62) and ask what variables are most strongly associated with positive work decisions. For this low parity grouping, SA modernity, as with non-Catholics, is the strongest correlate of employment (r = +.25). Next are TW and RLM modernity (.23, .22). Moreover, similar to non-Catholics and unlike Catholics, a status variable—in this instance husband's SES—is positively rather than negatively related to employment (.19).

Among higher parity wives (2 or more; n = 76). SA modernity, for the third time among these black wives, seems to affect full-time employment (r = .26). Next in strength is a positive ISC (r = .21). Thus even among wives with relatively high parity, and with many of their children probably quite young, this particular dimension of role modernity (SA) emerges consistently as a most critical factor in explaining work behavior. At the same time, a strong instrumental self-concept is also a potent factor in motivating higher-parity wives to enter the labor force, whereas those less instrumentally oriented are more likely to stay home.

Among wives with children (n = 78) the correlation between the age of youngest child and employment is a modest .10—identical to that for Catholics but below that for non-Catholics. Also like Catholics a husband status variable—in this case income—is negatively related to employment (−.25). But on the other hand these blacks resemble non-Catholics in that greater egalitarianism on both the IE and SA dimensions is linked positively with their employment (.20, .19). However, in a regression equation the strongest predictor of employment is husband's income (beta = −.33), followed at some distance by SA modernity and age of youngest child (betas = .15, .06).[12] Therefore, as with comparable subsets of white wives, age of youngest child does not seem so important as certain other factors in affecting employment decisions. Nevertheless these particular blacks appear more like Catholics than non-Catholics in that a socioeconomic variable is more potent than role modernity in deciding whether or not to work. Those who are relatively better off economically choose not to work. As this pattern does not emerge for the three subsets of blacks previously examined, it would seem that for blacks, in contrast to Catholics, income has this negative consequence only among women with children.

PROPORTION OF TIME IN THE LABOR FORCE

Earlier investigations have found an inverse relationship not only between parity and employment but also between parity and proportion of married life spent working (Whelpton *et al.,* 1966). We devised an index to measure the proportion of time (in months) since marriage that women in our sample had worked full time.[13] Table 3–8 presents the correlates of that index. For non-Catholics it is clear that parity is the strongest correlate of proportion of time employed, followed by education. Next is their AE ranking, then come several dimensions of sex role modernity and their instrumental self-concept.

Among Catholics parity is also the strongest correlate of proportion of time employed, followed at a great distance by their education. It is only when we move to blacks that we discover that several sets of role norms are more strongly related to proportion of life in full-time employment than is parity. And education has virtually no connection at all.

Did working more frequently influence whites to have fewer children, or did having fewer children influence them to work more often? Among blacks the causal sequence hinges not so much around parity but around role norms and work proportion. Although we shall leave a fuller discussion of influences on parity until Chapter Four, the issue of work proportion underscores again the processual nature of family fertility control in particular and of family structure and interaction in general. Women (black and white) who hold more individualistic or modern sex role norms are likely to be better educated, to work at more rewarding jobs, to work more frequently, and to plan for and to have fewer children. Subsequently, the fact that there actually are fewer children means that it is less costly to continue to work, or to commence it again, or perhaps to take it up for the first time. And more frequent work participation could very well enhance and reinforce more egalitarian or modern sex role norms, and so the cycle continues—all these highly interrelated factors constantly affecting and "feeding back" on each other in ongoing fashion.

Religion appears to make some difference in these complex processes, in that role norms seem to bear no connection at all to work-proportion for Catholics. Therefore though much of the process just described may exist in Catholic marriages, interconnections between sex role norms and work-frequency may be a relatively missing element. By the same token, among black marriages such interconnections may be more crucial and significant than even for white non-Catholics. Recall that in Chapter Two blacks were found to be less role traditional than whites over several significant dimensions.

STRUCTURAL CONTEXTS AND BIRTH INTENTIONS

EMPLOYED WIVES

Turning to Table 3–9 we find that among employed black women (as among whites) a dimension of sex role modernity (TW) is the single strongest correlate of birth intentions: the less traditional and more egalitarian they are in terms of sex role norms, the fewer children they intend to have.[14] As with whites, preferences for individualistic rewards apparently tend to depress orientations towards familial gratifications. Moreover while education was negatively related to birth intentions for non-Catholics, here we find that in addition to education the wife's own SES and income reveal similar consequences. As was the case for whites, education is linked with greater sex role (TW) modernity ($r = .29$) and also with wives' SES (.41) and wives' income (.56). Moreover wives with higher SES are more TW-modern (.30), as are wives who earn more money (TW = .28, RLM = .29). In short these black wives reveal that sex role modernity, education, SES, and income are all positively intercorrelated, and that all four types of reward or resource-type variables tend to depress birth intentions.

Husband's job status also affects birth intentions as did husband's income among working Catholics. And like those Catholics, working for enjoyment also results in intending to have fewer children. In addition, that type of work motivation for blacks shows positive connections with education and income and with TW, TH, and PHA modernity (.30, .29, .24, .28, .20). It also relates to husband's income at .29. Black wives who themselves earn more money (and whose husbands do also) nonetheless are more likely to say they work mainly for enjoyment. Thus both the tangible and intangible benefits of occupational endeavor, in conjunction with more egalitarian sex role norms, apparently make the benefits of additional children less compelling and their possible costs more real insofar as their potential for undercutting those extrafamilial benefits is concerned.

AGE AT MARRIAGE

As was so for white non-Catholics, Table 3–9 shows that among working black wives marriage age is negatively associated with birth intentions. In turn Table 3–10 displays those factors related to deferral of marital gratifications. Although the two variables (education and premarital job) that correlate strongest with marriage age are the same as for whites, their relative order is reversed. For blacks it is that job rather than education which emerges as somewhat more influential. As with two subsets of Catholics in Table 3–7, not having a working mother encourages later marriage. Finally, Table 3–10 reveals even more strongly than for comparable whites a direct positive relationship between a sex role variable (RLM modernity or secularity) and later age at marriage. Therefore, given links between parental status, education, and sex role norms[15] it would appear that blacks in this particular situational context can be fitted under the model in Figure 3–1.

Nonemployed Wives

The same conclusion apparently applies to wives within the upper right panel of Table 3–9—those not currently working. Among whites the model was more problematic in this context than in the former one, but among blacks PHA modernity correlates negatively with birth intentions at virtually the same level that TW does for employed wives. Three additional role variables join PHA in depressing intentions, as does a stronger AE ranking. To be sure age at marriage and education are the strongest correlates of intentions, and Table 3–10 shows that education is the most potent force affecting marriage deferral. Yet as we have repeatedly seen better-educated wives hold more egalitarian sex role norms. For wives in this situation, the dimensions linked with education are TW (.27), RLM (.30), TM (.23), as well as a stronger instrumental self-concept (.32). Moreover these wives reveal a connection between education and working full time prior to marriage (.32), a second factor affecting marriage age. Therefore the argument can be made for wives in this context too that education and correlated role modernity along with employment defer the gratifications of marriage. Possessing educational resources (plus their potential for later occupational benefits), already having deferred marriage, and possessing more individualistic sex role norms, they are subsequently oriented towards fewer children.

Low to Average Education

Among less-educated women (lower left panel, Table 3–9) we find that two dimensions of role modernity correlate in the expected direction with intentions at about the same level as does age at marriage. Moreover, working full time depresses intentions—a finding that did not emerge for whites in this situational context. Their own marriage age reveals the strongest direct influence on intentions, and in Table 3–10 we find that by far having worked full time while still single was the most potent factor "causing" them to defer marriage. As was so often the case for whites, we could, in this situation, identify no variable that might have influenced that behavior, although in certain contexts (such as nonemployed wives) education appears to be associated with it.

In connection with white non-Catholics we speculated that women most likely not to work at that point in time are those that become pregnant. Data from a national sample of women aged 15 to 19 reveal that a substantially higher proportion of blacks than of whites have experienced premarital pregnancy (Kantner and Zelnik, 1973:31). Therefore, although among whites the chain of influences between pregnancy, employment, and marriage age may exist to a certain degree, among blacks the links may be relatively more powerful and more significant. As the literature reveals an inverse connection between education and premarital pregnancy, it is likely that sex role norms are related (at least indirectly) to the latter phenomenon as well. Future investigations should consider the extent to which preferences for individualistic gratifications among single women affect sexual behavior, use of contraception, and the likelihood of pregnancy.

HIGH EDUCATION

Because we find comparatively few cases of well-educated wives, our conclusions here must be considered quite tentative. This context is the first in which expressive self-concept has been linked at all to birth intentions. In contrast to the negative correlation which appears in Table 3–9 one might have expected that wives who are more "warm, quiet, gentle," and .the like would have had an affinity for greater numbers of children (Clarkson et al., 1970). Presumably children provide a vehicle for the "motherly exercise" of these kinds of personality traits. This would have been in contrast to Table 3–3, for instance, where instrumental self-concept predicted reduced intentions. Yet we discovered in Chapter Two that black women tend to see themselves as more strongly expressive than do white women. That finding may be part of the explanation of the relationship in Table 3–9. In any event it would appear that well-trained black wives who are more nurturant have less affinity for additional children than do wives who are less nurturant. It may be that the latter find in children the characteristics that they do not perceive in their own personalities. Or perhaps the more nurturant are more sensitive to the high costs of "quality" child-rearing and thus are more concerned to hold down their quantity.

An additional finding that contrasts with whites is the effect of economic satisfaction. White Catholics who were more satisfied wanted more children; blacks who are more economically satisfied want fewer. For blacks, perceived economic benefits are rewards that apparently function as alternatives to familistic rewards. Catholics on the other hand seem more likely to be persuaded by the pronatalist or "moral" norm that greater resources should make additional children possible.

Still a third contrast with whites occurs when we discover that two dimensions of modernity pertaining to husband role behavior relate to increased intentions. Recall that in Chapter Two we found that black wives tend generally to be more individualistic than white women with regard to male roles. At the same time, it may be that this "select subgroup" of educated black women are more willing than comparable whites to insist that their husbands should participate more fully in domestic and child-care duties. Thus while comparable whites who are "modern" on these dimensions might in turn reduce children as a strategy to reduce the likelihood of marital conflict over these issues, black women might be less prone to do so. They might intend to have additional children and still seek to bargain their husbands into fuller household participation. Interestingly, however, they do not apparently envisage such a situation in terms of their own role behaviors. The table shows that TW sex role norms correlate with birth intentions in the expected inverse direction. Moreover, it is not at all certain that they could get their husbands to concur with the household pattern that they might prefer. To the extent their own husbands are more IE-modern and TH-modern, the men might "hold out for" and insist on resolving the issues involved by having fewer children. Table 3–10 reveals similar ambiguities for wives in this context in that three sets of role norms are associated negatively with marriage age, while only one is associated positively. Results from both tables may simply be idiosyncratic because so few cases are involved, or it may be that among younger well-educated black women these variables are related to fertility control in ways that currently are not readily apparent.

Nevertheless, overall, Tables 3–9 and 3–10 plus our discussion of factors relating to full-time employment make it apparent that younger blacks too can be fitted within the model of Figure 3–1. There do not seem to be any significant exceptions as there were for Catholics (income), except that in one context with very few cases certain aspects of husband role norms may stimulate birth intentions. Basically it would appear that blacks coming from more advantaged homes get more education and that both education and egalitarian sex role norms reinforce each other over time. There is some hint that education might enhance obtaining a premarital full-time job and that in turn education, employment, and sex role modernity tend to lead to a deferral of marriage. Once married, current employment decisions appear to be affected by sex role norms perhaps to a greater extent than is true for whites. Taken together, all these preceding elements influence birth intentions, with sex role norms operating for blacks on intentions fairly homogeneously in all four situational contexts. As was the case for whites, these norms indicate that the more strongly black women seek modern, or individualistic, or egalitarian benefits for themselves, the less strongly they seek for the rewards (and the more strongly they seek to avoid the costs) of additional children.

Norms of Older Wives and of Husbands

Table 3–11 presents correlates of births wanted (explained earlier in the chapter) for non-Catholic older women and birth intentions for non-Catholic younger men.[16] The patterns in these data are also representative of those for older Catholic and black women, as well as patterns for older men. Although younger men reveal some correlations between sex role norms and birth intentions in the expected direction, the relationships are more modest and less consistent than for women. The pattern is not much different among older women. Although it is possible to construct possible paths of influence for younger men similar to those developed for younger women, to do so would be repetitious without adding much of substantive and theoretical significance to Figure 3–1.

In general, therefore, we may say that the model as it stands displayed in Figure 3–1 has comparatively less relevance to younger men and to older women. Concomitant changes in sex role norms and fertility orientations are most pertinent to younger women who, unlike older women, have both the great bulk of their childbearing period and many opportunities for individualistic pursuits still largely ahead of them. During earlier years when older women were in the initial stages of the childbearing period, they were probably more role-traditional than women who are currently in that period (see Chapter Two). Connections between role norms and fertility behaviors were simply less likely to have occurred during earlier years than at present. Consequently a reward-alternative model in which individualism is juxtaposed over against familism has less meaning for currently older wives.

Likewise, among men, being oriented towards greater or lesser individualistic interests for women seems to have much less consequence for their own birth orientations than it does for women. Apparently there is much less of a trade-off involved for husbands. If women seek egalitarianism and individualism, they apparently feel compelled (often non-consciously) to seek fewer children as well. But men can be amenable to certain changes in their own and in their wives' behaviors and still not necessarily have that significantly affect orientations towards children. However, it is not likely that men who hold more modern sex role norms would significantly oppose their wives' individualistic aspirations. Recall earlier in the chapter the correlations between perceived husband support and wife role modernity. Instead it seems more likely that better-educated, role-modern men are simply more amenable to their wives structuring their own occupational and fertility behaviors as wives themselves see fit (S. M. Miller, 1971). In that sense the model of Figure 3–1 would need to be modified to take younger husbands into account. We might expect that the more men's sex role norms are more egalitarian, the more they will reinforce wives' sex role egalitarianism, as well as wife employment behavior. Thus although husbands' own role orientations may affect their own birth orientations relatively minimally, such norms may maintain an indirect influence on wives' birth intentions through wives' sex role norms and occupational behaviors.

Summary and Discussion

The central issue of this chapter was to try to identify linkages between sex role norms and birth intentions. In spite of certain problems of interpretation, birth intentions are found to have substantial effect on later parity. For a variety of reasons, most important of which is that fertility control is an ongoing process containing feedback loops that may significantly affect birth intentions, it did not seem feasible nor valid to attempt to construct actual path diagrams. Nevertheless an attempt was made to reason in terms of possible paths of influence and to develop a flow chart (Figure 3–1) which accurately displays those influences. The model as it was developed applies to younger women (white Catholics and non-Catholics, blacks) but not so well to older wives or husbands. Among older women the kinds of issues that revolve around changing sex role norms were apparently not relevant to them when they were in the early childbearing years. And now that their childbearing is virtually behind them, sex role norms continue to be only minimally relevant in that regard. Likewise, for men the linkage between sex role norms and fertility control is a less striking characteristic than for younger women probably because having a child is less life-changing than it is for women. Therefore in terms of social change processes in general, it is to be expected on theoretical grounds that the segment of any subordinate group that has the most to gain from change is the first to exhibit it. Specifically, to the degree that younger women are actually more oriented towards individualistic rewards than older women, we may expect them to be more likely to behave in ways designed (often unconsciously, as we will see) to achieve those rewards.

Before continuing at this more general theoretical level, let us drop down to the specific variables which are part of the model in question. Parental status as indicated by years of education or by father's job status positively influence the woman's education, sex role modernity, and to some extent her age at marriage. Education and modernity are positively correlated and over the years prior to marriage have had incremental effects on one another. Education and role modernity tend to delay marriage age; and they also very likely reduce the probability of pregnancy, which also has some direct effect on delaying age at marriage. Pregnancy also may have substantial indirect influence on marriage age by affecting full-time employment. Young women who do not work full time —for whatever reason—tend to marry much sooner than women who do work. The only variable we measured that sometimes was related to premarital employment was increased education, which reveals still another influence on marriage age. Subsequently in the model, later marriage age negatively affects birth intentions. For whites this is especially true within the situational contexts of low education and non-employment, though sex role norms and instrumental self-concept negatively influence intentions there as well.

However, within the contexts of full-time employment and especially high education, sex role norms are generally the most powerful predictors of lowered intentions. Our respondents were subdivided by employment and education to let us detect if the operation of role norms is linked to particular situational contexts. The foregoing suggests that it is, and a longitudinal study might show how norms move women into particular situations, but how the situation influences the norms and related behaviors once they are in the situations. As the model is conceived here it is assumed that wives (especially non-Catholics and blacks) who are more sex role modern are more likely to seek full-time employment. In turn wives who work full time presumably intend to have fewer children, though in the several regression equations predicting intentions, that variable did not appear often.

Furthermore, there was evidence to show that among two samples of never-married university students, sex role norms are better indicators of lowered birth intentions than is religion, year in school, or status background. Thus, even among younger persons with similar levels of high education, variation in birth intentions can be accounted for by variation in sex role norms—a finding similar to that for married persons. Presumably those single women who are currently more modern or individualistic will defer marriage for a longer time, will work more frequently after marriage, and will maintain relatively lower birth intentions.

Moving from these specific empirical relationships, let us try to illuminate them by returning to the more general theoretical level. Recalling Holter's (1970) conceptualization of sex roles as a "distributive system" of rewards or interests, we may say that the various sex role dimensions identified here apprehend preferences for particular kinds of rewards. By implication they also indicate willingness to assume certain types of costs and willingness to forego certain alternative rewards. The rewards minus the costs spell out the type of "profit" that women seek from their sex role behaviors (Homans, 1961). The role norms indicate the degree to which women do or do not prefer individualistic interests, the costs inherent in attaining such gratifications, and the alternative rewards that are foregone in the pursuit of individualism. Individualism here is equated with sex role egalitarianism or with sex role modernity. Thus a woman who seeks individualistic rewards is in effect seeking the benefits of increased autonomy and egalitarianism within marriage, so that she can experience both phenomena outside of it. There may still be certain costs involved, such as increased time pressures, occupational demands, increased conflicts with her husband, and so forth. And she may forego particular benefits such as a degree of discretionary leisure.

The construct labeled familism subsumes those benefits attached to the bearing and care of children as discussed in Chapter One. The model developed here indicates an inverse link between individualism and familism. The more strongly individualistic rewards are preferred and sought for, the less strongly will familistic benefits be preferred and sought for, and the more willing wives will be to forego them. Behaviors such as premarital pregnancy, full-time premarital employment, age at marriage, postmarital full-time employment, education, and so forth may also be conceptualized as indicators of individualism. Women who are more individualistic tend to get more schooling, avoid premarital pregnancy, marry later (defer the gratifications of marriage), and work more frequently. They also intend to seek fewer familistic rewards. In terms of "net profit" younger women appear to make trade-offs (often unconscious) between the rewards and costs of individualism as over against those inherent in familism. One set of rewards and costs is alternative to the other in terms of achieving what is to them acceptable and reasonable profits in terms of their own sex role behaviors.

This theoretical framework rekindles certain questions that appeared in earlier chapters and which we hope to treat more fully in Chapter Six. One of these is the classical issue of how norms and behavior are interrelated. Our assumption has been that norms formed in childhood have affected age at marriage, work behaviors, and the total number of children intended. But that assumption triggers two related theoretical questions plus a related methodological matter. First, should not the process of family fertility control be treated in terms of a systems strategy? Sex role norms may very well affect behaviors, but in turn these behaviors may feed back on those same norms (Ryder, 1973). Next, could not this kind of process be examined in terms of the larger question of "adult resocialization" in which norms and behaviors are both altered over time not only because of their interplay but also as a result of other occurrences and happenings? Thus wives and husbands who begin marriage with a certain level of role modernity or traditionalism may experience movement in either direction for a variety of reasons. When spouses move at different rates or in opposite directions, we might expect system stability to be threatened. Finally, it is plain that these kinds of ongoing system processes can adequately be tapped only by the method of longitudinal design.

A second major issue has to do with the question of rational calculus. From a perspective of Homans' type (1961), one could argue that much of the trade-off process between individualism and familism is nonconscious. Wives may not be overtly aware of favoring certain gratifications, downgrading others, and moving in certain directions toward particular objectives, though in fact such phenomena may be occurring. Indeed for most women in their 30's, 40's, and beyond, fertility control processes may have been especially random, haphazard, and noncalculated because viable alternatives outside the home were simply not deemed meaningful to females. But for younger women—particularly those who are more individualistic—the motivation to attain individualistic rewards may be much stronger and greater than it was to older women. Therefore, conscious awareness of trade-offs—of actual costs and rewards—may be much greater as well. This is a matter for future research, but we would expect that the more conscious persons are of the alternative sets of rewards (and costs), the more likely they are to be most effective in actually attaining the kinds of utilities they desire—whether modern, moderate, or traditional in nature.

A third major issue centers around whether "liberated" women need to make a choice between children or occupational achievement. Why are not both sets of gratifications possible, either through greater husband participation in child care or else through widespread quality day-care centers? Day-care facilities of high quality are simply not yet available in large numbers in the United States. As to husband participation, recall from Chapter Two that women were generally less egalitarian when it came to men's roles than men themselves were—a finding corroborated by Steinmann et al. (1968). In short, whatever one might wish women to do, what actually appears to be happening is that the strategy of that subordinate group is not to maintain a high level of familistic rewards and to press for greater husband participation in child care. Instead they appear to be lowering the level of desired familistic benefits. This does not mean that role-modern women would not expect relatively greater male participation with their comparatively fewer children. (See Table 3–9 for a slight hint of this pattern among educated black women.) But it does appear that given the continued subordination of women as an interest group, the best bargain, or set of trade-offs, they can strike at present is the one described in these pages. What changes the future may bring in this bargaining arrangement is not yet clear.

However, a fourth major issue relates to the foregoing and centers around what benefits husbands are to receive if sex roles are actually undergoing the kinds of evolutionary changes described here. There is some talk in the media and by some scholars about "men's liberation," which term generally seems to refer to some release from achievement pressures and towards greater involvement with children. As men are the dominant interest group, if the status quo is to be altered significantly, then they must perceive it to be in their own best interests to change.[17] For instance, significant changes could be negotiated by women if men gradually came to perceive that marital rewards would be greater both at the socioemotional and socioeconomic levels if women were more autonomous and marriages more egalitarian. In Chapter Six we discuss this matter in greater detail.

A final issue is a methodological one, the question of the strength of the correlations and betas in the tables. It is always wished that such relationships could be stronger, but given the minimal variation in the dependent variables, it is remarkable they are as strong as they are. That is, birth intentions cover a very narrow span, as can be noted from Table 3–2. Age at marriage may cover a somewhat wider range of responses, but still within a relatively narrow band. It may be that in the future better measures of sex role norms will produce even stronger correlations. Moreover, measures of processes between husbands and wives—negotiation, bargaining, decision-making over role and fertility behaviors—may add considerably to our ability to predict fertility outcomes, but more of that in the following chapters.

Notes

1. Additional variables include the remaining role and self-perception dimensions, education, SES, income of respondent and spouse, economic and marital satisfactions, and wife's marital authority (multiple $R = .57$; $R^2 = .32$).

2. For purposes of consistency, simplicity, and clarity, in Table 3–3 and following, role modernity will always be read as "high" or "positive." Stronger instrumental or expressive self-concepts will be read similarly, as will a more positive AE ranking.

3. Physical affect: (a) How do you feel about the physical love and sex relations you experience with your (wife/husband)? Do you feel it's very good, O.K., or not so good? (b) Affiliativeness (Companionship): How do you feel about the companionship that you and your (wife/husband) have in doing things together during leisure or nonwork time—things such as movies, picnics, and so on. Do you feel the companionship is very good, O.K., or not so good?

   Index of primary relations: Range: 0–4; mean: women = 0.77, men = 0.68; Standard deviation: women = 1.02, men = 0.92. Low score = positive satisfactions; but in tables positive satisfaction will be understood and read as "high."

4. Intergenerational mobility was also modestly related inversely to the birth intentions of highly educated white non-Catholic women, aged 30 to 44 (r = − .17).

5. Index of economic satisfactions: (a) Expectations for future life style: Realistically speaking, how good do you think your chances are for getting ahead in life? Do you feel they are: excellent, fair, or somewhat limited? (b) Evaluation of present life style: How do you feel about the standard of living—the kind of home, clothing, car, opportunities for the children, and so on—that your husband's job allows you to have? Do you feel very satisfied, satisfied, or dissatisfied?

   The past literature on measures similar to this one suggest opposite but equally plausible arguments linking it to childbearing (Westoff *et al.*, 1963: 113–14). From one standpoint those who are more economically satisfied may sense less cost in another child and thus not be motivated to delay or prevent it. On the other side, those who are less economically satisfied may seek alternative compensatory rewards in the form of another child.

   Index range: 0–4; mean: women = 1.43, men = 1.61; standard deviation: women = 1.09, men = 1.11. Low score = greater satisfaction, but in the tables the index will be understood to mean that "high" reflects a "positive" or more satisfactory orientation.

6. Separate factor analyses for students produced dimensions very similar to those that emerged for married adults.

7. The item used to measure devoutness, borrowed from Ryder and Westoff .(1971), asks how often respondent receives communion: more than once a week, once a week, two or three times a month, once a month, a few times a year, once a year, less than once a year, never, other.

8. Additional variables in the equation are the same as those described above for non-Catholics (multiple $R = .63$; $R^2 = .40$).

9. If respondent said "enjoy," we probed further: "Is one of the reasons you work because your family needs the money?" If respondent says "yes," we probe: "Would you continue working if your family did not need the money?" If respondent said money was the main reason she worked, we also used the latter probe: "Would you continue . . .?"

10. Perceived husband reaction is based on a series of three items put to working wives: (a) "How does your husband feel about your working? Does he think it is a good thing or not so good?" (b) "Would he prefer it if you did not work?" (c) "Does your husband ever feel that your working keeps you from doing all he thinks you should do for him (and the children)?"

11. Authority in "conflict-resolution" was measured by first ascertaining the one thing respondent and spouse "disagree about most often," and then asking "who usually gets his way" ("you or your husband/wife") when they disagree over that one thing. See Scanzoni, 1970, Chapter Six, for further discussion of marital authority.

12. Additional variables in the equation are the same as those described above for non-Catholics (multiple R $= .61$; $R^2 = .36$).

13. The calculation is based upon the number of months out of the total number since marriage that the wife had worked full-time. For example, a woman who had worked 18 out of 36 months would be ranked the same as one who had worked 24 out of 48.

14. We restrict ourselves to simple correlations because of the limited number of cases.

15. Mother's and father's education correlate with women's education at .51 and .32, respectively.

16. The only variable in the table not yet explained is "empathy." Variables akin to our measure of empathy have been shown in past literature to be positively associated with fertility control (Hill *et al.*, 1959). Our measure of empathy (defined as "the intellectual identification with or vicarious experiencing of the feelings, thoughts, or attitudes of another . . . ," Scanzoni, 1970), is based on an index composed of the following items: (a) Communication: How do you feel about the ways you and your wife (husband) can confide in each other, talk things over, and discuss anything that comes up? Do you feel it is very good, O.K., or not so good? (b) Understanding: How do you feel about the way your wife (husband) understands your problems and feelings? Do you feel her (his) understanding is very good, O.K., or not so good?
    Index range: 0–4; mean: women $= 1.10$, men $= 0.98$; Standard deviation: women $= 1.2$, men $= 1.1$. (Low score $=$ positive satisfaction.)

17. This assumes that male-female conflict on both the macro and micro levels is geared to attain "maximum joint profit" rather than any sort of coercive domination.

Chapter 4.   Influences on Current Family Size

THE QUESTION TO BE EXPLORED IN THIS CHAPTER is what influence sex role norms have on current parity, the actual number of children born to younger wives in our sample. It would be most ideal to be able to follow these persons in order to trace the effects of role norms on timing and spacing decisions (or lack of decisions) and on their contraceptive behavior. In turn, we would then be able to investigate how those decisions and their implementation might influence sex role norms. In particular, we would want to observe how the birth of the first child, or second child, and so on might alter or perhaps reinforce those norms.

Lacking that ideal design, our aim here is to develop a model that incorporates key factors that help to account for current parity. It will be presented visually as a flow chart in Figure 4–1 and can be considered as complementary to Figure 3–1. A cross-sectional design requires us to keep the two models separate, though there is some degree of overlap in the variables used for both models. The separation is required mostly because of uncertainty regarding particular temporal sequences and also because the measure of birth intentions is built partially on actual parity as explained in Chapter Three. Thus in a cross-sectional design one could not use intentions to predict parity. However, as Figures 3–1, 4–1, and 5–1 provide the bases for hypotheses to be tested in a panel design, the most significant elements of the three models could be combined by using that approach.

Table 4–1 reveals the actual numbers of children born to date as reported by whites first as a combined group and then separated according to religion, and by blacks at younger and older ages. Descriptions of parity levels for younger wives by employment are reported in Table 3–2. Among persons aged 18 to 24, blacks have more children than whites of either religious category; but among persons 25 to 29, Catholic women report more children than do black women. Moreover, in the oldest age

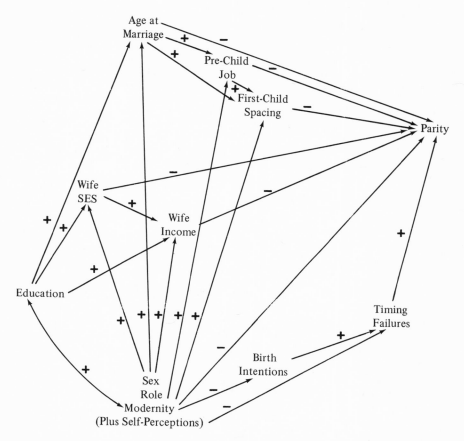

FIGURE 4-1. Flow Chart Showing Factors That Influence Parity for Wives Aged 18–29

category Catholic men and women both reveal that they have more children than black men and women, followed by white non-Catholics. Thus the difference that religion makes is obscured when we compare whites as a whole category with blacks, for then it appears that older whites in general have fewer children than older blacks.

In 1971, census data on white wives 18 to 24 years old showed that the mean number of their births to date was 0.9 (*Current Population Reports*, P-20, No. 232). This figure is less than the 1.16 reported for comparable wives in our sample. However, as discussed in Chapter Three in connection with birth intentions, the difference in parity figures is in part the result of our excluding wives not presently living with their husbands. Nevertheless the 1.9 figure reported by white wives 25 to 29 years old in our sample is identical to the mean parity for comparable wives at the national level (*ibid.*). On the other hand, black women 18 to 24 years old in our sample report more births to date than the 1.4 figure reported by black wives nationally in 1971 (*Current Population Reports*, P-20, No. 263). Yet the national sample of black wives 25 to 29 years old reports a figure of 2.5 births, which is greater than the comparable number in Table 4–1 (*ibid.*). These variations among blacks may be due in part to the fact that we have relatively fewer cases of blacks, as well as to the fact that we include only black husband-wife households.

Parity of White Non-Catholic Wives

STRUCTURAL CONTEXTS AND PARITY LEVELS

Chapter Three investigated variables related to wife employment and there is no need to repeat them here in studying non-Catholic wives aged 18 to 29. We plan to follow the convention described there of sorting wives first by employment, then by education. Therefore, in spite of lacking a longitudinal design, we can be sensitive to the effects that structural or situational contexts might have on sex role norms and thus in turn on parity levels. By way of reminder, the labels for the sex role dimensions refer to the following: TW = traditional wife; SA = self-actualization; PHA = problematic husband alterations; IE = institutionalized equality; TH = traditional husband; RLM = religious legitimation of motherhood; TM = traditional mother. ISC refers to instrumental self-concept and ESC to expressive self-concept, while AE indicates evaluation of wife skills and abilities.

WORKING WIVES

If we examine the last column in the top row of Table 4–2 we discover that age at marriage is the strongest correlate of parity: The later these wives married, the fewer children they currently have.[1] Recall from Table 3–4 that we explained marriage age as the result of preferences for certain alternative kinds of gratifications.[2] Women who preferred individualistic or modern-type gratifications were more likely to defer the gratifications of marriage than were women who were less individualistic and more traditional. Specifically, education was a powerful influence on marriage age, but it was highly intercorrelated with sex role modernity and over time probably stimulated by it. We may therefore say that the longer wives are willing to defer the gratifications of marriage, the fewer familistic gratifications (children) they actually have. And willingness to defer those gratifications seems to rest on preferences for and possession of alternative types of rewards.

Note too that the same third column indicates that working fulltime prior to the birth of any children is also related to fewer current children. The first column in the top row of Table 4–2 reveals variables most strongly related to that type of employment behavior. Note that age at marriage and education are most strongly related to working: Wives who are better educated and who waited longer to marry were more likely to work at that point in time. Likewise wives who rank themselves more positively on the AE index and who are more role-modern in TW or TH were also more likely to work. The same holds if they worked prior to marriage. Therefore, at the more general theoretical level, we may say that the more strongly wives are oriented towards individualistic rewards and possess greater levels of educational benefits and the longer they defer marital gratifications, the more likely they are to seek and obtain the tangible and intangible gratifications of employment early in marriage and prior to children. "Economic need" factors as measured by variables such as husband's job status at time of marriage or his income bear no relationship to that sort of employment decision. Instead, it is clear that wives who are less "needy" as measured by their own education (which correlates positively with husband's education and SES) are more likely to be employed. Rather than dollars, it would seem that other more subtle kinds of gratifications are operating to motivate them. Moreover, wives who seek those kinds of gratifications at that point in time are subsequently more likely to possess fewer familistic benefits.

Past literature (Whelpton *et al.*, 1966) has indicated empirical relationships between age at marriage and parity and between pre-child employment and length of first-child spacing as revealed in the second column of the top row of Table 4–2. However, there has been little attempt to conceptualize these linkages in any sort of over-arching theoretical framework such as the one envisioned here. Moreover, the temporal sequence between early employment and first-child spacing has not been clearly established. For example, it is possible that certain wives who, for whatever reason, do not bear a child though they do nothing to prevent it might eventually take a job simply because they have time and there are no costs of children involved.

Nevertheless, if we look at the second column of the top row we find that, besides a full-time job, education and role modernity are also positively associated with delay in having that first child, that is, with the number of months between marriage and first child. There is no theoretical reason why education and sex role norms should be related to first-child spacing if the main direction of influence has been from a longer interval towards the work decision. Conversely, if we assume that among wives under 30 (the opposite may have been more true for older wives in former years) the work decision has influenced a longer first-child interval, such behavior elaborates still further the theoretical framework in view. We may say that wives who prefer employment gratifications and who are more individualistic, or sex role modern, are more likely to defer the gratifications of children. As the third column of the top row reveals, the longer such gratifications are delayed, the fewer children younger (employed) wives are likely to have. Therefore, first-child spacing becomes part of the reward-alternative framework we are seeking to develop. As Figure 4–1 indicates, we may suggest that the correlated benefits of education and preferences for individualistic interests lead to a deferral of marital gratifications. The former function as alternative rewards to the latter, and deferral of marriage stimulates desires for imminent employment as do education and sex role norms. The benefits of education and job along with those norms function as alternatives to the onset of children, and subsequently the postponement of their onset operates to reduce the actual numbers of children.

On the one hand, therefore, are the long-standing kinds of highly significant rewards that women have traditionally sought—the security of early marriage, the prestige of an early child, and the importance of a large number of children. These benefits, which serve to make her totally dependent on her husband and to center her life in the family, are part of the syndrome labeled "familism." On the other hand, modern sex role norms prescribe benefits gotten from the larger society and in particular from the educational and occupational structure. These resources reduce dependence on her husband and enable her to function more as an individual outside the family. It would appear that one set of benefits is alternative to the other. Though not inherently (extensive day-care facilities and substantial male involvement might affect the association), those who prefer familism opt less for individualism, and vice versa.

Table 4–2 also indicates that the variables that measure the working wife's own achievements are directly related to lower current parity: the greater her education, her own job status, and her own income, the fewer children she has. These elements themselves may be conceptualized as alternative gratifications to children. Both tangibly and intangibly education, job position, and earnings supply benefits that undercut the motivation to have children (Cain and Weininger, 1973). Concomitantly, as Figure 4–1 indicates, each of these variables maintains strong associations with sex role norms and with instrumental self-concept. Moreover, the table reveals that wives who rank themselves higher on the AE index have fewer children, and AE is also connected with these three status variables. For example as already shown in Chapter Three, education is positively linked with modernity on the TW, RLM, PHA, and TH dimensions (.41, .39, .21, .20). Wives who are better educated are more AE capable (.32), have higher SES (.60), and earn money (.48), as do wives with higher SES (.46). At the same time, higher SES is linked with a stronger AE ranking and with greater egalitarianism on TW, TH, RLM, and TM (.39, .36, .26, .30, .20). Income also correlates positively with AE, TW, and RLM (.34, .26, .27). Wives with greater SES and income also possess stronger instrumental self-concepts (ISC: .22, .23). Finally, AE relates positively to ISC, TW, and RLM (.46, .24, .24).

Therefore, although sex role norms do not maintain direct influence on the number of children that these younger, employed wives currently have, the argument can be advanced that they do maintain indirect influence through these status variables, as well as through marriage age, pre-child job, and first-child spacing. Wives who are more sex role modern, who see themselves as more instrumental and task-capable are likely to value more strongly the tangible and intangible rewards of occupational endeavors and achievement. They prefer the rewards and gratifications of greater marital egalitarianism alongside the occupational benefits that egalitarianism makes possible. Besides these benefits as alternatives to children, the children are also perceived (unconsciously perhaps) as costs that could undercut both sets of benefits. Therefore their number is reduced. It is quite likely that by the end of their childbearing period wives in this younger cohort will reveal meaningful correlations between completed parity and sex role norms. Over the years, there are likely to be strong differences in childbearing patterns and related employment behaviors between those who are most individualistic and those who are less so. The differences that role modernity makes in birth intentions, as identified in Chapter Three, are important indications of likely differences in completed family size. At the present stage of the life cycle, however, it would appear that the consequences that sex role norms have in reducing actual family size—in functioning as alternatives to familism—operate mostly through key "marital-events" and, for these employed wives, through key status variables as well.

Interestingly, one hint that with the passage of time and events direct links between role norms and parity become more evident emerges when we consider younger working wives with at least one child ($N=78$). Here we discover that wives who are more TW-modern and TM-modern have fewer children than those who are more role-traditional (r's $= -.20, -.20$). We might predict that as time goes on and more children are eventually born to younger women, the inverse correlations between sex role norms and parity will continue to grow stronger as women who are more traditional bear more children than those who are more individualistic and egalitarian. Although our assumption is that role norms exercise a major influence on family size, we obviously cannot rule out the hypothesis that the presence of one or more children could "feed back" on norms to alter them in either a more traditional or a more modern direction.

Recall that Table 3–3 revealed a negative link among highly educated wives between intergenerational mobility and birth intentions. Following Featherman's (1970) suggestion that "select subgroups" might reveal mobility–fertility relationships, Table 4–2 shows that those among these working wives who have experienced greater job mobility have fewer children. Job mobility is defined as the difference between their own father's job status and their own current job status. Earlier tests of the fertility–mobility hypothesis have focused exclusively on the husband's mobility, which made sense when most women were not seriously committed to occupational achievement. However, changes in women's sex role norms may lead them to view occupational endeavor much differently than in the past. They may come to define it much as men do, not because occupational achievement is intrinsically "masculine" or "male", but rather because women as persons may simply come to prefer as strongly as other persons (males) the kinds of rewards that the occupational system of a modern society has to offer. To the extent this is so, one way in which the fertility–mobility hypothesis will need to be carefully reexamined is in the light of what we call "job mobility".

Without following the wives in Table 4–2 over time, we cannot be certain whether they have experienced greater mobility because they had fewer costs of child care or whether because they wanted to rise as much as they could they therefore limited the level of familistic costs as much as possible. Given our earlier discussion of the positive connections between sex role modernity and job status, we would expect that wives who aspire to more rewarding positions strive to limit their family size accordingly. However, because they have fewer domestic responsibilities they are also freer to fulfill the demands of higher-status positions. In turn, those gratifications probably motivate them to maintain lowered family size, and so the process continues.

PREVIOUS BIRTH PLANNING

In the chapter following, we explore connections between sex role norms and current contraceptive behaviors and consider factors that influence expected future contraceptive efficacy. In this chapter we want to give attention to a phenomenon that is considerably more difficult to measure in valid fashion: How do respondents assess their previous contraceptive efficiency? Let us consider first the question of unwanted children, or what has been labeled "excess fertility" (Whelpton et al., 1966), or "number failures" (Ryder and Westoff, 1971). These are past pregnancies and/or live births that the respondent says he/she did not want at all. To measure this phenomenon, we utilized a series of questions quite similar to those used in the 1970 National Fertility Study.[3] However, a major procedural divergence from earlier studies is that we do not have information on pregnancies that did not result in live births. Those earlier investigations probed for an exhaustive array of all pregnancies, some of which may have been terminated by spontaneous or induced abortions or resulted in a stillbirth. The fact that we have contraceptive information only on live births means that our results may not be strictly comparable to earlier efforts.

The major similarity in those cross-sectional designs and ours is that we rely on retrospective judgments of the respondents. That is, months or years after the child has become a vital part of the household, the parent is asked whether or not the child was wanted at all or wanted in general but not planned for when it actually arrived. As Ryder and Westoff (1971) observe, this technique is less than ideal because the parent may not remember the truth or may falsify and rationalize that the child was planned when it was not. Therefore, those investigators argue that unless we ask persons beforehand about their birth planning we may get systematic underreporting as to the number of unplanned children.

As it turns out, the proportion of younger women reporting "number failures" is so small that it renders the validity of any analysis quite suspect. For example, among this entire cohort of younger employed women there are only 5 cases who report a number failure. If we look at wives with proven parity (one child or more), we find the same 5 cases and no more. Among younger non-Catholic wives not currently employed, 14 cases (6%) report a number failure, and again that figure does not change when we consider nonworking wives with some children. Nonetheless, if a much larger cohort of currently younger wives were followed over time until, say, near the end of their child-bearing period, it is likely that the proportion of unwanted children would be large enough for meaningful analysis. In addition, we would expect that sex role norms would eventually come to be associated with number failures. Given conclusions from Chapter Three, plus the information we have considered so far in this chapter, and especially given the information on current and expected future contraceptive behavior in Chapter Five, we would predict that wives who are more sex role modern or egalitarian would experience fewer number failures than wives who are more role-traditional. As the costs of an unwanted child are greater to wives who have stronger extrafamilial interests, we can expect that, over the long term, they will be more highly motivated than more traditional wives to avoid those costs. At the same time we would not rule out the possibility that an unwanted child could alter sex role norms. Its presence could prove more costly to a hitherto traditional woman than she had imagined. Hence, that event could move her towards greater role egalitarianism to ameliorate or lessen those costs, especially in terms of preferred changes in her husband's role behaviors in the direction of greater participation in household and child-care responsibilities.

The whole issue of the validity of retrospective data for contraceptive efficacy and birth planning has been subjected to thorough critiques by those sympathetic to it (Ryder, 1973) and those considerably less sympathetic (Blake and Das Gupta, 1973). However, all investigators concur that a longitudinal design is essential to capture adequately beforehand how wives and husbands calculate the timing and existence of a child (or children) not yet conceived and how their concomitant contraceptive behavior squares with those prior calculations. The problem of retrospective statements would seem especially acute in trying to assess what are labeled as "timing failures." As long as persons have not had the total number of children they say they intend to have, it seems that many couples are unconsciously less contraceptively cautious or rigorous than they know they should be or indeed could be (Whelpton et al., 1966; Blake and Das Gupta, 1973). Should a conception and birth occur under such circumstances, instead of being labeled a genuine failure of timing or an unplanned birth, it might in certain instances be equally valid to think in terms of a couple's uncertainty about when it would be "best" or "least costly" to have the children they want to have.

This last question becomes especially pertinent to younger women with individualistic aspirations during an era of societal changes in sex role patterns. As was noted in Chapter Three, almost all American women want to have children. But when will children be least costly to these females' individualistic interests and occupational endeavors? Early in marriage before they become highly involved in extrafamilial interests? Or later on once they have become more established in those pursuits? Judging from actual birth rates among women generally and in particular among the better educated, it appears that many younger women are opting to postpone their childbearing for now and instead pursue other gratifications (Current Population Reports, P-20, No. 254). But at what point do they commence the deferred childbearing that Campbell (1973) predicts will occur in spite of current low birth rates? No matter how modern-oriented a childless woman in her late twenties or early thirties may be, if she wants a child or two but, because emerging patterns of women's life styles remain relatively uncharted, is not sure how a birth might affect her occupational interests and thus how to time the child, she may simply, as Blake and Das Gupta put it, "more or less ease into exposure to the risk of pregnancy by becoming increasingly careless in birth control practice" (1973:681). If a child were then born, could that legitimately be labeled a "timing failure" even though she was not certain that she wanted it precisely at that time and though it perhaps made little difference to her individualistic interests? In particular, if the mother makes arrangements such that the child is not costly to her occupational (or other) pursuits, then its significance for her preferred life style is relatively minimal.

Clearly, the need has been present for some time to investigate birth planning and contraceptive behavior through a longitudinal design. The evolution of sex role patterns to their present level of increasing egalitarianism, plus concommitantly lowered birth rates and thus the possibility of new patterns of deferred childbearing and related emerging life-styles, makes the need for such investigations even more pressing. In terms of the question of rational planning, which seems to underlie the notion of the so-called timing failure, perhaps a more significant issue to research is the rational planning that goes into coping with the possibility of a child. If a couple feels beforehand that they could "manage" a child if it "happened" to come along—that is, it would not interfere with the wife's career aspirations—that situation could be assessed as representing a reasonable degree of rational planning and not necessarily a failure. Conversely, if they feel that a child would be a serious cost or interference, then one that was born anyway might more reasonably be labeled a failure in their overall level of rational planning. This type of notion is hinted at in the Ryder and Westoff retrospective items by asking if the respondent "cared" or not about a particular "failure." But in the future it will surely need to be probed far deeper than that, and in terms of the theoretical context just described.

Our items are limited to the existing modes of establishing whether a particular live birth was a "timing failure" or not. Using those techniques, we found that 16% of those working wives report a child in that category, and when we consider only those with at least one child, the figure rises to 29%. This change in percentages is corroborated by Whelpton *et al.* (1966), as well as by Ryder and Westoff (1971), who observe that the proportion reporting more "successful" birth-planning tends to decline among those with proven parity, compared to categories which include wives at parity zero. They suspect that part of the reason for the change may be that some wives in the latter category have difficulties conceiving or bearing children for psychological or physiological reasons. In any case they suggest that in examining contraceptive failure the major focus be placed on wives with proven parity. Consequently, Table 4–3 is constructed on this basis, and in the upper left panel of that table we find that working before having any children and greater TH-modernity are the strongest correlates of reduced timing failures.

In other words, wives who worked early in marriage were less "careless" then in their handling of contraceptives. We have already examined the individualistic-type variables that help to account for early employment. In addition, wives who are more egalitarian and modern on the TH dimension (also on the TM) have also been more "careful." Moreover their own job status, income, and deferred marriage age—which all correlate with role modernity and education—have also apparently motivated them to be more rigorous planners. Therefore to the degree we accept the validity of this type of retrospective measure of past contraceptive efficacy, the argument can be made that preferences for individualistic rewards motivate employed wives to be more careful birth-planners. Sex role norms, employment, education, dollars, job prestige—all of these highly interrelated rewards that are alternatives to familism (as defined in this and prior chapters) appear to stimulate wives to behave contraceptively in ways that will reduce familistic costs (and rewards).

As Table 4–3 also shows a positive relationship between timing failures and current number of children, we have included this variable in Figure 4–1. The patterns of influence charted there suggest that the more strongly wives prefer individualistic gratifications the less careless they are in timing intended children and that the less careless they are the fewer children they have.[4] Thus, as with other segments of the model, individualism and familism continue to be inversely linked, only this time the influence is exerted through contraceptive efficacy. Given the enormous intrinsic importance of contraceptive management within the total schema of family fertility control, these are theoretically significant findings. Much earlier literature has made the point that effective contraception is fundamentally a matter of motivation. In addition, the prediction had been made that persons holding more modern sex role norms should be motivated toward greater contraceptive efficacy (Scanzoni and McMurry, 1972). Within this subgroup of wives, that prediction is apparently valid. Of course it is possible that being more effective has led to being more egalitarian. No doubt over time greater modernity and greater effectiveness positively reinforce and feed back on each other in incremental fashion.

AN ENLARGED MODEL

One consequence of parity noted in earlier literature is its negative impact on measures of marital satisfaction (Rainwater, 1965; Clausen and Clausen, 1973). Among all younger non-Catholic working wives we found that the more children they have the less satisfied they are with the levels of empathy and primary relations (described in Chapter Three) they receive from their husbands ($r's = -.28, -.21$). We also found that number of children is negatively related to economic satisfaction ($r = -.35$). As we have shown elsewhere (Scanzoni, 1975), the wife's economic satisfaction is positively influenced by her husband's social position. Here too we find that the higher her husband's job status the more economically satisfied she is (.34). Table 4–2 reveals that the higher the husband's status, the fewer children they have. Moreover our earlier investigations indicate that wives who feel more economically satisfied report more positive empathy and primary relations. In short, there appear to be important interconnections between the variables displayed in Figure 4–1 and economic and marital satisfactions. Figure 4–1 traces the ongoing influences among an array of variables of which education and sex role norms are initial factors. The underlying premise is that familism (parity) exists in inverse proportion to individualism and to related status variables. But familism also appears to be inverse to economic and marital satisfactions.

Therefore in an ongoing study we would need to enlarge Figure 4–1 to take into account an additional series of what are undoubtedly significant feedback loops. Wives who are more sex role traditional and less well-educated and whose husbands have lesser status have more children. Having more children means greater demands on finite economic resources, and thus they are less satisfied with their economic situations. Likewise additional children put strains on marital interaction and reduce that type of satisfaction too. Simultaneously, wives whose husbands have lesser status are less economically and maritally satisfied because of that status. If we conceptualize economic and marital satisfactions as important rewards that wives possess to a greater or lesser degree, the question becomes what the consequences of those rewards' levels are. Those who have fewer rewards may seek alternative compensations in the form of additional children. Those who perceive more economic and marital rewards may be less likely to seek alternative familistic gratifications. In brief, current parity may influence subsequent parity through its impact on these kinds of economic and marital gratifications. To the degree this process occurs it provides additional insight into the explanation for continued higher parities among lower-status couples (Blau and Duncan, 1967:427). Those higher parities are the result not only of being sex role traditional and of having fewer educational and occupational alternatives but also of lower levels of the two basic kinds of rewards that women have traditionally learned to expect from their husbands.

NONWORKING WIVES

The bottom row of Table 4–2 presents findings that enable us to suggest that younger non-Catholic wives who are not currently working can to a certain extent be fitted under the model displayed in Figure 4–1. Missing of course are wife SES and income, but recall from Table 3–4 that sex role norms (highly correlated with education) may have helped to influence deferral of age at marriage. Recall too that better-educated wives worked prior to marriage, and in the first column of Table 4–2 we learn that that variable, along with marriage age and education, influences early postmarital employment. The second column assumes that the latter behavior influences a lengthier first-child spacing (rather than the other way around). In turn, explanation of parity itself seems to rest most strongly on deferral of marriage, deferral of the first child, and education. But as the flow chart suggests, modern sex role norms may be operating on reduced parity through education and age at marriage, as well as through first-child spacing which itself is affected by age at marriage and education.

Of additional interest here is the inverse relationship of instrumental self-concept to parity, analogous to its influences on birth intentions in Table 3–3. ISC is strongly correlated with AE (.52), which is also linked with parity. Clarkson *et al.* (1970) report similar inverse links between instrumentality and parity. Thus even though these wives are not now in the labor force, those who define themselves as more "active" and "competitive" and who see themselves as more task-capable actually have fewer children. Presumably such wives are more oriented toward individualistic interests and thus are minimizing familistic costs now so that perhaps at a later date they might be less impeded if they choose to enter the labor force.

Overall, however, when we compare the two rows in Table 4–2, the presence of sex role variables is more evident among wives who work. Recall from Chapter Three that nonworking wives already have more children and that they are generally more role-traditional. Therefore, although we may conceptualize that age at marriage, early employment, and first-child spacing indicate preferences for gratifications other than the familistic and although we may be able to trace the influence of sex role norms on parity through them, as well as through education, the pattern is less consistent, less evident, less strong. The relatively minimal direct links between role norms and parity within this context may also in part be a reflection of the fact that these women are currently in the early stages of the childbearing period. Were we to follow them over time we would likely find stronger role–parity relationships as suggested by ISC and AE dimensions. However, at this stage of their lives, we may conclude that younger non-Catholic non-working wives can be less readily subsumed under the rubric of Figure 4–1 than can their employed counterparts.

TIMING FAILURES

Likewise, if we examine the lower left panel of Table 4–3 we find another important divergence from working wives. Of those in the panel, 32% report timing failures. In trying to account for timing failures among nonworking wives we find that sex role variables do not emerge but that birth intentions do. Wives who intend fewer children have had fewer timing failures. Similar conclusions are reported by Whelpton *et al.*

(1966). The factors that influence the birth intentions of these wives are reported in Table 3–3. Thus, to the degree that variables such as role modernity, instrumental self-concept, and deferral of marriage depress the birth intentions of these wives, to that degree are timing failures also depressed, and those paths of influence are shown in Figure 4–1. Wives in this structural context who intend to have more children appear to be more contraceptively "careless" during the early stages of childbearing. However, Ryder and Westoff (1971) suggest that contraceptive failures may affect birth intentions. That is, each unplanned-for pregnancy may increase the target number of children. This possibility would seem to be most likely in the case of number failures rather than timing failures.

Subsequently, the strength of the positive relationship between timing failures and parity is much greater among nonworking than working wives. We would interpret this difference to mean that among nonworking wives, the level of current parity has been reached more by what Kammeyer (1973) calls "nonpurposive" means. There has evidently been less "rational planning", and perhaps less "calculation." Contraceptive failure and childbirth are more likely simply to "happen." In contrast, among (working) women who evidently seek more strongly for alternatives to familism, current parity levels are more the result of "purposiveness" and apparent "rationality." Contraceptive behavior obviously affects the parity of working wives but within a larger framework of rewards that motivate them to make contraceptive behavior more rigorous because its outcomes tend to be defined as less gratifying and more costly.

LOW TO AVERAGE EDUCATION

Conclusions similar to those for nonworking wives emerge when we examine the top row of Table 4–4. Even among less-educated wives we may once more conceptualize premarital employment, age at marriage (Table 3–4), pre-child employment, and first-child spacing as behaviors that indicate strength of preferences of alternative gratifications to familism. Nevertheless as we learned from Chapter Two, these wives are strongly role-traditional. Therefore, the effects of sex role norms per se upon these marital events and upon current parity itself appear to be problematic. The same holds even when we examine wives with proven parity. It may be that over time some of these wives might become more egalitarian, and perhaps such a change could influence their completed parity. For example, the third column of the top row in Table 4–4 shows that variation in education among these wives, along with instrumentality, were related to fewer children. Thus it may be that some high school graduates in this cohort might at some point become quite amenable to and develop an affinity for more individualistic sex role norms and that this could possibly significantly reduce their childbearing as compared to those who remained more role-traditional.

HIGH EDUCATION.

In contrast, while less-educated wives can be fitted only partially under Figure 4–1, Table 4–4 indicates that better-educated wives can be fitted much more comfortably. Recall from Table 3–4 that TM was the strongest predictor of their marriage deferral. The bottom row of Table 4–4 reveals that in turn the longer these wives deferred marital gratifications, the more likely they were to work before having any children. Next we assume that willingness to defer the gratifications of the first child is related to possession of the tangible and intangible benefits of a job. In addition wives who are more AE-capable, more role-modern, and more instrumental also lengthened that interval. Subsequently, early employment and longer spacing (plus their determinants) mean fewer actual children. Concomitantly, wives who rank themselves stronger on the AE index and who are also more SA modern also have fewer children. A strong instrumental self-concept has as strong a negative effect on parity as their prior willingness to defer marriage. Variation in their own education is not as important an influence on parity as any of the preceding variables.

When we examine the fourth column of the bottom row (wives with proven parity), we find that all seven sex role dimensions show meaningful inverse correlations with parity and that the TM-modernity correlation is stronger than any other single variable, including marriage age and spacing. The ISC and AE dimensions also continue to exercise a firm negative impact on current family size. Indeed, compared to any of the three earlier situational contexts, the direct impact of sex role norms on actual parity is greatest here. Even among currently employed wives the influence of individualism operated more indirectly that otherwise. Better-educated women have access (actual or potential) to the most gratifying and rewarding kinds of occupations. Thus the structural potential for attainment of those gratifications is present. But even within this structural context, wives who are more strongly individualistic are oriented towards fewer familistic benefits. For optimum reduced parity it is not sufficient to be in a situation where alternatives to children are feasible. It is also necessary to posses the strong motivation to seek those alternatives. Sex role norms provide the basis for that motivation. Even among wives who are better educated, those norms affect marriage age, subsequent important fertility-related events, and actual family size. And were we to follow even these highly advantaged wives over time, it is quite likely that here, as in the former contexts, the inverse correlations between individualistic and familistic gratifications would probably grow even stronger than they are at present.

Table 3–3 revealed an inverse link between birth intentions and the intergenerational mobility of these wives. Similarly, among all educated wives that type of mobility and actual family size are also negatively related. However, among wives with proven parity that relationship disappears and what emerges instead is an inverse association between intragenerational mobility and number of children. The greater the difference between their husband's job position at marriage and their present SES, the fewer children these wives have. In both instances, apart from following respondents over time and applying measures of consumption goals and related life-style aspirations (Easterlin, 1973), it is uncertain whether having fewer children enabled them to be more mobile or whether because they wanted to be mobile, they had fewer children.

Theoretically, the issue to be resolved by future research is the extent to which the phenomenon of social mobility can be integrated into the reward–cost framework being suggested here. To what degree is the perceived "profit" of mobility (rewards minus costs) an alternative "profit" to children? What are the ongoing causal links not only between mobility and fertility control but also between mobility and individualistic gratifications (indicated by sex role norms and behaviors), marital satisfactions, and economic satisfactions? At least in the case of educated wives in column three who have experienced the greatest intergenerational mobility, they reveal positive links between that movement and sex role modernity (RLM = .26, PHA = .27, TW = .27, education (.50), and economic satisfaction (.22). In short, there appear to be meaningful associations between preferences for individualistic benefits, having fewer children, and experiencing greater mobility.

TIMING FAILURES

Finally, if we examine Table 4–5 we discover contrasts similar to those in Table 4–3. Among less-educated wives, 33% report timing failures. Higher intentions have apparently influenced increased timing failures, and failures have had a positive effect on parity. The direct effect of sex role norms on failures is not much in evidence. Conversely, among better-educated wives, 25% report timing failures. TH-modernity has the strongest impact on failures (a negative one) along with first-child spacing (explained in Table 4–4), instrumental self-concept, income, and TM-modernity. Educated wives who are more sex role egalitarian and instrumental and who possess greater economic resources have been more rigorous and careful in their contraceptive behaviors. In turn, those with fewer failures have had fewer children. Simultaneously, if we look back at the lower far right panel of Table 4–4 there are other variables (the sex role dimensions in particular) that have had greater direct impact on parity than have timing failures. In short, similar sets of individualistic reward-alternative elements seem to influence both contraceptive behaviors and actual family size, as displayed in Figure 4–1.

Parity of White Catholic Wives

STRUCTURAL CONTEXTS AND PARITY LEVELS

Working Wives

As discussed in Chapter Three and noted again in Table 4–1, Catholics still tend to want and have more children than non-Catholics. Therefore, to what extent can these younger Catholic wives (18 to 29) be fitted under the model in Figure 4–1? If we examine the third column in the top row of Table 4–6, we find that the current family size of Catholic working wives is explained by variables similar to those used for non-Catholics. Age at marriage, for example, is the strongest correlate of reduced parity, and we recall from Table 3–6 that the wife's own education is the most significant predictor of marriage deferral. And as was so for non-Catholics, education and TW-modernity are positively related (.26), and we can assume that the norms that make up TW (the preferences for individualistic rewards) have helped to delay marital gratifications. Furthermore, the table shows that the more years of schooling her husband has, the fewer children they have. There are even more dimensions of the wife's sex role modernity related to her husband's than to her own education (TW = .31; SA = .32; RLM = .33; TM = .20).

Wife's own income is next in its relative impact on reduced family size, and we find that wives who earn more dollars are more egalitarian on the innovative IE dimension (.31), and that they also score higher on AE (.39). It would be fascinating and important to ferret out the causal sequences here. It is likely that wives who are more AE-capable and IE-modern feel that they have the potential to earn higher salaries and also that their husbands would and should make alterations in their own role behaviors to support wives in their attainments. Over time, wives who have more dollars probably have more bargaining power with their husbands to get them to actually behave in terms of IE, with greater actual sharing of domestic and child-care tasks.

Compared to non-Catholics, wives' own job status is less strongly related to having fewer children. The same holds for their own education. Yet both variables maintain some connection with having fewer children, and wives with greater SES are—like non-Catholics—more individualistic (TW = .33; TM = .24). Catholics are also similar in that working prior to children and lengthening the first-child spacing interval both mean lower current parity. However, unlike non-Catholics, the table reveals that it is not possible to identify direct links between greater role modernity and either early employment or spacing. Interestingly, Table 4–6 indicates that the more education the wife's mother had, the shorter was her own spacing interval. This is the only hint throughout the top row that these working wives fit conclusions from earlier literature (Whelpton *et al.*, 1966) that higher-status Catholics behave in ways that result in higher parities. Instead, the data here are analogous to those in Table 3–5, wherein wife's intentions and husband's income were inversely related. Moreover, her actual parity is also inversely related to status variables, including the education of their own fathers and their husbands' SES.

Moreover, if we shift to the fourth column of the table (wives with proven parity) we learn that the inverse correlation between husband's SES and parity is considerably stronger than it is in column three. The same holds for their intergenerational mobility. At the same time, the greater their degree of mobility the more role-modern they are (TW = .33, TM = .23); and they also possess stronger instrumental self-concepts (.29). Even more markedly than for non-Catholics, two dimensions of maternal sex roles become more strongly related to family size in column four than they are in column three. Among Catholic working wives with proven parity, to hold individualistic norms for both their maternal roles is to have fewer children. Therefore, as with non-Catholics, we would expect that as time goes on the effects of sex role norms will become even more pronounced in influencing family size. Those who are more traditional will tend to have more children. Nevertheless, we cannot rule out the effects of a child or children on sex role norms. It could very well be that the costs (tangible and intangible) of, say, the first child could contribute towards increasing the preferred egalitarianism of younger Catholic women, thus making them more desirous of individualistic gratifications.

Overall, therefore, we may conclude that younger Catholic working wives can be fitted under the rubric of Figure 4–1. Deferred marriage, early employment, and deferred childbearing can be conceptualized as indicating preferences for gratifications other than the marital and the familistic, i.e., for the individualistic. To the degree they are present, actual familistic gratifications are decreased. Education and correlated preferences for individualism influence marriage deferral, which in turn decreases parity. A variety of status variables indicating actual tangible and intangible gratifications also seem to reduce the motivations to have additional familistic gratifications. Sex role norms presumably operate on parity through and in conjunction with status factors. Especially among wives who have at least one child, individualistic norms and familism are firmly and clearly inversely related.

CONSEQUENCES OF PARITY

Among non-Catholics we considered the notion that a longitudinal design would reveal feedback loops between parity and economic and marital satisfactions. The entire cohort of Catholic working wives reveal a similar positive link between husband's status (education) and their feelings of economic satisfaction ($r = .51$), and a negative one between parity and economic satisfaction ($r = -.34$). Thus wives whose husbands are better-educated not only hold more modern sex role norms and have fewer children, but they also feel more economically satisfied. Being more satisfied stems from the status of their husbands and also from having to allocate finite resources to care for fewer children. Concomitantly, wives whose husbands are better-educated and who feel more economically satisfied report more satisfactory empathy (.29, .49). In addition, parity has a modest negative effect on empathy ($-.16$) but a much stronger negative impact on primary relations ($-.30$). The latter variable, like empathy, shows a positive link with husband's education (.25) and with economic satisfaction (.42). As with non-Catholics its most powerful association is with empathy (.62).

Therefore among Catholics too the question arises whether over time among wives who are less economically advantaged, and thus less economically and maritally satisfied (and also more sex role traditional), does a minimal level of economic and marital satisfactions help to account for motivations to have additional children as compensation?

NONWORKING WIVES

Recall that, among non-Catholics, wives who did not work fitted the model in Figure 4–1 less well that those who did. However the contrast in Table 4–6 between employed and nonemployed Catholics is perhaps somewhat less marked (except for parity) than it was in Table 4–2. What does stand out in the bottom row of Table 4–6 is the positive association between husband's income and current famliy size. The relationship is even stronger here than it was in Table 3–5 for birth intentions. At that juncture we indicated that Catholics apparently hold more strongly than others to the notion that "good people should have as many children as they can afford." That discussion may also be tied to the earlier one in this chapter regarding timing failures in connection with the wife's individualistic interests. This same general schema may be broadened to include a couple's economic interests. Given that they have not yet reached their target number of children and given that they feel a child would not interfere with family life-style or consumption patterns, or at least that reasonable rearrangements could be made to manage it, they might be more likely to ease into pregnancy through what an investigator might label "carelessness." That same investigator might also consider the pregnancy a timing failure and might conclude that Catholics have more of these than non-Catholics. But on the other hand, if more advantaged Catholics believe they should utilize the rewards of dollars to enjoy additional familistic gratifications, then perhaps the label of timing failure should be restricted to situations where the child might be perceived as a serious cost to or significantly interfere with the current or planned economic life style of the couple.

Both in Chapter Three and now here, this positive income–fertility linkage does not occur among working wives. As we learned from Table 3–2 husbands of nonworking Catholic wives earn significantly more money than those of working wives. Thus younger Catholic women who are more economically advantaged are less likely to experience the gratifications of employment and more likely to be willing for additional familistic gratifications. Presumably the economic resources make occupational rewards less attractive, and those resources also reduce the costs of children. At the same time absence of their own occupational rewards makes the alternative benefits of children seem that much more attractive.

Nonetheless, there are other reward factors that operate to make the alternatives to children less compelling and attractive. Table 4–6 (bottom row) indicates that their own education is one such variable, and we recall from Table 3–6 that education also influenced deferral of marriage. Education is positively related to TW-modernity and to RLM-modernity (.26, .22) and to a higher AE ranking (.30). In turn marriage deferral affected working before having children and also resulted in fewer children. Moreover wives who are more egalitarian in terms of PHA sex role norms have fewer children, as do wives who are less devout. Devoutness relates negatively to RLM-modernity (−.33).

In short there appear to be two contrasting forces operating among younger nonworking, relatively advantaged Catholic wives. One is a kind of reward–stimulus model. That is, the presence of economic rewards stimulates or encourages willingness for or perhaps "actual purchase" of familistic gratifications. The other model is one that also applies to non-Catholics and to working Catholics—a reward alternative model in which education, deferral behaviors, and sex role norms indicate preferences for benefits other than familistic. And although because of this second set of forces these non-working Catholics can be partially fitted under Figure 4–1, it is clear that at the present stage in their family life cycle the former model is operating in very powerful fashion. Which set of forces will eventually become more predominant in the future could be only ascertained by reinterviewing these wives, but even now when we examine those with proven parity (at least one child) the pattern observed in Table 4–6 remains unchanged.

TIMING FAILURES.

In Table 4–3 the percentage of Catholic working wives who report timing failures is 32; among the unemployed the figure is 37%. The data for employed wives are similar to those for working non-Catholics in that their own job status and incomes are negatively related to timing failures. The same holds for their father's job status and their husband's income. Thus socioeconomic benefits seem to have motivated wives in this context to be less careless contraceptors. But surprisingly there are two dimensions of role modernity that are linked positively with timing failures, as is intergenerational mobility. Equally puzzling is the finding that wives who are more devout have had fewer failures, whereas earlier literature (Ryder and Westoff, 1971) might have suggested the opposite. Similarly, among nonworking wives (bottom row) we again find that several sets of sex role norms show positive associations with timing failures.

There are at least two possible interpretations to these positive relationships between modernity and timing failures. One derives from our earlier discussion that during this era of changing patterns in marital structures and childbearing, many role-modern wives may not be at all certain as to when to have the total number of children they intend eventually to have. Should they time them early in the childbearing period or later on? Which would be least costly to their individualistic interests? White non-Catholics are apparently resolving that issue by deferring children. Earlier investigations (Whelpton et al., 1966) suggest that Catholics in general have not leaned in the direction of deferred childbearing patterns. It may be that younger role-modern Catholic wives are to some extent continuing that orientation. Nevertheless, compared to earlier cohorts of Catholics and to their more role-traditional contemporaries, they should reach the end of their childbearing period with fewer total children. It may be that over time role-modern Catholics will alter their timing behaviors to conform more to the predominant pattern exhibited by white non-Catholics. But for the present it appears as if such Catholics (perhaps unconsciously) are "easing" into pregnancies during the early stages of their marriages so that later on there will be fewer costs and punishments involved in pursuing individualistic (extra-familial) interests.

An alternative interpretation is that timing failures and the resultant live birth(s) occur to wives who are role-traditional but that the costs involved are substantial and traumatic enough to cause them to change or redefine their sex roles. That is prior to the "failure" they were only mildly egalitarian in terms of what behaviors and concessions they expected from their husbands and as to how fully their own interests should be realized. However, the resultant demands and pressures on them, likely rearrangement of employment behaviors, and even chagrin at contraceptive ineptness—i.e., the total range of subsequent punishments—could pressure them into placing "demands" on (or at least making requests to) their husbands to "allow" greater egalitarianism and individualism.

Both interpretations are open to testing within the context of a longitudinal design. Theoretically, we would lean towards the former explanation primarily because it fits better the models of Figures 3–1 and 4–1, which assume that sex role norms are shaped prior to marriage and have consequences for subsequent marital events. On the other hand, Catholics may fit those models less well than non-Catholics. It may be that processes of significant adult resocialization regarding sex roles occur among Catholics to a greater extent than is so for non-Catholics.

CONSEQUENCES OF PARITY

Pursuing further the implications of the reward-stimulus model, recall that for working Catholics parity had a negative effect on economic and marital satisfactions. Here among nonemployed Catholics its consequences for economic satisfaction are nil ($r = -.02$), while for marital satisfactions the relationships are more modest than above, especially for primary relations (empathy, $-.13$; primary relations, $-.17$). Hence it would appear that, in this situational context, where additional children may be more strongly perceived as a "moral good" and therefore highly significant and rewarding, children are less likely to undercut perceived economic and marital satisfactions.

Yet religious values cannot be the whole of it, because when we examine nonworking non-Catholics we find that there too parity has virtually no effect on economic satisfaction ($-.07$), empathy ($-.08$), or primary relations ($-.01$). It may be that time demands of full-time wife employment added to whatever time demands are made by children help to account for the negative effects of parity on marital satisfaction in employed-wife households of both religious categories. If wives do not work, the time demands of children by themselves do not seem to undercut husband-wife gratifications. But why would economic satisfactions not be affected where wives do not work, given that they have more children and probably in many instances lower family (not husband) incomes? It may be that certain wives have high life-style aspirations that help to account for why they work. Additional children may subvert hopes for attainment of those aspirations and thus negatively affect their economic satisfactions. Conversely, wives who have lower life-style aspirations (and, partially as a result, do not work) may also be less likely to perceive children as having an adverse affect on their economic situation.

Clearly, we need to learn how these several factors affect each other in feedback fashion. In what ways do economic and marital satisfactions and life-style aspirations interact with sex role norms to motivate wives to make decisions about labor force participation or about that first or next child? In what ways does the presence of a certain number of children influence subsequent satisfactions and sex role norms for wives in particular situational contexts—working or not working? What are the subsequent effects of these variables for childbearing patterns and so forth?

LOW TO AVERAGE EDUCATION

Shifting to the top row of Table 4–7, we examine that structural context in which all wives have average or less education. As was the case for non-Catholics the consequences of sex role norms are much less apparent where education is low and parity higher ($\bar{x} = 1.5$), than in the bottom row of the table where education is high and parity lower ($\bar{x} = 1.0$). Nonetheless the third column (top row) indicates that lowered parity is accounted for by deferring the gratifications of marriage and of the first child and also by seeking the benefits of full-time labor-force participation prior to children. Gratifications inherent in the wife's education have the same consequence, but as with nonworking wives, more dollars supplied by their husbands seem to stimulate familistic rewards and make the economic costs involved appear "manageable."

HIGH EDUCATION

Looking at the bottom row of Table 4–7, we find that aside from the negative effects of TM-modernity and education on pre-child employment, these wives can fit quite reasonably into the model of Figure 4–1. For instance, three dimensions of role modernity help account for a lengthier first-child spacing interval. In turn that variable results in fewer current children. The strongest of the three sex roles in terms of spacing is PHA-modernity and we recall from Table 3–6 that PHA was the single strongest correlate (and presumably influence) on their marriage deferral. Now, marriage deferral also lengthens spacing and has directly affected reduced parity levels. Furthermore, PHA also has direct bearing on parity (along with SA and TM) in tending to lower it.

But the single greatest influence on reduced family size is their self-evaluations of their task and skill capabilities (AE): the more positively they view themselves, the fewer children they have. Presumably, wives who are more task-capable want to utilize those skills beyond the confines of the home (as well as within it). Hence they tend to limit current familistic costs so that they are more free to exercise those skills both now and in the future. As we have seen before, higher AE relates positively to ISC, SA, RLM, and PHA (.46, .27, .29, .21). Thus AE-capable wives are also more instrumental and more individualistic—characteristics which tend to reinforce their AE perceptions and thereby help reduce their parity levels as well. Finally, as in two prior contexts of Tables 4–6 and 4–7, we find that here too the more dollars their husbands earn the more children they tend to have.

Aside from the effects of income, educated Catholic wives reveal patterns leading up to current parity that are very similar to those shown by educated non-Catholic wives. Individualism and familism appear to be inversely related in the terms portrayed by Figures 4–1. To the degree that education, sex role norms, and a variety of critical "marital-event" behaviors reflect preferences for individualistic benefits and concomitant willingness to defer marital and familistic gratifications, to that degree are actual familistic rewards and costs minimized.

TIMING FAILURES

Nonetheless, Table 4–5 makes plain that Catholics, regardless of education, diverge from non-Catholics when it comes to the relationships of role norms to timing failures. However, educated Catholics reveal that deferral of marriage and of the first child have influenced greater contraceptive rigor, and we have already seen the positive effect of role norms on those crucial events. At the same time, based on our earlier discussion it is possible that role-modern, younger Catholics have been less careful early in their marriages in order to permit greater freedom, autonomy, and flexibility to pursue individualistic interests when both they and their children have aged.

Also of interest in the lower middle panel of Table 4–5 is the strength of the correlation between birth intentions and timing failures, a correlation greater than in any of the three preceding situations for Catholics. Recalling from Table 3–5 the effects of role norms on their intentions, it may be argued that modernity reduces intentions, which in turn reduces timing failures. This particular process, along with the one traced through marriage age, tends to minimize failures, while the direct effect of role norms is to increase them. Obviously, compared with non-Catholics there is less consistency in terms of an overall reward-alternative framework to account for Catholic fertility control. The same holds with regard to the contrasting effects of husband's income. Therefore, analogous to the discussion in Chapter Three, although there are trend data showing convergences in Catholic–non-Catholic fertility patterns (Ryder and Westoff, 1971), until the kinds of inconsistencies identified here are modified we may continue to expect Catholics to report higher parities than non-Catholics at all stages of the life cycle.

Parity of Black Wives

SITUATIONS AND PARITY

The same question is asked of black wives 18 to 29 as was asked of white Catholics: To what degree can blacks be fitted under the model displayed in Figure 4–1? Table 3–2 showed that both working and non-working black wives have more children than comparable whites. However, unlike whites, blacks reveal no significant differences in parity levels whether they do or do not work.

WORKING WIVES

Looking at Tables 4–8 and 4–9 we observe that overall the patterns that emerge there are similar to those found earlier for whites. For example, insofar as working wives are concerned, we recall from Table 3–9 that education and role modernity helped to explain deferral of marital gratifications. In turn, Table 4–8 (top row) shows that marriage deferral and role modernity have influenced working after marriage and that employment at that time has resulted in deferring the gratifications of children (column two).

Finally, column three shows that deferring marriage helps to reduce the levels of current familistic rewards (and costs), as do the benefits of education. TW-modernity is associated with education (.29) and presumably operates on parity through it. Note too that wives who say they work mainly for enjoyment have fewer children than those who state that money is their major motivation. In the last chapter we found that Catholics and blacks who gave enjoyment as their major work motivation also intended to have fewer children. At those points we also explored the positive correlations between enjoyment motivation and role modernity. In short, sex role norms may operate on parity not only through education but also through work motivation. Black wives who are more individualistic are more likely to seek the intrinsic gratifications of employment, and those types of benefits are likely to motivate them to have fewer children. Such intrinsic benefits function as compensations or alternatives to additional children. Simultaneously, additional children could undercut attainment of those gratifications and they seek to avoid such costs. Moreover, as we would expect, the table shows that wives who are more egalitarian or modern in terms of the innovative "self-actualization" (SA) dimension currently have fewer children, as do those who earn more money and whose husbands are better educated. And as was so for whites, higher earnings are positively related to sex role modernity (TW = .28, RLM = .28, TH = .23) and to having a stronger instrumental self-concept (.27).

NONWORKING WIVES

Just as Figure 4–1 can subsume black wives in a situational context of full-time employment, it appears also to hold for those in a context of nonemployment. The bottom row of Table 4–8 reveals that a positive AE perception and premarital employment [the latter correlates with AE (.26) and with education (.32)] have apparently had a strong influence on the decision to work before having children. Their father's education and their own sex role norms have a similar consequence. The assumption here, as before, is that that particular work decision provides gratifications which motivate wives to defer benefits of children for a longer period of time (column two). Being more egalitarian on the PHA aspect of husbands' role behaviors also seems to delay that first child, as does being more instrumental and AE-capable. Blacks, like whites, show a strong positive link between ISC and AE (.47). Lastly, the actual level of current familistic gratifications (and costs) experienced by black nonworking wives is related inversely to a variety of indicators of individualism. Marriage deferral (influenced by education and correlated sex role norms) is one such indicator, along with education, child deferral, working prior to marriage, and ISC, AE, and RLM.

TIMING FAILURES

Reference was made in Chapter Three to Westoff and Westoff's observation (1971) that the realm of contraception behavior contains perhaps the greatest divergence between black and white patterns of fertility control. However, the younger black women in our sample did not report percentages of "number failures" substantially greater than those reported by whites (4% to 5%). Similarly, among employed black wives represented in Table 4–3, 31% report "timing failures," while among those who do not work the figure is 38%. Thus, although wives in the former situation diverge somewhat but not substantially from what we observed earlier for whites, wives in the latter context diverge most of all. Among all younger wives, blacks who are not now working seem to have experienced the greatest proportion of timing failures.

But perhaps more significant than proportion per se is the pattern that appears in Table 4–3. Blacks closely resemble Catholics, and both categories stand in contrast to non-Catholics. Among blacks who work, for instance, the wive's own higher job status and greater social mobility relate inversely to timing failures, but two sets of sex role norms indicate that egalitarianism and "failures" are positively correlated. Recalling the caveat as to the validity of retrospective assessments regarding whether an intended child came at the "wrong time" or not, we are then faced with the same kinds of questions that surfaced for Catholics. Do some wives view an untimed live birth as such a shock or trauma in terms of costs that its punishments force them into becoming more egalitarian, into making greater demands on their husbands and asserting more rights for themselves? Or do some black (and Catholic) wives who are more individualistic "not mind" having their intended "quota" early in the life cycle, believing that as a result they will be less hindered later on in achieving their individualistic interests.

The latter interpretation appears more plausible for reasons previously discussed. One of these reasons is indicated by the finding in Table 4–3 that lower birth intentions are related to fewer timing failures. Table 3–8 revealed that modern sex role norms help to lower birth intentions. Thus black working wives who are more individualistic want fewer children overall; and wanting fewer means they have been more contraceptively rigorous. Nonetheless, while their individualism probably means they will eventually end up with fewer children, apparently it does not indicate that younger blacks (and Catholics) had been strongly concerned to postpone their earlier intended childbearing by rigorous contraception. At least this may have been the case during the present era when sex roles and childbearing patterns appear to be in a state of transition. Were we to venture a prediction, we would say, given increasing convergences in other sorts of fertility control patterns (Ryder and Westoff, 1971), that over time Catholics and blacks will develop the same positive links between sex role modernity and contraceptive rigor already reported by non-Catholics. (In Chapter Five, we discover evidence for a convergence in that blacks resemble non-Catholics insofar as the explanation of current contraceptive practices is concerned.)

The lower right panel of Table 4–3 shows a variable that in all prior contexts has demonstrated virtually no correlation with timing failures. Here we see that the greater the empathy the less the likelihood of failure. Hill *et al.* (1959) report that the phenomenon measured by empathy—capability of spouses to communicate and understand—is strongly related to contraceptive efficacy. Being able to "talk" in general apparently has some impact on being able to deal more effectively with the specific issues that may arise between spouses regarding contraception. However as we learned earlier for whites, there appear to be complex causal interconnections between parity, empathy, economic satisfactions, and wife employment. Blacks reveal similar kinds of associations[5] and the empathy–timing failure relationship. Therefore, future investigations of the process of fertility control should, in both racial groupings, examine those factors that early in marriage and prior to children influence empathy in a positive direction—factors such as feelings of economic satisfaction. In turn, the consequences of both these variables on contraceptive behavior and on parity should be considered, followed by investigation of the subsequent effects that timing failures and parity levels have on both economic and marital satisfactions such as empathy.

LOW TO AVERAGE EDUCATION

The upper row of Table 4–9 indicates that wives in a situation of lesser education do not differ markedly from the reward-alternative model being developed here and portrayed in Figure 4–1. To be sure, as we noted for whites in similar situations, the direct effects of the sex role dimensions may be less apparent here than in certain other contexts. Nevertheless, if we compare the third and fourth columns we find that wives with proven parity show stronger associations between sex role norms and family size than do wives taken as a whole. Indeed the direct negative impact of sex role modernity on actual parity is even more evident among these particular black wives that it is among either set of white wives with comparable education.

HIGH EDUCATION

Shifting to wives with high education (Table 4–9, bottom row) we must caution as in Chapter Three that as cases are few, conclusions must be tentative. Insofar as explaining pre-child employment and first-child spacing are concerned, these wives fit the model well, especially in terms of spacing. Four dimensions of sex role norms relate to child deferral in the expected directions—the more egalitarian, the more months between marriage and the first child. The same positive relationship appears for their instrumental self-concepts. Nevertheless when we examine current parity we discover that two dimensions of husband-role modernity plus SA relate positively to higher parity.

Similar unexpected findings occurred in Chapter Three in connection with the birth intentions of these wives. The results both there and here may simply reflect the paucity of cases. On the other hand, they may intriguingly suggest a tendency among educated black wives for the number of children they have to stimulate preferences (perhaps demands) for greater rights and privileges for themselves and for greater concessions on the part of their husbands. For instance, IE and SA are the most innovative of the seven role dimensions we identified, and these are the dimensions, along with "problematic husband alterations" (PHA), that relate to parity. In Chapter Two we discussed some of the historical factors that might help to account for greater egalitarianism among black women in general. Furthermore, educated black women, owing to the range of economic opportunities open to them, are even more individualistic than their less-educated sisters. Therefore, these women for reasons both historic and current may, more than any other category of white or black wives, press their husbands towards taking greater responsibility for child and domestic care, i.e., towards granting wives greater rights, privileges, autonomy, and flexibility.

This pattern does not necessarily imply that they will attain completed family sizes greater than those for educated white Catholics or non-Catholics. Instead, blacks may simply have to bear fewer domestic responsibilities or costs at comparable parities. In any case, it would be necessary to follow educated women and observe differences by race in the impact that role norms have on parity and the influence that the presence of children makes on the subsequent definitions of these norms. Does race make a difference in the ways in which those role norms and behaviors are renegotiated so as affect attainment of the wife's extra-familial interests and objectives?

Timing Failures

To add further complexity to these matters, the lower right column of Table 4–5 reveals that two dimensions of role modernity (RLM and TW) affect timing failures in ways similar to their effects on non-Catholics: the more modern, the less probability of failure. Yet the "extreme" IE dimension shows an opposite relationship. Thus, the notions of genuine equality inherent in IE may make these wives more indifferent to timing failures early in marriage. Nonetheless, the notion of secularity intrinsic to RLM and acceptance of the individualistic notions in TW may serve to make them more cautious and rigorous.

Overall, fitting educated black wives into the model of Figure 4–1 is somewhat complicated, at least insofar as the direct relationship between parity and role norms is concerned. It is also problematic because of the limited number of cases available to us. Nonetheless, enough relationships emerge in the expected directions (e.g., certain role relationships with timing failures and first-child spacing) to indicate that this subset of wives can reasonably be subsumed under that larger rubric, if we make clear that future research may well dictate important refinements in the model which are unique to them.

Summary and Discussion

The purpose of this chapter is to seek to account for current family size, using but expanding the reward-alternative framework developed in prior chapters. Our major goal throughout the entire book is to develop a theoretical model of fertility control that is coherent and systematic. In that model are included variables we have already measured, as well as additional variables hitherto overlooked but identified as essential to further theory development. Throughout the chapter the major and recurring methodological problem, a hindrance to theory development, has been uncertainty regarding temporal and thus causal influence. The most significant variables that were missing were those that measure negotiation, bargaining, and decision-making, especially as they pertain to changes in sex role norms and to changes in birth intentions. These missing measures of negotiation and the like also pertain to decisions regarding wife's labor force participation, contraceptive behaviors, and domestic and child-care responsibilities.

In spite of the cross-sectional nature of the data, we have nonetheless interpreted them in terms of a set of ongoing influences as displayed in the flow chart of Figure 4–1. Even that chart is not complete, because it does not indicate feedback loops that the variables maintain among themselves, nor does it include variables for which parity itself may have significant consequences. In certain respects, Figure 4–1 overlaps with Figure 3–1, and in certain others it omits variables that are nonetheless implicitly assumed to be operating, such as parental status and current wife employment. From a systems theory perspective, all of the variables in those two figures and in Figure 5–1, as well as variables not now included, would be interrelated in a much more definitive fashion than is presently possible. The hypothesized linkages for such a systems approach are derived from findings in the several chapters.

At a more general level all the variables in the system are conceptualized as indicating preferences to attain certain kinds of rewards and to avoid certain kinds of costs. In this way we tie this model to a growing literature in economics, sociology and psychology (Fawcett, 1972, 1973) in which reward–cost frameworks are being increasingly utilized to explain not only fertility behaviors but also a wide range of other varieties of human behavior. We assume that certain rewards are alternative to others —that preferences for one set tend to reduce preferences for another. Moreover, in an effort to approximate the different structural and situational contexts and conditions that an ongoing systems approach would identify, we categorized our respondents first by employment and then by education. In certain contexts the model applies more fully and more validly than in others—for example, where women work full time or where they have high education.

The main variables in the model discussed in this chapter include sex role norms and self-perceptions, working full time prior to marriage, age at marriage, full-time employment subsequent to marriage and prior to any children, number of months between marriage and the first child, past contraceptive behavior—specifically timing failures—job status and income of employed wives, husband's social position (education, SES, income), types of social mobility, actual parity, economic satisfactions, and marital satisfactions (empathy and primary relations). All these elements may be placed on a continuum of familism (traditionalism) to individualism (modernity). The familistic end of the continuum reflects a high premium placed on group (familial) interests and loyalties. Wives found at that end place collective interests far ahead of individualistic interests, and they find those interests rewarding and gratifying. There are costs involved in making those choices, but whether perceived or not, the costs are assessed as less important than the rewards. The result of subtracting the former from the latter is a net profit.

Conversely, wives found at the other end of the continuum place individualistic or personal interests far ahead of familistic or collective interests—for them individualism and marital egalitarianism are rewarding and gratifying. Obviously most young American wives today would be found clustered towards the center of the continuum instead of at either end. Younger women who were extremely individualistic might find themselves in serious basic conflict with their husbands and might sometimes divorce them, or they might never marry in the first place. As our sample excluded single and separated persons, as well as those who had ever been divorced and/or remarried, we may very well have excluded many of those women who were most individualistic. Had they been included we might have discovered much more variation than we did in our measures of sex role norms. Perhaps we might also have discovered that such persons reveal much stronger relationships between those norms and fertility control behaviors (including parity) than women in stable marriages.

In any case the model (Figure 4–1) begins with full-time premarital employment, which appears to be influenced positively by education. Employment, education, and sex role modernity combine to increase age at marriage. Each of these factors tends to increase the likelihood that wives will work full time after marriage and prior to children. In turn these cumulated factors tend to increase the spacing interval between marriage and the first child. Next, all the preceding reduce the number of children born to these younger wives. Sex role norms, greater education, employment behaviors, deferral of marriage and of the first child—all reflect preferences for individualistic gratifications. The stronger these preferences are, the fewer children or familistic gratifications these wives have. In contrast, the weaker those preferences the greater their level of familism. One set of rewards functions as compensations or alternatives to the other.

Moreover, both the intrinsic and tangible rewards of their own job status and income also function to reduce familism. The same holds for their husband's SES and income, except in the case of nonemployed Catholics (also both educational categories), where husbands' income is apparently a stimulus rather than an alternative to children. Where social mobility was identified, it was related inversely to number of children born. However, Catholics gave some indication that mobility might have influenced earlier contraceptive carelessness. Education and SES of both spouses and income of wives tend to be positively correlated with role modernity. Thus apart from the income of Catholic husbands, status or socioeconomic benefits have the same consequences as sex role norms. The construct *individualism* may be thought of as broad enough to subsume the tangible and intangible benefits that wives achieve through their own education, SES, and income as well as the kinds of benefits that may accrue to them as a result of greater marital egalitarianism. Thus when we say individualism exists inversely with familism, the former includes a wide range of gratifications that wives potentially have access to or actually receive outside marriage and certain gratifications and interests they can attain within it. Wives who seek those kinds of benefits and costs tend relatively to forego both the costs and benefits of children, and vice versa. In either instance the particular behaviors are based on the type of net profit sought.

An important element in this model is the earlier contraceptive behavior of these wives, measured by retrospective techniques. Employed and educated white non-Catholics reveal that the more sex role modern they are, the fewer timing failures they have had. Other non-Catholics indicate that modern sex role norms lower their birth intentions and that the latter then reduce timing failures. In turn, wives who have experienced more failures currently have more children. Significantly, Catholics and most often blacks indicate that timing failures and sex role norms are positively associated. It may be that wives in these two categories are more willing to incur familistic costs early in their marriages, in order to be less impeded in their individualistic pursuits later on. In this connection it became evident that future research will have to probe more deeply into coping mechanisms that couples may or may not have to manage children that in the past have been labeled timing failures. When mechanisms are present that render the child nonpunishing to individualistic or to status-consumption aspirations, then perhaps such children ought to be classified differently than children who are punishing to either set of aspirations or behaviors.

In contrast to less-educated blacks, black wives with high educational levels revealed that certain sex role dimensions affected timing similarly to non-Catholics, while other dimensions fell in a pattern similar to Catholics. Educated blacks also tended to show positive links between certain role norms and parity, an anomaly that may be accounted for by the relatively few cases involved. Apart from these divergences, Figure 4–1 tends to apply with fairly equal validity to non-Catholics, Catholics, and blacks.

Moreover, parity itself, as well as timing failures, may exercise causal influence on a variety of factors including degree of sex role traditionalism or modernity, employment, birth intentions, and economic and marital satisfactions. Those with more children are less satisfied on the last two variables (working wives in particular), and that lack of satisfaction could motivate them to seek additional children as compensation. On the other hand, wives who are more economically and maritally satisfied seek fewer alternatives (children) as a source of gratification. In addition, lowered empathy (one aspect of marital satisfaction) may impair effective contraceptive behavior, further increasing parity levels.

Aside perhaps from fixed events such as age at marriage, at any point in the model a variable that has been caused by preceding factors can act back upon those same factors that "caused" it or upon any other factors. Theoretically, future analysis of ongoing systems of family fertility control can be subsumed under the type of reward–cost framework suggested here—one in which individualistic and familistic rewards (and costs) are inversely juxtaposed and thus presumably influence various types of decisions, motivations, and behaviors at each point in the system.

Notes

1. The wife reports that both she and husband are currently fecund. The same large array of variables listed in Chapter Three is examined for potential relationships with dependent variables. Those with the strongest possible correlations are listed in the tables. Usually this means .20 or better, but sometimes we must drop below that figure.

2. Regression equations are not used in this chapter because of a degree of uncertainty regarding the numerous issues surrounding causality and temporal sequence, as discussed in the text. Parity, for example, may very well influence some of the variables we have designated to try to explain it. We do, however, hypothesize paths of influence and interpret the data in terms of an ongoing "systems" model in which feedback loops maintain a very significant function.

3. Our procedure was first to determine number of live births and then to try to ascertain planning behavior prior to each birth (if any) and in the interval between births, and in what Ryder and Westoff (1971:223) call the "open interval" (the one terminated by the interview). Had the couple used any method of birth control during one of these three time segments? If "yes," did the wife become pregnant "because you *and* your (spouse) deliberately *stopped* using a method in order to have a child; or did it happen even though one or both of you *did not want* that pregnancy?" If the response is the former, this pregnancy is classified as a timing success; if the response is the latter, then the pregnancy is classed as a failure. If no method had been used the question was "Was the main reason you did not use any method then because you and your (spouse) wanted a baby as soon as possible?" An affirmative response indicates a nonfailure, a negative response

a failure. In the case of a failure (whether through use or nonuse the respondent was asked, "just before (the wife) got pregnant that time, did *you* yourself want a child *later*, or did you really want (no/no more) children?" If respondent said she wanted the child "later" it was classified as a timing failure. If the response was that no more were wanted it was classified as a number failure.

4. Figure 4–1 omits additional influences on timing failures in order to avoid making the visual display more complex than it appears at present.

5. Employed wives: parity correlates with economic satisfactions, empathy, and primary relations at −.21, −.14, −.28; Nonemployed wives: *r*'s, respectively, −.19, −.08, −.17.

Chapter 5. Current and Future Contraception

We come now to the third and final theme in our examination of changes in marital patterns and their consequences for fertility control. Chapter One laid the theoretical base for all that follows. The second chapter was devoted to detailed theoretical and empirical explication of our measures of sex role structures and self-concepts. Chapter Three explored those factors that influence age at marriage and orientations toward numbers of children. Chapter Four considered a series of "marital events" that lead up to and help account for current family size. One of the events to which we gave attention was the respondent's retrospective history of earlier timing failures.

Past "success" or "failure" involved, of course, the effective use of contraceptives, but in Chapter Four efficacy was only one segment of the larger issues examined. In contrast, the central concern of this chapter is contraceptive behavior, and we shall examine it from several related perspectives. Theoretically, however, the framework for explaining past "timing success" and current contraceptive behavior is the same. Wives who are more egalitarian or modern-oriented—who prefer greater individualistic gratifications and are willing for resultant structural changes in wife, husband, and mother roles—such persons should be more motivated to practice more rigorous and careful contraceptive behavior in the present (and future) just as they tended to do in the past.

Of course, as we recall it was white non-Catholics—the employed and the better-educated in particular—who best fit the general theoretical model. Wives in those contexts who were most role-modern had been least subject to timing failures. Among Catholics and blacks the possibility emerged that those who were more modern-oriented were not adverse to having their intended number of children early so that later on they might be less hindered in pursuit of their individualistic interests. In many of the remaining contexts it could be argued that wives who intended more children had in the past been more contraceptively careless. As we saw from Chapter Three, higher intentions were affected by sex role traditionalism. Thus sex role norms may have influenced timing failures through birth intentions. The basic problem in this discussion is that it may not be legitimate to label certain occurrences as timing failures, not merely because these are retrospective assessments (and thus their reliability is uncertain) but perhaps even more importantly because we do not have enough information about the total situation surrounding the event which the investigator labels as "failure." In certain situations, handling contraceptives carelessly might not necessarily be a failure if, for example, a resultant live birth is not costly to wives' individualistic interests or to the couples' consumption aspirations.

Unfortunately such information is not available to relate either to past or to present contraceptive behaviors. Therefore in the analyses that follow we continue to lean heavily on the assumption that to a large extent contraceptive behavior reflects the degree to which persons are indifferent to the costs, and perhaps unconsciously desirous of, the benefits of pregnancy and live birth. We are aware that other factors—e.g., an overall schema or plan regarding life style into which a child could be adequately incorporated at minimum cost even though it was not specifically planned for at that precise time—are probably intrinsic to the total "syndrome of indifference." But in spite of lacking data of that sort, we shall nonetheless seek to explain current and expected future contraceptive behavior in terms of the same reward-alternative framework utilized in prior chapters. We would expect that greater individualism (as reflected in particular by more modern sex role norms) will continue to emerge as inversely related to stronger familism (as reflected by less rigorous and effective contraceptive behaviors). Wives most oriented towards individualistic rewards should be most likely to be motivated to behave consistently and effectively in reducing the level of unintended familistic costs and rewards.

Fecundity

The obvious first step in determining whether persons are at risk of an unintended pregnancy is to ascertain their physiological capacity to reproduce. Among our respondents slightly less than 16% (n = 488) report that together with their spouse it would be "physically impossible to have a(n) (additional) child." These persons were than asked the reasons for their nonfecundity and were allowed to respond to more than one if it applied. Only 3% of the nonfecund responded that their condition was due to the wife being at menopause, a finding to be expected given the age of wife (44) beyond which households could not be included in the sample.

At the same time, some 66% of these particular respondents indicated that the wife in the household had had "an operation," and 22% reported that the husband had had "an operation."[1] Westoff reports that "one of the most dramatic findings in the 1970 *National Fertility Study* is the fact that voluntary sterilization—typically, tubal ligation for women and vasectomy for men—has become the most popular method of contraception currently used by older couples (in which the wife is aged 30–44)" (Westoff, 1972: 10). According to Westoff, 12% of older husbands and 13% of older wives had undergone contraceptive sterilization. He interprets these figures to mean that "one-quarter of all older couples who were currently practicing contraception had been surgically sterilized." Findings among our older respondents suggest similar conclusions regarding the popularity of the contraceptive operation for voluntary sterilization. Among households where the wife was aged 30 to 44, some 23% of those "practicing contraception" had had a contraceptive operation (11% of husbands; 12% of wives).[2]

By comparison, only 20% of all older persons in our sample were using the pill (oral contraceptive), 8% were using rhythm, 12% the condom, 4% withdrawal, 6% the diaphragm, and 2% or less some other methods. Westoff reports that 21% of older persons in their national sample reported using the pill, virtually identical to our 20% figure (1972:11). Likewise, 47% of all younger (wife aged 18 to 29) persons in our sample report using the pill,[3] which is very similar to the 49% figure Westoff reports for younger persons nationally (1972:11). Also, among younger persons in our sample the closest competitor to the pill in terms of popularity is the condom (9%), which was also second among younger persons in popularity nationally (17%) (1972:11).

By contrast, a recent major fertility survey in England reported the condom to be more popular than the pill overall, but that the pill was becoming more popular among recently married couples. Within a representative sample of both ever-married and never-married women, 36% of those at risk of pregnancy were using the condom, while only 25% were using the pill (Bone, 1973). But among those married between 1966 and 1970, 38% were pill users, compared to 31% for the condom. For those married between 1961 and 1965 the figures were 30% and 35% for the pill and the condom respectively. In another contrast with American patterns the English study goes on to report that the contraceptive operation is much less popular in Britain, where only 4% of married couples reported using it, compared to an overall 11% figure for American married couples.

Whelpton *et al.* (1966) found that in the past the contraceptive operation for women (tubal ligation) was more common if education was limited. Presser and Bumpass (1972) indicate that this continues to be the case. However, they also report that the male contraceptive operation (vasectomy) is becoming increasingly common (as is tubal ligation) but, significantly, that vasectomy is positively correlated with wife's education (see also Bumpass and Presser, 1972).

In the future it may be that increasing numbers of well-educated couples may choose to control fertility by the vasectomy route. Compared to tubal ligation it is only minor surgery, requires no confinement, and is less painful and is inexpensive. This technique might be especially welcome among some persons who choose to remain childless (see Chapter Three). We saw that such persons preferred marriages based on sex role equality. Such persons strongly prefer the individualistic as well as other sorts of gratifications that such marriages can provide. Therefore, in order to achieve maximization of those kinds of rewards they (as well as those wanting only one or two children) may increasingly turn to this radical means of birth control. In either case (childlessness or minimal child-bearing), among the most modern and individualistic couples, vasectomy may become an increasingly popular tool to maximize desired net profit in terms of individualistic versus familistic costs and rewards. Unfortunately among the 34 younger persons and 192 older persons who reported contraceptive operations, we were unable to identify any meaningful pattern of variables (not even education) to account for that behavior. Given its apparent increasing popularity, future studies will need to probe in greater depth both the antecedents and consequences of voluntary sterilization.

CONTRACEPTION AMONG THE FECUND

If couples are physically capable of reproduction they are at risk of unintended pregnancy except under two conditions: First, the wife is currently pregnant. Second; the wife is not pregnant but in response to a question as to why she is not now using any contraceptive technique, she replies that she "wants to have a baby as soon as possible." [4] In the text and tables that follow we exclude these two classes of wives and focus instead on all other fecund women who are at risk. As we shall see, as most of these wives are using some sort of contraceptive method, we assume that they do not want a child at this particular time. Furthermore, for the minority who are not using some technique we make the same assumption because they have specifically asserted that their reason for non-use is not their desire for another child.

The Choice of Effective Contraceptives

Respondents who report currently using a method were asked what method it is. Of the full range of contraceptives used, the oral contraceptive commands major attention because of its three-fold significance: (1) With regard to social policy, it appears to be one major factor in recent reductions of national birth rates; (2) substantively, Ryder and Westoff (1971) maintain that the pill is responsible for what they term a "contraceptive revolution" and hence students of fertility must give it special attention; and (3) theoretically, for our purposes, it would seem that because it is so efficient those younger women who are most determined to limit familistic gratifications might perhaps be most likely to use it.

Besides age, another factor which enters into our understanding of pill use is the physiological side-effects (real or imagined) certain women suffer from it (Allingham et al., 1970). Thus, some wives who might wish to use the pill find themselves physically unable or extremely hesitant to do so. Of this number, those most concerned about effectiveness would be likely to use the diaphragm or jelly or both—methods which were the most widely used, along with the condom, prior to the sixties (Ryder, 1970).

In comparing the relative effectiveness of contraceptive methods, Tietze (1970) states that oral contraceptives are what he labels "most effective," what he also calls Group 1 methods. "Failures are exceedingly rare (approximately 1 pregnancy in more than 10,000 cycles or 0.1 pregnancy per 100 women per year) if all tablets are taken according to prescription. Tablets missed during cycles of medication have accounted for about one pregnancy per 100 women per year in published studies" (p. 269).

In a separate category which he labels "highly effective," (group 2) he places such methods as the intrauterine device (IUD), the diaphragm with cream or jelly, and the condom (p. 270). These have "a failure rate of between one and five pregnancies per 100 women per year" (p. 270). Finally Tietze describes a third and fourth group of methods, labelled as "less effective" and "least effective" (pp. 272–73). Group 3 includes jellies or creams (without diaphragm), foams, suppositories, sponges, tampons, withdrawal, and rhythm. The fourth category consists of postcoital douching and prolonged breast-feeding.

Based on the theoretical perspective developed to this point, an argument can be made that, because of the extraordinary effectiveness of the oral contraceptive, as sex role modernity increases, so will the use of the pill, precisely because it guards so well against unwanted familistic costs. Were it not for two related phenomena, that proposition could be developed without hesitation. Because of the physiological complications cited above and also because of the high effectiveness of Tietze's Group 2 methods, our predictions require qualifications. Persons who are individualistically oriented and not troubled by the pill's physiological implications—both current and future—will probably gravitate toward its use. But persons who are equally modern but for one reason or another are troubled by these questions may be expected to gravitate toward Group 2 techniques and, what is more, be motivated to make them work. Perhaps it requires less motivation to make the pill work than to make Group 2 methods work.

Significantly, several feminist spokeswomen have criticized current female oral contraceptives precisely because of their possible physiological hazards. Some have gone a step further and alleged that the absence of comparably sophisticated male contraceptives implies a certain degree of chauvinism on the part of mostly male biological researchers (Segal, 1972). This latter issue aside, the main point is that strong preferences for female autonomy and individualism by no means implies automatic and unquestioned acceptance of the female oral contraceptive.

The point would seem to be that, theoretically, the major gulf is not between pill users and all other users, but between users of what Tietze labels Group 1 and 2 methods versus users of Group 3 and 4 methods. The high effectiveness of Group 2 techniques suggests that they are not mutually exclusive or qualitatively different from oral methods insofar as the central theoretical issue here is concerned, the effects of modernity on the processes and outcomes of contraceptive behavior. The more fundamental difference, when it comes to the theoretical link between modernity and technique efficiency, is between those who choose the less or least effective methods and those who go beyond to a level of greater effectiveness. It can be assumed that persons using techniques from Groups 3 and 4 are not strongly motivated to prevent familistic events. Although less than totally indifferent (as nonusers might be assumed to be) they evidently do not feel the same cost–reward constraint that persons do who use techniques from either Group 1 or Group 2.

Discussion of pill use and the Ryder-Westoff (1971) characterization of it as a "contraceptive revolution" again raises the question of how central motivation is to fertility control, as over against technology. We gave some attention to this theoretical and policy issue in earlier chapters. The issue can be placed on a continuum, with some investigators and planners leaning toward the technology end, while others lean toward the motivation end. Most are probably somewhere between, realizing that fertility control is a complex combination of both technology and motivation.

In this regard, Campbell argues that the declines in American birthrates up to 1973 represent delays in childbearing "that will be made up later" (1973:112). His argument, in part, appears to be that motivational components that influence birth timing combined with highly efficient technologies were largely responsible for these birth declines. Furthermore, he contends, certain motivational components can be expected to bring about subsequent birth increases. To this position we would add that to the extent such increases actually occur, they should vary by degree of role modernity. That is, we would expect that those who are more role-traditional or less individualistic will contribute most heavily to any future fertility increases that might take place. Thus both Campbell's position and our elaboration of it suggest that although technology is irrefutably vital to effective fertility control, motivation is prior to it in both theoretical and policy significance. Although we shall consider this question further in Chapter Six, the point to keep in mind now is that the following discussions of methods assume intrinsic linkages with certain motivational components.

Methods of White Non-Catholic Wives

STRUCTURAL CONTEXTS AND CONTRACEPTIVE BEHAVIOR

We shall examine first the contraceptive behavior of the non-Catholic wives aged 18 to 29. The first column in Table 5–1 displays those variables (out of the complete array available) that show the strongest correlations with use of the pill. Recall the earlier theoretical reasoning that we should expect important contrasts between pill users and those who use techniques from Groups 3 and 4. Based on that reasoning, column 1 includes all cases that report using the pill or methods from Groups 3 or 4.

Working Wives

If we look first at employed white non-Catholic wives (row 1, column 1, Table 5–1) we discover that our theoretical expectations are verified. (Recall the meanings behind the role dimension labels: TW, traditional wife; SA, self-actualization; PHA, problematic husband alterations; IE, institutionalized equality; TH, traditional husband; RLM, religious legitimation of motherhood; TM, traditional mother. ISC refers to instrumental self-concept, ESC to expressive self-concept, and AE to evaluation of wife abilities.) The correlations might even be stronger were it not for an additional complication that should be introduced in trying to explain pill use. Because of widespread publicity given to the pill, willingness of physicians to prescribe it, and its overwhelming public acceptance, many wives are coming to adopt it (Bumpass, 1973). As a result, it may be difficult to isolate variables that meaningfully discriminate its use. Other studies have indicated a positive relationship between education and pill use, but for these wives, neither education, job status, nor income for themselves or for their husbands relate directly to use of the pill.

Nevertheless, we see from the table that TH modernity is quite firmly related to pill use, along with two additional dimensions of modernity. TH is related to other dimensions of modernity (TW:$r = .32$, RLM: $r = .24$), and to wives' job status ($.32$). In turn, wives' SES is linked to greater education and more income of their own ($.60, .45$). We may thus suggest that working wives who prefer more modern and individualistic role structures and who have greater objective status benefits are the ones most strongly motivated to use the most efficient contraceptives available to control familistic benefits and costs. Rewards that are alternative to childbearing and caring are apparently more compelling than are traditional gratifications.

The second column in Table 5–1 presents those variables that show the strongest correlations with use of Group 2 techniques. An index was constructed for all current users (except those on the pill) based on whether or not they were using one (or more simultaneously) of the three "highly effective" Group 2 methods.[5] Using the same theoretical reasoning as described for the pill and its correlates, we expect important contrasts between those who use a Group 2 technique and those who do not. Based on that reasoning, column 2 includes all cases that report using methods from Group 2 or from Groups 3 and 4. Therefore the question answered by column 2 is, what correlates positively with choice of a Group 2 method? At that level the question is similar to the one answered in column 1 as to what correlates with choice of the pill. But at a more general level, the two questions are identical: "What are the correlates of the choice of efficient or effective contraceptive techniques?

When we examine column 2 of the top row of Table 5–1, we find that two dimensions of role modernity (TH, RLM) relate firmly to use of Group 2 techniques. Husband's education also emerges as directly and positively related to Group 2 use, and husbands' education and wives' role modernity are strongly related (TW = $.42$, RLM = $.43$, PHA = $.37$). Hence, for whatever reasons (physiological or otherwise), these particular users do not employ the pill, nonetheless the same theoretical perspective applies in attempting to explain selection of highly effective means to control pregnancy. The gratifications of education and preferences for individualistic gratifications combine to increase the motivation to reduce the risk of a birth that could be defined more as cost than as reward.

At the same time, wives who are more instrumental are not being efficient in their contraceptive behavior. We shall observe a similar phenomenon in the second row of the table in connection with the AE dimension. It may be that wives who see themselves as more instrumental are more likely to believe they can manipulate whatever methods they might use to prevent a child. Or it may be that their instrumental self-concept leads them to believe that if an unintended pregnancy should occur, they could cope with whatever costs might arise from it.

Nonworking Wives

Turning to nonworking wives, in the second row of Table 5–1 we find that among these particular cases, 55% employ the pill, less than the 64% reported for working wives. There is, apparently, some connection between full-time employment (i.e., its benefits) and use of the most efficient means available to prevent an occurrence that could hinder continued employment and the resultant acquisition of material and nonmaterial benefits. Surprisingly, we discover that AE capability is correlated with non-use of the pill. Moreover, overall task-capability (AE) is strongly related to greater instrumentality (.50). Why the negative relationship between AE efficiency should emerge is not at all clear. We may suggest that we are observing these young nonemployed wives at a particular, perhaps unique, point in their early childbearing years. For a variety of reasons their very capability and instrumentality may lead them to believe that they can manipulate techniques from Groups 3 and 4 (known to be less efficient) to control conception. Their self-confidence, however, may be ill-founded, and they may eventually find themselves confronted with an unwanted pregnancy. Another possibility is that high-capability, highly instrumental wives who are not working are more indifferent to a (another) conception. They may feel that their skills and personality characteristics would enable them to cope with such an eventuality.

Simultaneously, however, three aspects of role modernity all relate to increased likelihood of greater efficiency (pill use), as does intending no more children. All three of the role dimensions listed in the table are positively linked with wives' education (.21, .32, .34). Hence, role modernity (in its different aspects) helps to explain pill use among currently nonemployed as well as employed wives. In both categories, presumably, preferences for extrafamilial gratifications help to motivate wives to want to control as efficiently as possible the timing and number of familistic rewards.

Education

When we shift to the situational context represented by the third row of Table 5–1 (low to average education), we find that sex role norms are only modestly linked with pill use. (As the results in columns two for Group 2 use in Tables 5–1, 5–2, 5–4, and 5–6 tend to be similar to results shown in columns one, we shall hereafter not comment on them in any detail in the text.)

Significantly, it is when we move to the bottom row of Table 5–1 that we discover the strongest and most consistent evidence of relationships between sex role norms and method efficiency (five role dimensions each affect both Group 2 and pill use). Were we to follow these wives over time it is possible that at certain points choice of a method could influence degree of role modernity. However, based on the theoretical reasoning developed throughout these pages, our assumption is that the major direction of influence runs the other way. Wives who are the most oriented towards egalitarianism and towards individualistic gratifications are the ones most likely to use those contraceptive techniques known to be most effective in preventing unwanted familistic costs. Their motivation to attain one type of gratification leads them to behave in such a way as to reduce the likelihood of another type of benefit.

Analogous to findings in Chapters Three and Four, this specific instance of the more general link between individualism and familism occurs most strongly where wives are best-educated. They are the ones who potentially have greatest access to the most rewarding (extrinsically and intrinsically) kinds of extrafamilial gratifications. Once we move out of that context, the consistency and strength of this specific individualism–familism relationship holds fairly equally whether wives work or do not work. However, the consequences of sex role norms for contraceptive efficiency are most problematic where wives have least potential access to gratifying extrafamilial pursuits—those with low to average education. There an unintended pregnancy is relatively much less costly or punishing than it would be to their well-trained counterparts.

We remarked that it was surprising to find the AE dimension related negatively to method efficiency. Among well-educated wives it is similarly surprising to discover empathy related negatively to efficiency when earlier literature (Hill *et al.*, 1959) indicates it should have been otherwise. However we did suggest that among younger wives AE (and ISC) could stimulate the attitude that they could somehow cope with an additional child should it occur, or that they could successfully manage less reliable contraceptives to prevent its occurrence. The same may hold for empathy. Feeling they can "communicate" might lead them to believe that either they can make less efficient methods work or that the "positive relationship" they have with their husbands could somehow help them to overcome potential familistic costs.

Methods of Older Wives

While in earlier chapters we found, for a variety of reasons, that older wives could not easily be fitted under the models that applied to younger wives, Table 5–2 represents an exception. In terms of method efficiency (selection of the pill or of Group 2 techniques), it is clear that numerous dimensions of sex role modernity relate positively with it. This conclusion is most apparent among working wives and those with most education. It also holds to some degree where wives are less well trained and holds least among nonworking wives. Interestingly, in contrast with younger wives, older women who see themselves as more AE-capable and more instrumental use more efficient techniques. Perhaps experience has taught them that their skills and capabilities could be used most effectively in manipulating efficient technologies rather than by attempting to cope with less efficient methods or in trying to cope with an actual child that was born partly as a result of unreliable methods.

In any event the major conclusion is that older (as well as younger) non-Catholic wives reveal strong linkages between modernity and efficiency. (Such relationships do not appear for older Catholics and older blacks.) The more strongly they prefer individualistic rewards for themselves—or the more sex role egalitarian or modern they are—the more likely they are to choose those methods that reduce the risk of unintended pregnancy or unwanted familistic costs. Apparently, older wives who remain at risk and who possess aspirations for extrafamilial, individualistic gratifications are more likely to use efficient techniques than are wives who do not possess those aspirations. For the latter women an "accidental" pregnancy may not be all that traumatic and life-changing, whereas for more role-modern wives it would be and thus they become more strongly motivated to avoid it.

The intriguing question is whether these older wives have shown this type of relationship ever since marriage or whether certain events over the years brought about a linkage that did not formerly exist. Has their selection of efficient methods contributed to their egalitarianism, or is the casual influence more as we have posited it—in the opposite direction? Has the recent revival of feminism contributed in any way to the existence of these relationships? Have they decided that since they are now older and have devoted many years to husband and children, it has finally become appropriate and legitimate to seek other kinds of alternative satisfactions and fulfillments? Are they prepared to "launch out" for the first time (or in many years), and as part of their program do they want to assure themselves that an unintended pregnancy does not occur? It is of course exceedingly difficult to answer these questions insofar as they pertain to past events. But it does seem significant that among older wives, most of whom have all the children they intend to have, we are able to identify this modernity–efficiency linkage at all. The link provides additional indication of the pervasiveness of sex role norms insofar as they pertain to fertility control among both younger and older non-Catholics. As with younger wives it is likely that were we to begin to follow these older women over time we would discover mutual causation or feedback loops, in which modernity stimulates efficiency which encourages modernity, and so forth.

EXPECTED CONTRACEPTIVE EFFICACY

Ryder and Westoff, for their 1970 National Fertility Study, devised a measure which can be labeled as: the respondent's own perception of how likely she is to have an unwanted pregnancy. They kindly shared this measure with us and the following is our slightly modified version of it:

> Suppose you decide *not* to have any (more) children. What would you estimate are your chances of getting pregnant anyway, on the basis of your experience? Would you say you: (1) would be certain to get pregnant; (2) would probably get pregnant; (3) would probably *not* get pregnant; (4) would be *certain* not to get pregnant.

The perception of one's own likelihood to have an unwanted future pregnancy reflects several important considerations in the control of human fertility. First, it reflects past experience and the degree of rigor and success in handling contraceptives; it reflects the image the respondent has of her own degree of contraceptive management. Second, it may be a kind of self-fulfilling prophecy in that persons who state they would have an unwanted pregnancy are perhaps more likely to have one, and those who state they would not might be less likely to have one. Besides these important substantive considerations there is a third issue—the theoretical question of the linkage between this type of perception and individualistic reward-seeking. Women who are more modern-oriented might be expected to perceive themselves as being more "successful" than those who are less modern. Irrespective of whether or which methods are employed, preferences for individualistic benefits might be expected to enhance the perception that when they wish to they are able to control pregnancy in "rational" fashion.

This kind of perception arises out of their greater motivation or determination to be more successful. In Ryder's terms (1970) "the perceived gravity of the consequences of failure" is presumed to be greater among those persons who are more concerned about individualistic, extrafamilial gratifications. For at least three reasons, therefore, this type of item becomes extremely important to the overall thrust of our study, and we shall attempt to explain it using regression procedures.

One other study that utilized a similar item was Rainwater's (1965). He sought to measure "attitude toward likelihood of success in limiting family to desired size." Three classes of expected success were built: (1) planful and self-assured, (2) hopeful but unsure, and (3) passive and fatalistic. He found that 63% of middle-class Protestants fell in class 1 and 37% in class 2. Among middle-class Catholics the percentages in the three categories were 23, 63, and 14, respectively. Upper lower-class persons (black and white) ranked at 18%, 58%, and 24%; while lower-class blacks and whites showed 5%, 32%, and 63%, respectively (p. 200). Clearly, persons who are more rewarded socioeconomically are the ones most likely to believe they can effectively ward off unwanted familistic costs; those least rewarded see themselves as least capable of doing so. Moreover, Rainwater indicates that there would be no meaningful differences between middle-class persons if it were not for the "sense of conflict between religious beliefs and middle class values" that Catholics experience (p. 202).

To get the distribution of the four responses to our inquiry about the respondent's own perceptions, we examined only marriages in which both partners are fecund; the item was put solely to such persons, as it makes sense only for them. Therefore among white men the percentages in the four categories (1, 2, 3, and 4 respectively) are 6%, 17%, 50%, and 24%, while 3% were undecided.[6] Among white women the figures are 7%, 15%, 49%, and 26%, and 3% undecided.[7] For black men they are 10%, 22% 44%, and 17%, and 8% undecided; for black women the percentages are 9%, 22%, 40%, and 22%, and 7%.[8] Clearly, the majority of fecund husbands and wives, black and white, place themselves in category 3—"would probably *not* get pregnant." The smallest number put themselves in the "certain pregnancy" row.

However, the major differences between blacks and whites are that blacks are more likely than whites to place themselves in rows 1 and 2 and less likely to place themselves in rows 3 and 4; and blacks are also more likely to be more undecided. As noted in Chapter Four, earlier studies indicate that historically blacks have had difficulty in gaining access to the most effective contraceptives, as well as with contraceptive efficacy generally. These discouraging experiences may help to account for the percentage differences here. Moreover, to the degree that fertility control in general consists of important motivational components, it is plain that blacks have been denied access to socioeconomic rewards. We may assume that persons (black or white) who have been excluded from those kinds of gratifications will be motivated to seek out other sorts of benefits —including familistic ones—and thus be relatively less motivated to practice rigorous contraception. However, the percentage differences are small and therefore merely suggestive, and later in the chapter we shall encounter a more significant generalization, both theoretical and relative to policy, that is, the processes that account for degree of perceived future efficacy are basically the same in both racial groups.

If we sort whites by religion we learn that male non-Catholics reveal the following percentages respectively for each of the four categories: 4, 14, 53, and 26 (3% undecided).[9] For Catholic men the figures are 8, 21,

45, and 22 (4).[10] For non-Catholic women they are 5, 14, 51, and 28 (2).[11] Among Catholic wives they are 9, 17, 47, and 22 (5).[12] Thus, as Rainwater, we discover that non-Catholics (men and women) tend to expect that they will be somewhat more efficacious than do Catholics, and probably for the same reasons.

WORKING WIVES

In Table 5–3 we examine the determinants of expected future contraceptive efficacy for younger non-Catholic wives within four different situational contexts.[13] Looking first at currently employed wives we find that four dimensions of role modernity are correlated strongly in the expected direction with expected efficacy: The more modern or individualistic or egalitarian these wives are, the more efficacious or successful they expect to be. This outcome was predicted because theoretically wives who prefer individualistic gratifications should be more strongly motivated to behave rigorously in preventing unwanted familistic costs. In this case the item wording makes clear the cost is in the form if a number failure—exceeding their targeted number of children. Wives who are more sex role traditional can be expected to be less concerned to prevent unwanted familistic costs; they are more indifferent to the costs and more casual about individualistic gratifications. Conversely, wives who are more sex role modern cannot afford to be casual or indifferent on either count if they are actually to fulfill their own individualistic aspirations, whatever those may be. By itself the TW dimension accounts for 9% of the total explained variance; no other single variable approaches that figure.

Nonetheless, the panel reveals that a dimension of birth orientations, desires, is more strongly correlated with expected success than any of the sex role variables. Too, both birth desires and birth intentions reveal stronger beta weights than any of the role dimensions, though the TM beta follows directly behind birth intentions. The birth desires variable was discussed in Chapter Three, where several points were made. First, the work of Ryder and Westoff (1971) suggests than an intentions measure is preferable to a desires measure for use in fertility studies. One reason is that the wording that measured desires may reflect more of a sense of wistfulness than does the measure of intentions. The desires item may tend to produce more inflated figures and be less linked to reality. Table 3–1, for example, showed that the mean number of children desired was consistently greater than the number intended. Specifically among these working wives, the mean number of children desired is 2.4, while the mean number intended is 2.3. However, Ryder and Westoff (1971) indicate that desires and intentions are highly intercorrelated and obviously not mutually exclusive theoretically or empirically. Among these working wives the correlation is .69. Furthermore, just as birth intentions was explained in Chapter Three by sex role norms, the same may be concluded regarding desires. For example, the more modern these wives are on TM, PHA, SA, TW, and TH, the fewer children they desire (r's = $-.36$, $-.19$, $-.22$, $-.36$, and $-.23$).

Therefore, in Figure 5–1 it seems reasonable to treat desires and intentions as fairly equivalent measures of birth orientations. As the flow chart indicates, a path of influence is assumed to exist from sex role modernity to birth orientations. As in Figure 3–1, the former tends to have a negative effect on the latter. In turn there is a path of influence from birth orientarions to expected efficacy, and this influence too is negative. As Table 5–3 indicates, the higher the birth orientations (desires and intentions), the less effective they expect to be. In other words, younger women who desire and intend more children (or familistic rewards) find it more difficult to perceive themselves effectively minimizing those gratifications. By comparison to the satisfying outcomes of children, their costs seem less salient and significant. In that sense the birth desires variable may not necessarily reflect as much wistfulness as may at first appear—"It would be nice to have x, but realistically I have to settle for x minus 1." Wives who think "it might be nice" to have that additional child may in fact behave in such a way (being less careful in their contraception) as to bring it about.

Figure 5–1 also displays a direct path of influence from sex role norms to expected efficacy: The more individualistic the norms the greater the expected success. Thus it may be said that sex role modernity influences

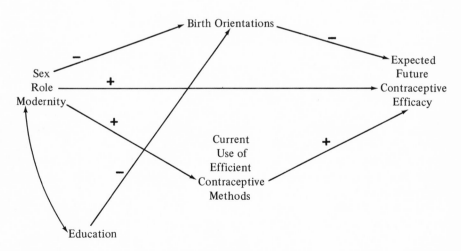

FIGURE 5-1.   Flow Chart Showing Influences on Current Contraceptive Behaviors and Future Contraceptive Efficacy

efficacy directly and also indirectly through birth orientations. In addition, Figure 5–1 reveals a path of influence from sex role norms to current use of efficient contraceptive techniques as represented in Table 5–1 by both the pill and Group 2 methods. We created a new variable by assigning scores on the basis of whether respondents were using those types of more effective methods or instead were utilizing the poor techniques from Groups 3 and 4.[14] The upper left panel of Table 5–3 reveals a connection between use of more efficient methods and greater expected efficacy. (There is also a more modest connection between use of any method and efficacy.) As we might predict, persons who use methods proven to be effective are more likely to perceive that they will be able to prevent an unwanted familistic event, and Figure 5–1 indicates a path of influence from method efficiency to expected efficacy. But here too sex role norms have presumably influenced choice of method and thus once more those norms indirectly affect expected efficacy through method efficiency.

Incidentally, it is worthwhile noting that this latter "technology variable" is not so strongly related to efficacy as are the role variables and the birth orientations variables, or what can be labeled "motivational" factors. As indicated earlier in the chapter, both strong motivation and sophisticated technology are requisite to optimal fertility control. Nonetheless the data in this panel and throughout the table suggest that motivation stimulated by cost–reward trade-offs may be prior in significance to technology. The stronger the motivation to achieve alternatives to familism, the less critical perhaps becomes the technology because highly motivated persons will make relatively less effective techniques work for them. Conversely, the weaker those motivational components, the more crucial becomes technology.

Nonworking Wives

Moving to the upper right panel of Table 5–3, we find that the flow-chart model of Figure 5–1 is applicable there as well. TM modernity has the strongest positive influence on expected efficacy among these non-working wives. Next in potency comes birth desires, followed by method efficiency and SA modernity. The two role variables by themselves account for 8% of the total explained variance. Although TM modernity has only a modest effect ($r = -.10$) on desires, the latter is strongly correlated to birth intentions (.45). Intentions are negatively related to RLM and to SA modernity ($-.24$, $-.20$).

Overall, therefore, we may conclude that wives in this situational context who are more individualistic expect that they shall be better able to prevent unwanted familistic costs. Sex role norms have this kind of impact directly, and also indirectly through lowered birth orientations and increased method efficiency, as shown in Table 5–1.

Low to Average Education

These same conclusions hold once more when we shift to wives with less education (lower left panel). Birth desires and TM modernity are the strongest predictors of expected efficacy. Desires are related inversely to TM modernity (−.19). Thus preferences for individualistic rewards may again be said both to depress familistic orientations and to enhance perceived contraceptive rigor. Conversely, husband's income has the effect of making wives appear more casual and less rigorous. Evidently the more economic resources they possess the more likely they are to feel that they could possibly afford to be careless even to the extent of "allowing" an unwanted child to occur. However aside from this element (and a modest modernity–efficiency link) the model in Figure 5–1 generally applies to wives with fewer years of schooling.

High Education

Finally, among highly trained wives, Table 5–3 reveals that six of the seven sex role dimensions are strongly correlated in the predicted direction with expected efficacy. TW is especially strong, accounting for 19% of the explained variance. Method efficiency also shows a strong correlation with efficacy, and we recall from Table 5–1 the effect of sex role norms on that sort of behavior. As before, birth desires are negatively associated with TW, SA, PHA, and IE modernity (−.37, −.33, −.34, and −.19). The one variable that has not appeared in any of the preceding contexts is what was described in Chapter Four as "timing failures." Recalling the complex issues surrounding that particular measure, we nonetheless note that the more timing failures wives have had in the past the less successful they expect to be in the future even when what is at stake is a number failure. Recall from Table 4–5 that wives in this context with at least one child reported that sex role traditionalism was strongly related to timing failures. Among this subset of wives, being less instrumental also seems to have had some stimulative effect on past contraceptive carelessness (−.28).

Therefore, although we shall not insert the timing failure variable into Figure 5–1, it represents still another pattern in which sex role norms reveal an additional path of influence on future contraceptive efficacy. To the degree that role modernity and instrumentality depress timing failures they evidently enhance the chances for future success. Furthermore, with regard to Figure 5–1 it seems apparent that among educated wives sex role norms exert direct influence on efficacy, plus indirect influence through birth orientations and through choice of sophisticated technologies.

In sum, more so perhaps than in Chapters Three and Four, non-Catholics in the diverse situational contexts of Table 5–3 seem to display rather congruent patterns. In general terms, the inverse link between individualism and familism appears with relative force in each setting. Wanting certain rights, benefits, privileges, flexibility, and autonomy for themselves—i.e., their own interests—leads them not only to seek fewer familistic events which could be defined as costs undercutting those interests, it also increases their motivation to determine that in the future they will use the best contraceptives effectively so as to assure minimization of these costs. Finally, it is quite likely that, over time, wives who determine to be more effective find that efficacy reinforces their egalitarianism, which in turn enhances their future efficacy.

Methods of White Catholic Wives

We turn next to Catholic wives aged 18 to 29 in order to continue the strategy of testing our basic theoretical approach on a wide variety of settings in order to establish its reliability and thereby to be able ultimately to place greater faith in its validity.

Catholics, of course, represent a special phenomenon when it comes to contraceptive behavior. They are by far the largest religious group in America for whom "artificial" contraceptives of any sort, including the pill, are up to now officially prohibited and declared sinful. Trend data, in spite of these bans, indicate increasing convergence between Catholics and non-Catholics with respect to contraceptive behavior (Ryder and Westoff, 1971). We might therefore expect to find linkages between individualistic reward-seeking and patterns of current (and future) contraceptive behavior that are at least somewhat similar to those just observed among non-Catholics. Nonetheless, recall from Chapter Four that sex role norms were related to earlier Catholic timing failures in a manner directly opposite to that of non-Catholics. Although non-Catholics who were more egalitarian had experienced fewer timing failures, Catholic egalitarianism and timing failures were positively associated. Therefore it is possible that we may once again discover somewhat similar divergences as we move into consideration of current contraceptive behaviors.

STRUCTURAL CONTEXTS AND CONTRACEPTIVE BEHAVIOR

WORKING WIVES

Turning to column one (top row) of Table 5–4, we note that among working wives the percentage of cases (80%) who employ the pill is actually greater than the figure observed among comparable non-Catholics. These figures verify the conclusion of Ryder and Westoff (1971) that church influence specific to pill use is declining among Catholics. However, in contrast to younger non-Catholics the same column reveals that husband education and three dimensions of sex role modernity are linked with non-use of the pill. Method efficiency, in other words, is related to sex role traditionalism rather than to modernity. Past literature (Whelpton *et al.*, 1966) has indicated that higher-status Catholics tend to be less effective contraceptors, especially during the early childbearing period. Here wives' own modernity is related to husband's education (SA = .37, RLM = .23, PHA = .20, IE = .23).

Furthermore, if we glance at the second row of Table 5–4 we find that, in contrast to the top row, SA modernity is linked positively with the pill use among the nonemployed. The latter have more children than working wives, and it may be that one reason for the absence of an individualism–efficiency link among higher-status employed wives may be greater indifference to additional children. As Catholics intend more children overall than non-Catholics, they may have longer to go before the costs of children are perceived as grave or as outweighing their benefits. Nonworking Catholic wives may have already reached the point where the number of children present does help to make salient the use of efficient contraceptives so that alternative benefits can be pursued.

In an era of changing sex role norms, one key to understanding differences between Catholics and non-Catholics in these matters is the issue of when to time children so they will be least costly to wives' individualistic aspirations (see Chapter Four). Whether consciously or not, younger non-Catholics who hold more modern sex role norms seem to behave in such a way as to defer the costs (and rewards) of children until a later point in time. But Catholics who are more egalitarian appear (nonconsciously, perhaps) to behave so as to undertake the costs of children early in marriage and thus be less impeded later on. Ideally we would want to follow these couples over time and identify changing situations that could make preferences for individualistic gratifications either more or less salient. It is likely that in such a study we would discover that individualism and method efficiency becomes positively linked sooner in non-Catholic than in Catholic marriages. It probably takes the occurrence of greater levels of familistic costs to stimulate notions among Catholic wives that if individualistic alternatives are actually to be attained, then efficient contraception becomes requisite behavior. Nonetheless, we would likely find that at the conclusion of the childbearing period Catholic wives who are more individualistic would probably have fewer children than Catholics who are more traditional.

NONWORKING WIVES

This expectation is reinforced by column one in row two where, as just discussed, wives who are oriented toward self-actualization (perhaps with future employment in view) are also more likely to be pill users in order perhaps to enhance their aspirations or at least to prevent those aspirations from being undercut. Wives who are more SA-modern are also less devout ($-.27$), and the panel shows that lesser devoutness tends to influence pill use as well. The effect of SA is the exact opposite from what emerged among working wives and tends to support the generalization that the individualism–efficiency link operates more strongly among Catholic wives once mean family size is somewhat increased.

Nevertheless within this column we learn that wives with relatively lower parity are pill users, while those with more children are using the poor-efficiency techniques from Groups 3 and/or 4. We might have expected higher-parity wives to be most concerned lest they conceive additional children, but apparently they are somewhat indifferent to or would not mind additional familistic gratifications.

Parity had the opposite effect in connection with Group 2 use among Catholic working wives (compare also Table 5–1). Futhermore, as we go on in the chapter we shall continue to observe inconsistencies in the effect of parity on contraceptive behaviors. The conclusion that tends to emerge is that parity by itself is not a consistent predictor of contraceptive behavior. Whether the wife works or not and other factors that influence parity must also be considered when seeking to account for contraceptive practices. In short, merely knowing the quantity of familistic gratifications (or costs) does not by itself appear sufficient to indicate the degree of determination to avoid, or degree of indifference toward, additional familistic events that could be defined as either reward or cost.

Column one also indicates that nonworking wives with better empathy are not pill users. We might have expected that better communication and understanding would have resulted in selection of the pill. But it is the case that persons who are more economically satisfied also experience higher empathy ($+.44$). Therefore, it may be that for them the particular combinations of perceived economic and marital rewards make them believe they can cope with the "costs" of an additional child. Children for them may be more affordable in the sense discussed in the previous chapter. Incidentally, 68% of wives in the second panel of row two utilize the pill—a figure less than that reported for working Catholics. Recall that a similar kind of difference emerged between working and nonworking non-Catholics.

One finding worthy of note in column two, row two of Table 5–4 is the negative effect on method efficiency of both intragenerational and intergenerational mobility. Evidently nonemployed Catholic women who have experienced the greatest levels of increases in socioeconomic benefits, compared to what they enjoyed as adolescents and especially at marriage, tend to be most casual about the kinds of contraceptives they utilize. It may be that the relative increase in economic gratifications makes them more amenable to the costs of children and thus undercuts their motivation to choose efficient contraceptive technologies (Easterlin, 1973).

LOW TO AVERAGE EDUCATION

Rows three and four of Table 5–4 lead to conclusions basically similar to those for rows one and two, plus some additional generalizations. Among less-educated wives more modern sex role norms bear some positive associations with reduced risk-taking in terms of the selection of more efficient techniques such as the pill or Group 2 methods. In addition, having a full-time job promotes selection of the pill. Yet economic benefits and resources such as feeling economically well-off, greater husband's job status, and greater social mobility all tend to promote increased risk-taking through use of ineffective techniques. One additional variable that has not yet appeared in either Table 5–1 or 5–4 is birth intentions. Less-educated wives who intend more children are more likely to be risk-takers. From Chapter Three we recall that three dimensions of sex role modernity were used to predict the birth intentions of these wives. And among the particular wives in both columns one and two of row three, the correlations between more modern sex role norms and lowered birth intentions are considerably stronger than they were in Table 3–6.[15] The argument could be made for Catholic wives in this particular situational context that sex role norms influence birth intentions and that level of birth intentions influences degree of permissible risk-taking.

HIGH EDUCATION

Of particular interest in explaining both pill and Group 2 use among the well-educated are the opposite effects of the three husband-role dimensions. Both PHA and IE modernity are related to selection of inefficient techniques; but TH modernity is related to method efficiency. The more that highly trained Catholic wives are committed to ideological equality between wives and husbands (TH), the less likely they are to be risk-takers. Yet behavioral innovations for husbands are related to greater risk-taking. Why this contrast should occur is not totally clear; however, in Chapter Four we allowed the possibility that the experience of timing failures could stimulate sex role modernity among Catholic wives. A similar pattern could be occurring here. That is, the more educated Catholic women take greater risks, the more egalitarian they become. Especially with regard to husbands sharing specific household tasks (PHA, IE), Catholic wives who take risks and thus become potentially subject to greater familistic costs expect that their husbands would share in those costs. The risk-taking may increase their preferences for greater concessions on the part of their husbands; it may lead them to expect from their husbands greater fulfillment of female interests, rights, and privileges.

In short, there may be a kind of nonconscious "bargain" occurring (at least from the wives' standpoint) in which risk-taking is traded off for greater male egalitarianism.

To determine the existence of such complex causal sequences would obviously require following these married couples over time. It would be particularly crucial to ascertain husbands' perceptions and behaviors in regard to these phenomena. Do husbands become more egalitarian as a result of risk-taking and increased familistic costs? Do they or their wives actually perceive any sort of legitimate trade-off between risk-taking and egalitarianism? In this regard in column one of row four (Table 5–4) we find that the marital authority variable emerges for the first time in this chapter. Wives who perceive their husbands to hold greater authority are less likely to be risk-takers. To what degree do relative differences in marital authority and in decision-making influence changes in sex role norms and behavior, and changes in contraceptive behaviors? To what degree do sex role norms and behaviors and contraceptive behaviors feed back on and influence marital authority?

EXPECTED FUTURE EFFICACY

WORKING WIVES

Just as there were substantial differences between Tables 5–1 and 5–4, so do different patterns emerge when we compare Tables 5–5 and 5–3. Many Catholics do not fit Figure 5–1 quite so well as do non-Catholics. The latter displayed three major influences on perceived efficacy: sex role modernity, birth orientations, and method efficiency. But among Catholics who work full time the strongest influence on expected efficacy is their work motivations. Wives who work primarily for the intangible rewards of fulfillment and satisfaction are more likely to be determined and successful contraceptors than those who work primarily for monetary benefits. Yet wives who work mostly for the former kinds of benefits have husbands with higher SES and incomes (.24, .24). Moreover, such wives currently have and also intend to have fewer children overall (−.25, −.27).

Hence in terms of these variables, employed Catholic wives can, at a more general level, be fitted under the same reward-alternative framework that subsumed non-Catholics. The same can be said when we examine the consequences of religious devoutness. As Table 5–5 reveals, wives who attend Mass less frequently expect a greater level of contraceptive success. As we saw earlier, reduced devoutness is related to greater sex role modernity (RLM = −.32, TH = −.22, PHA = −.22). So here too we may conclude that wives who are less exposed to religious teaching are more likely to prefer individualistic gratifications for themselves; and that such wives are more likely to expect to minimize unintended familistic costs.

Besides work-motivation and devoutness, the table also shows that TH modernity also has a direct but more modest impact on enhancing expected efficacy. The same holds for their AE rankings.

However working wives who have experienced the greatest job mobility (their own compared to their father's SES) expect the least success. Here again we witness the now-familiar pattern in which various sorts of socioeconomic benefits contribute towards less rigorous Catholic fertility control. In this instance because they have already come so far in status, they apparently feel that they can manage the costs of unintended children, whether monetary or individualistic. Likewise their education has a negative impact on expected success, and probably for the same kinds of reasons. Interestingly, while the correlations from their job status and incomes are also negative, the betas become positive, though very modest in strength. Finally, intending additional children is related to less expected success. The figures show continued evidence of countervailing forces: TW modernity and less devoutness influence them to want no more children ($-.20$, $-.22$), whereas greater education, job status, and income have the opposite effect ($.26$, $.30$, $.39$).

In sum, paradox and ambiguity towards effective fertility control continue to surface among Catholic wives. Intangible occupational gratifications, alongside less formal religious participation and some indication of preferences for more egalitarian husband role structures, result in greater certainty that unwanted familistic costs can be avoided. But socioeconomic gratifications—especially their own status achievements—lead them to be more casual about costs.

NONEMPLOYMENT AND LOW TO AVERAGE EDUCATION

The upper right and lower left panels of Table 5–5 also are fitted under the rubric of Figure 5–1 with difficulty. In both situational contexts by far the strongest determinant of expected efficacy is whether or not they intend to have additional children. More than other kinds of reward (or cost) alternatives, simply intending to have additional familistic gratifications makes these wives see themselves as more careless. While they still have some targeted children to attain, it is apparently quite difficult for them to stand back and objectively assess how careful they would be once they might actually reach that target. This pattern emerged modestly for working Catholic wives but not at all for non-Catholics. Evidently this kind of question means something very different to wives in the two religious categories. Among non-Catholics, whether or not the target has been reached is unimportant compared to the effects of more significant reward–cost factors. To many Catholics—especially those not working or with less education—whether the target has been attained seems to overwhelm other considerations.

Among nonworking wives the only variable that helps explain wanting more children is current parity: the more children present the more likely they are to want no more ($-.45$). Among wives with less education, parity again has this consequence ($-.51$), but so does TW modernity ($-.29$). Having more children and being more sex role modern leads them to want no additional familistic costs.

High Education

It is when we turn to well-educated Catholic wives (Table 5–5) that we discover most conclusive evidence of a fit with the model of Figure 5–1. First off, greater TM modernity and lesser devoutness are virtually equal in their positive impact on expected contraceptive efficacy. TH modernity also has a similarly positive but less powerful impact. And as we might expect, devoutness is strongly related in an inverse fashion to six of the seven dimensions of sex role modernity (TM, TW, SA, PHA, TH, RLM; r's $= -.31, -.46, -.44, -.40, -.35, -.59$). As with non-Catholics, method efficiency also enhances expected success. Nonetheless a divergence from non-Catholics that might be expected from Table 5–4 is that both PHA and IE modernity are related to reduced method efficiency ($-.30, -.29$). Next, Table 5–5 also reveals that lowered birth desires influence greater expected efficacy. This particular convergence with non-Catholics continues as we note that lowered desires are strongly affected by sex role modernity (SA $= -.47$, RLM $= -.26$, PHA $= -.24$, TW $= -.24$). Deferral of marital gratifications (explained in Chapter Three) also enhances efficacy as do, surprisingly for well-trained Catholics, two socioeconomic dimensions. The benefits of higher job status for their husbands and the gratifications of greater social mobility both tend to increase motivation to avoid unwanted familistic costs. As we might expect, both socioeconomic dimensions are related positively to sex role modernity.[16]

It seems clear, therefore, that we can place this subset of Catholic wives under Figure 5–1, with some minor modifications. Modern sex role norms influence efficacy directly, as well as having a direct impact on birth orientations. Through the latter variable, sex role norms maintain an additional indirect impact on efficacy. A variable not present in the model for non-Catholics is devoutness, and although it tends to influence Catholic efficacy, sex role norms via devoutness maintain yet another path of influence on expected efficacy. The two status variables would also have to be inserted into the model for Catholics, but once more their effects do not exist apart from preferences for role egalitarianism. The major divergence from non-Catholics lies with the different link that method efficiency has with sex role norms. Nevertheless, in both religious groupings being more efficient leads to more optimistic perceptions of future contraception. Thus at a general theoretical level we may conclude that for well-educated

Catholics individualism and familism are inversely related in a fashion comparable to non-Catholics. Familism (as represented by the costs and rewards of potential unintended children) is depressed to the degree that alternative individualistic and status rewards are present, and appropriate technologies are utilized.

Nevertheless, given many of the remaining findings in Table 5–5, it is apparent that Catholic fertility control, especially in two contexts, continues to diverge from that of non-Catholics. (The divergence is less among working wives.) Therefore the conclusion reached in Chapters Three and Four that Catholics will probably continue to maintain higher parities than non-Catholics for at least some years is supported by data from this chapter. Yet, as in prior chapters, that subset of well-educated Catholic wives provides the most extensive evidence of convergence with dominant patterns. We would expect that to the degree increasing numbers of women in general—and Catholic women in particular—attend college and become involved in highly rewarding occupations that religious divergences appearing here and in prior chapters will steadily continue to diminish.

Methods of Black Wives

Blacks, like white Catholics, have in the past given evidence of diverging from the fertility patterns of the white non-Catholic majority, especially in the realm of contraceptive behavior (Westoff and Westoff, 1971). As we examine our findings about these black wives aged 18 to 29 and compare them with those of other fertility studies, it is especially crucial to keep in mind that our sample includes only husband–wife households. It is clear that this form of the black household is in many respects quite different from black female-headed households, and one of these differences is the lower fertility of the husband–wife household (Scanzoni, 1971). In short, by including only husband–wife households, our results for blacks are likely to diverge somewhat from those studies that include households with only one parent (usually the woman) present.

STRUCTURAL CONTEXTS AND CONTRACEPTIVE BEHAVIORS

WORKING WIVES

Some 94% of these black working wives are users of some method, a figure that is somewhat higher than for young white working wives in either religious category (non-Catholics = 88%; Catholics = 86%). Thus whatever divergence may have existed in the past between blacks and whites with respect to method use, these particular black wives give indication that such differences are disappearing. They seem to be equally anxious as whites to avoid the kind of risk-taking that could give rise to an unplanned familistic event (or cost).

In column one of the top row of Table 5–6 we note that 87% utilize the pill, a proportion which is once more greater than for comparable Catholics or non-Catholics. It is therefore abundantly clear that young, employed black wives do not hesitate to choose this most efficient of contraceptive technologies. And as with white non-Catholic wives, individualistic reward-preferences inherent in SA and RLM modernity maintain major functions in motivating behavior of this type. Working chiefly for enjoyment has a similar effect, and this important variable is connected with SA and IE modernity and with wives' education (.29, .34, .29).

Nevertheless, we find that working wives with more education and higher SES tend not to be pill users. Both these variables correlate with several aspects of sex role modernity and with lowered parity as well.[17] Therefore what may be operating here is a pattern in which, in the past, individualistic and status rewards have resulted in fewer familistic benefits, and sex role norms continue to have the same consequence through method efficiency. But the combination of greater economic benefits and fewer children apparently make them more causal toward preventing pregnancy. Thus we find evidence here too (albeit a different pattern from Catholics) of correlated rewards operating in diverse fashion. Individualism is tending to depress familism, whereas material factors are tending to stimulate it.

NONWORKING WIVES

Shifting to the second row of Table 5–6 we note that the proportion of these wives who use any type of method is only 74% which, while high in absolute terms, is much lower than for black working wives and less than for both sets of white non-working wives (non-Catholics = 95%; Catholics = 98%). Full-time employment apparently makes much more difference among blacks than among whites in stimulating method use and hence the reduction of risk-taking. Thus the black–white divergence seems to occur most noticeably when we compare nonworking black wives with whites, but it does not occur at all when we focus on black wives employed full time.

Furthermore, 67% of wives in column one (row two) use the pill, which is also less than the figure for black working wives. Yet when it comes to explaining use of the pill and of Group 2 methods, the row reveals that modern maternal sex role orientations, along with status benefits provided by husbands, and by wives' own education, exert strong positive influences on method-efficiency. This conclusion applies equally well to the extraordinarily efficient oral and highly efficient Group 2 technologies. Likewise, wives (in both columns) who want no more children tend to use more effective contraceptives; and the more sex role modern they are, the more likely they are to want no additional familistic rewards and costs.[18] Similar to "additional intended children" is "total births intended" (same as "birth intentions" in Table 5–4 and in Chapter Three). Both columns reveal that the greater their total intentions the less rigorous these wives are. As we have seen repeatedly, wives who are more sex role traditional intend to have a larger number of children than wives who are more modern.

In addition, columns one and two of row two also tell us that expressive self-concept explains method-efficiency in the expected direction: wives who are less expressive are more likely to be users of efficient procedures. Wives who are more nurturant and the like apparently are more likely to perceive an affinity with infants and small children and thus be less strongly motivated to behave in rigorous fashion to prevent children. Their own expressiveness makes children appear to be more rewarding than they are to wives who are less quiet, gentle, and so on.

Overall, therefore, among nonworking blacks, more rigorous and efficient contraceptive behavior is clearly and positively linked with individualism and with indicators of current social status, just as it was for non-Catholics. Though these influences on efficiency were sometimes muted or else reversed for Catholics, these blacks resemble non-Catholics much more than Catholics in verifying our theoretical expectations. However, one area where blacks are like Catholics is in with the negative effects that intragenerational mobility seems to have on method-efficiency. Nonworking black women who have been more mobile tend to be greater risk-takers, perhaps because they feel that the relative increases in economic benefits they have enjoyed make additional familistic costs that much more "affordable" (Easterlin, 1973).

EDUCATION

The results presented in rows three and four do not differ substantially from those in rows one and two. Fulltime employment enhances method efficiency. Expressive self-concept has precisely opposite consequences. Social mobility tends to increase casualness; so does income among the less educated while among the better educated it increases rigor. However, for wives in both situational contexts various dimensions of role modernity all have the expected outcome: The more modern or egalitarian they are, the more rigorous is their contraceptive behavior with regard to method efficiency.

In an overall comparison of blacks with whites in terms of method efficiency, the striking feature is how much blacks are like non-Catholics, and how much Catholics differ from both other categories. When in Chapter Four we examined the correlates of timing failures, blacks seemed to be somewhat closer to Catholics than to non-Catholics throughout the patterns that emerged. Both here and there younger Catholics give evidence that sex role modernity does not increase their degree of contraceptive rigor early in marriage. Presumably were we to follow Catholics over time we would discover that sex role norms eventually influence movement towards greater rigor, and thus toward smaller family size. By way of contrast, non-Catholics especially, but blacks as well, give strong and consistent evidence that early in marriage individualistic and egalitarian sex role norms move them in the direction of greater contraceptive caution, rigor, and efficiency. Thus in spite of alleged increasing secularity in American society, Catholic religion apparently still maintains enough influence on its younger adherents to cause their fertility behaviors to be identifiably different from those of non-Catholics, both black and white.

EXPECTED CONTRACEPTIVE EFFICACY

Therefore, as we turn to Table 5–7 we expect that the patterns there will also resemble non-Catholics more than Catholics. And in at least several major respects this is indeed the case. TM modernity especially, and also SA modernity reveal strong correlations with perceived efficacy in each of the four panels in the table. In two of them (upper right, lower left) TM is the strongest correlate of contraceptive success, and among employed wives SA shows itself virtually equal to the strongest correlate. In addition PHA modernity is positively related to expected success among the nonemployed and less-educated. Furthermore, in two of the three contexts where regression equations are used, TM modernity reveals the third strongest beta in predicting expected success; and among less educated wives it is the single strongest predictor of contraceptive success. Thus in terms of fitting younger black wives under the model in Figure 5–1 we may say that they do reveal consistent, pervasive, and strong paths of influence from sex role norms to expected efficacy. What is more, as with non-Catholics, this influence emerges in all four structural situations, not chiefly among the well-educated as was the case for Catholics. Blacks too reveal that the more modern or egalitarian they are in terms of their own sex role norms (TM, SA) the better contraceptors they expect to be. Preferring individualistic rewards motivates them to expect to be more efficacious in preventing familistic costs so that, presumably, they will actually be freer to pursue those desired rewards.

Another segment of Figure 5–1 that applies to blacks is the impact that method choice has on efficacy. If black women do not work or are highly educated, use of the pill itself increases their expectations for contraceptive success. The broader method-efficiency variable, which includes Group 2 techniques and which emerged in Tables 5–3 and 5–5, is not meaningfully related to black efficacy. Apparently the uniqueness of the pill provides its black users with considerable optimism regarding contraceptive success in a fashion and to a degree that is not matched even by "highly effective" Group 2 methods. In any case we know from Table 5–6 that modern sex role norms affect pill selection. Therefore with respect to Figure 5–1, we may say that, for blacks in at least two contexts, role norms positively influence pill use directly and through that use positively stimulate efficacy indirectly.

An additional influence in Figure 5–1 that applies only to nonworking blacks is the negative consequence that higher birth intentions have on efficacy. And blacks in this subset who hold higher intentions are also more traditional on PHA and TM ($-.27$, $-.22$). Hence, as Figure 5–1 indicates, role norms influence their birth orientations and through the latter have the predicted outcome on expected success.

However, there are some additional variables in Table 5–7 that are virtually unique to blacks in explaining contraceptive success. For instance, in each of the four panels their father's job status (SES) has a strong positive effect on efficacy. Throughout earlier chapters in general and in Figure 3–1 in particular, considerable stress has been laid upon the generational links which are intrinsic to the complex processes of family fertility control. Ever since Moynihan (1965) there has been speculation about the lack of resource-provision by lower-class black parents for their offspring. Both our earlier study of black husband–wife households (Scanzoni, 1971) and this one confirms that at least beyond the lower class black parents provide ample resources both tangibly and intangibly. In Table 5–7, for example, we may argue that the greater the level of socioeconomic resources provided to the women by their fathers while they were growing up, the more strongly motivated they now are to prevent unwanted familistic costs. Presumably those resources motivate them to seek, instead of children, additional socioeconomic benefits.

Moreover, as we have seen, fathers who have higher job status apparently socialize their daughters into more individualistic sex roles. Among working wives, father's SES is positively related to TM and to SA (.21, .19); where they do not work the correlations for the same two variables are .22 and .24. In addition, instrumental self-concept is positively linked with father's SES (.29) and, as the upper right panel of Table 5–7 indicates, to be more instrumental is to be more efficacious. Among less-educated wives correlations of father's SES with ISC, SA, and TM are .24, .19, and .18. Among the better educated we find that SA, PHA, RLM, and TM are related to father's job status (.32, .22, .30, and .31), along with instrumental self-concept (.33). In the latter context too ISC stimulates more effective contraceptive manipulation. In short, father's job status provides not only economic rewards to enhance black efficacy, it also results in stronger preferences for individualistic rewards and in a more instrumental (or active) definition of oneself. Subsequently, wives who hold these preferences and definitions tend to be more oriented towards actual individualistic satisfactions and extrafamilial gratifications and are therefore more determined to minimize unwanted familistic costs (and benefits) that could undercut those alternative benefits.

However, at the same time we note in three of the panels of Table 5–7 that intergenerational mobility is related to less expected success. Moreover, the same holds among working wives in terms of their own job mobility. It turns out that there are strong negative correlations between their father's SES and the degree of their generational and job mobility.[19] The further they have moved socially, the lower was their father's job status. Such wives, therefore, expect to be less rigorous for at least two reasons. One, the contrast in the level of material resources they possess now relative to what they had while adolescents apparently makes them more casual about contraception in the sense that owing to their relative abundance they feel can surely somehow manage the financial costs of an unplanned-for child. Two, because they came from lesser-status homes they tended to learn more traditional sex role norms. Such norms also influence greater contraceptive carelessness as we have seen. Women from higher-status backgrounds do not experience marked contrasts in socioeconomic rewards between past and present. The reward level has been fairly constant and relatively great and motivates them to expect to practice rigorous contraception. Their more modern sex role norms accomplish the same end. On the other hand, the contrast in resources felt by mobile women and their learned traditionalism combine to reduce their expected rigor and efficacy.

It seems significant that father's SES and wife's intergenerational mobility have contrasting consequences for efficacy among blacks, but that such a contrast does not occur among whites. This may in part be owing to the greater relative economic disadvantage that blacks experience compared to whites (see Table 3–2). In any case, to validate these processes which we have tentatively identified would require a study in which whites and blacks would be followed and compared in terms of the causes and consequences of extensive upward mobility. How do sex role norms and early economic position stimulate aspirations for mobility? In turn, how does mobility influence those norms, definitions of their new economic situation, and their subsequent fertility control?

One additional socioeconomic factor that appears in Table 5–7 is the positive impact that husband's income has on expected efficacy among well-educated wives. Significantly, that income bears no relationship to any measures of social mobility, but wives whose husbands earn more are also more sex role modern (TM = .39, RLM = .34, SA = .25, PHA = .20). In two of the contexts in Table 5–7 a more positive AE ranking enhances expected efficacy, as we might expect; but twice we note that deferred marriage has the opposite consequence, something we would not expect.

Also worthy of mention is the positive impact that perceived husband reaction to their employment has had on their expected success (upper left panel). Wives who feel their husbands support them in their job endeavors are more motivated to prevent unwanted familistic costs so that they can continue those endeavors unimpeded. Where husbands are less supportive, there is less motivation to be rigorous. In the latter circumstances wives are evidently more willing for unwanted familistic costs than for ongoing costs emanating from husbands' negativism towards their working. Presumably that negativism would be terminated if wives became pregnant and left the labor force. As we noted in previous chapters, it is better-educated wives with higher job status (who are also more role modern and married to similarly educated men, who are also more role modern) who perceive that their husbands are more positive towards their employment.[20]

Finally, among working wives and among those with less education we learn that expressive self-concept relates positively to expected efficacy. This is surprising, given its negative impact on method-efficiency in Table 5–6. Nevertheless in spite of a presumed affinity between nurturance and children, wives in these contexts who perceive themselves as more expressive expect to be more rigorous contraceptors. Just as in the remaining two situations, where instrumental self-concept stimulates their perceived ability to manage contraceptives, in these two being expressive has the same effect.

Overall, aside from the distinctive elements that appear in Table 5–7, the conclusion seems to be that by and large blacks are comparable to white non-Catholics and to educated Catholics when it comes to determinants of expected contraceptive success. All four situational contexts of blacks give evidence of being able to be fitted under the model in Figure 5–1. Sex role norms are pervasive in all instances. Familism, as represented by a casual and haphazard evaluation of future fertility control, is once more inversely linked to individualism and to the kinds of rewards and gratifications that are inherent in it. Efficient technologies, as represented in particular by the pill, shore up their confidence; but the motivation to utilize that technique is stimulated by their desires for individualistic benefits. A final pervasive element stems from gratifications provided through their families of orientation. Both the socioeconomic benefits and the greater stress on role egalitarianism supplied by their parents make them less oriented towards the kind of contraceptive casualness that tends to result in larger familistic costs as well as rewards.

Summary and Discussion

A major aim of this chapter has been to examine the contraceptive behaviors actually practiced by younger wives at risk of pregnancy. A second prime consideration was to evaluate their assessments as to how competent and rigorous they expected their contraceptive behaviors to be in terms of warding off unwanted children. Both issues were subsumed under the larger theoretical framework utilized in former chapters. We constructed a flow-chart model which overlaps with and is complementary to Figures 3–1 and 4–1. Current contraceptive behavior can be placed on a continuum of risk-taking. Wives using no method are obviously at the "extreme-risk" end of that continuum. As it turns out, the great majority of wives are substantially removed from that end through the use of some sort of contraceptive technique. But the type of technique employed may vary considerably and affect where wives should be placed on the risk-taking continuum. Wives who rely on rhythm, for instance, are high risk-takers, because that technique is known to be extraordinarily unreliable and inefficient in preventing pregnancy. Users of the pill are low risk-takers because of its great efficiency. Users of other techniques fall in between these two extremes.

At a more general level we may say that risk-taking level reflects degree of indifference to the costs of children and also what we might call affinity for, orientations toward, or even preferences for their rewards. Theoretically we had predicted beforehand that that such indifference and affinity would exist inversely to preferences for individualistic gratifications, as represented by our measures of sex role norms. The mere use of contraceptives or behaviors at one extreme of the continuum was not strongly explained by this schema, probably because so many wives consider themselves to be users and because use of some technique by married persons has become so strongly institutionalized throughout all segments of society. Therefore we focused most of our attention upon users and examined the relationships between degree of efficiency (reduced risk-taking) and sex role modernity. Among non-Catholics (both younger and older wives) and among blacks we found that role norms and method-efficiency were related in the expected direction: The more modern they were the more likely they were to choose efficient techniques. (Efficiency, incidentally, includes methods besides the pill such as the condom, IUD, or diaphragm with jelly.) The more oriented those wives were towards individualistic rewards—or alternatives to familism—the more motivated they were to select those technologies most likely to prevent familistic costs in the form of unintended or unwanted children.

These findings are not only substantively important; they are also theoretically significant not only because they were predicted beforehand but also because they provide firm evidence of associations between norms and behavior. Recall that in Chapter Two we discussed the problematic nature of such associations, especially in connection with sex role norms. Chapters Two and Three also provided indications of links between sex role norms and behaviors (age at marriage, employment, first-child spacing, timing failures, and so on). But the association here suggests perhaps more vividly than those others that sex role norms have an impact on those motivational components that are so fundamental to fertility control. If fertility control is basically a matter of motivation, or "profit motive," then costs and rewards signified by those norms tend to be traded off (nonconsciously perhaps) with the costs and rewards of childbearing and caring. This conclusion does not imply that causality is one way. Over time "efficient behaviors" may have reciprocal or feedback impact on sex role norms.

The question of causality leads us to discuss Catholics, because, as in previous chapters, they provided results different from those of non-Catholics and blacks. Though there was occasional indication of a positive link between modernity and efficiency, most generally the association was negative. The interpretation is unclear as it was in Chapter Four in connection with timing failures. Do Catholics who are more egalitarian tend to be contraceptively careless while they are young in order to attain their targeted number of children early in marriage and thus be less hindered later on in their pursuit of individualistic gratifications? Or in connection with method-efficiency does the use of less reliable methods prompt Catholic wives towards greater egalitarianism, towards expecting more concessions from their husbands? Does the risk-taking and potential for additional children (as well as higher current parity) move them to seek concessions and even to make demands? Future research will have to devise sophisticated measures to probe these questions in depth.

For both whites and blacks, other variables were linked with method-efficiency, and most of these (education, father's job status, full-time employment, whether or not more children were intended, and so on) are correlated with sex role modernity and can be fitted under the general theoretical reward-alternative framework being developed here. However, in Figure 5–1 for purposes of simplicity we show only the major path of influence between sex role norms and method-efficiency. Significantly, where they appeared (among Catholics and blacks), measures of social mobility were most often negatively related to rigorous fertility control. Apparently there is some connection between moving a rather large social distance—having come from relative economic disadvantage and the learning of rather traditional sex role norms—and being more careless and casual towards contraceptive efficiency.

The second major issue to which the chapter was devoted was the degree to which these younger wives perceive or define themselves to be efficacious contraceptors. Theoretically we had expected that wives who were most highly motivated to avoid the costs of a "number failure" would be most strongly oriented towards sex role modernity—individualism and egalitarianism. Substantively, this kind of measure is most important because not only does it represent the respondent's evaluation of how "good" a contraceptor she is, it also functions as a type of self-fulfilling prophecy. Wives who think they will be relatively successful probably will be; those who are less optimistic about success will likely be less successful. Thus the item may be an additional valid predictor of future contraceptive behavior.

Among non-Catholics this expectation was fulfilled within all four situational contexts; and Figure 5–1 reflects that path of influence. Simultaneously, the method-efficiency variable we just explained also influences expected success or efficacy in the expected fashion, and that too is displayed in Figure 5–1. Non-Catholic wives who use methods proven to be effective expect to avoid unintended pregnancies, and the selection of those techniques is influenced in part by sex role norms. The latter also influence birth orientations (see Chapter Three), and Figure 5–1 indicates the chain of influences from the norms to the orientations to expected efficacy. In passing, we observed that efficiency level as an indicator of technological sophistication never outweighed the impact of the role variables in determining expected efficacy. We therefore concluded that although technology level is an important consideration for optimum fertility control, the motivational component is probably more fundamental and basic. This seems to be true both in choice of sophistication level and in successful management of whatever level is selected.

All that we just concluded for non-Catholics applies to well-educated Catholics as well. Even the mobility of those wives leads them to expect to be more rigorous contraceptors. However, among the three remaining categories of Catholics the applicability of the model in Figure 5–1 is more problematic, though there are various indications of its validity. One of these is among working wives, where an "enjoyment" motivation stimulates efficacy. That kind of motivation is positively related to sex role modernity. An additional element which, of course, is unique to Catholics is frequency of participation in the Mass, or devoutness. For working and educated Catholics limited participation is related to sex role modernity, and less participation had a significant effect in stimulating expected contraceptive rigor.

Among black (as among non-Catholic) wives sex role norms are pervasive in their influence on efficacy in that they appear potently in each of the four structural situations. Equally pervasive for blacks is their fathers' job status which, of course, has a positive impact on degree of sex role modernity.

Overall, therefore, we may conclude that the model in Figure 5–1 applies with reasonably equal validity to non-Catholics, blacks, and educated Catholics. To be sure, the latter two categories exhibit some variations from the model which are cumbersome to represent in one figure, yet which do not undermine its essential thrust. The model is complementary to those discussed earlier, and in an ongoing longitudinal design it would be essential to incorporate measures of method-efficiency and expected efficacy to identify the full range of both their causes and consequences. Theoretically it seems apparent that these two factors, along with those from earlier chapters, could be subsumed under a general reward-alternative framework. Both efficiency and efficacy represent degrees of preferred familistic rewards and indifference to related costs. The strength of these preferences and indifference is related inversely to the strength of preferences for alternative gratifications (and related costs) in the form of marital egalitarianism and resultant flexibility and autonomy to pursue individualistic interests outside of the family.

Notes

1. The wording of the complex series of items used to measure fecundity is based on items drawn from the 1970 *National Fertility Study*. A close approximation is found in Ryder and Westoff, 1971.
2. Men: n = 836; women: n = 862.
3. Younger persons: n = 1240.
4. Based on Ryder and Westoff (1971).
5. Values were assigned to use or non-use of these three methods. Any case could have a range from zero (all three methods) to three (none of these methods). Among users (excluding pill users) the mean Group 2 score reported by men was 2.45 (standard deviation = 0.52). For women the mean was 2.41 (standard deviation = 0.42). (Lower mean score indicates greater degree of method efficiency; though in the tables for purposes of simplicity and clarity, increased use is "high" or "positive.")
6. (n = 983) (wording altered for husbands).
7. (n = 946).
8. (Men: n = 294; women: n = 386).
9. (n = 665).
10. (n = 315).
11. (n = 592).
12. (n = 350).

13. An index of expected future contraceptive efficacy was built in which each valid case was assigned a value ranging from zero to three. For men from households where both spouses are fecund, the mean efficacy score is 1.89, standard deviation = 0.82. For women from such households, mean = 1.91, standard deviation = 0.84. (High mean score equals greater perceived efficacy.)

14. The possible range of scores is from zero (high efficiency) to four (low efficiency). Among all male users the mean "efficiency score" was 3.22 (standard deviation = 0.49). Among all female users the mean score was 3.20 (standard deviation = 0.45). In the tables, for purposes of simplicity and clarity, increased use is "high" or "positive."

15. Column 1: PHA = −.25, RLM = −.20. Column 2: PHA = −.24, ISC = −.37.

16. Mobility and: TW (.21), SA (.33), PHA (.31), RLM (31), and TM (.24). Husband's SES and: SA (.28), PHA (.42), ISC (.22), RLM (.33), and TM (.20).

17. Education and: TW (.23), TM (.20), parity (−.31). Job status and: TM (.24), TH (.18), parity (−.21).

18. Column 1: PHA = −.40, TM = −.43. Column 2: SA = −.41, PHA = −.23, RLM = −.34.

19. Working wives: generational = −.58; job = −.74. Less educated wives: generational = −.69. Better educated: generational = −.58.

20. Correlations of their own education and job status with perceptions of husband support were .22 and .25, respectively.

Chapter 6. Toward Theory and Policy in Fertility Control

THEORY GIVES US CAPABILITY TO UNDERSTAND and to make certain predictions regarding behavior. Once we understand how something operates we can decide whether or not we want to alter it in any way and, if so, in what direction and by what means. The purpose of this chapter is to try to show how we can interrelate theory and policy with respect to sex roles and family size.

There is of course no universal consensus when it comes to policies on fertility control. There are numerous interest groups with spokesmen and would-be spokesmen. There is the Catholic Church, for example, which issues official statements from the Vatican regarding contraception, and there are its local parish priests who may utter things quite different. Then there are varieties of views held by Mormons, liberal and conservative Protestants, Jews, groups for and against abortion, groups for and against the Equal Rights Amendment, women's liberationist groups, and black groups concerned with population and political power, and so on. Of course, the federal government maintains considerable interest in population matters, as evidenced by its continued funding of much research in the area and its recently sponsored Commission on Population Growth and the American Future.

Until recently those groups favoring pronatalist policies prevailed in the United States, as in most societies. Then during the late sixties and early seventies there arose a great concern for environmental and ecological problems and what continued population growth meant for the depletion of the earth's natural resources. In 1974, viewing the record-low 1973 American birthrate (15.0 per 1,000 population; *Monthly Vital Statistics Report*, Vol. 22, No. 13), some spokesmen were warning against the "dangers" of zero population growth. These dangers ranged from declines in important consumer markets to problems connected with continuing increases in the median age of the population and to matters such as alleged societal stagnation and hesitancy on the part of those who are younger, but fewer, to bear the costs of supporting the greater numbers of older persons.

For example, government officials in East European communist countries were in the late 60's quite anxious over sharp declines in their birth rates. In Romania from 1957 to 1967 the crude birth rate dropped from 25.5 to 14.6. As a result in 1967 tight controls were placed on abortions, and according to data from the World Health Organization, the Romanian birth rate jumped for a while to be the highest in Europe (Prinz, 1973). But the outcome of that was overcrowding in the Romanian school system, and by 1984 the likelihood of "severe unemployment or an out-migration of surplus labor . . ." (Westoff, 1974). And in Argentina, where abortion has not been legally available (Berelson, 1973:154), the late Perón's concern over insufficient population growth led him to make "oral contraceptives illegal" and to "remind Argentine women of their maternal responsibilities" (Westoff, 1974).

Clearly, population policies remain as live issues, and throughout the chapter we shall attempt to make policy inputs based on our findings. Moreover, we shall not restrict policy discussions solely to developed societies but seek to spell out implications for developing nations as well. But first a summary and integration of our findings.

Theoretical Perspectives

The fundamental assumption with which we worked is summed up in this statement (Blake, 1972:3):

> In order to understand the long-run determinants of birth rates, insofar as these relate to motivational . . . factors, one must translate birth rates into the operational context of reproduction. People do not have birth rates, they have children.

Human reproduction is inextricably bound up with the sociology of the family, and family structure and process is inextricably related to the opportunity structure of any given society. For at least 170 years Western conjugal family structure has been oriented around a system of reward-allocation which defined the husband as unique provider and the wife as "expressive hub." The husband has sought to achieve his major life satisfaction, identity, and self-worth within the occupational sphere. The wife has gained major satisfactions by identifying with and sharing in her husband's attainments and also by bearing and caring for children.

This description, however, does not imply that marital structure has been static. It does assume that children have provided an important source of gratifications to wives as well as to husbands but that occupational behaviors (including achievement) function as another source of rewards. In a modern society these latter kinds of gratifications take on enormous significance not merely in their material aspects but even more so in their intangible senses. The whole thrust of modern societies over the past several hundred years has been from what has been termed traditional to rational behavior patterns—or, put another way, from familistic to individualistic. White men have had access to individualistic rewards proffered by modern society and the kind of independent status, autonomy, and identity they supply. One of the outcomes of the Feminist Movement that began early in the nineteenth century was to generate aspirations among women for these same kinds of highly valued resources. And though one of the fruits of the counter culture has been to question materialism and frenetic striving after conspicuous consumption, there is little if any evidence that the importance of occupational achievement itself has declined among American youth. Williams' (1968) distinction between achievement as means and material success as ends is critical here, for it is the latter and not the former that is being seriously reassessed by both women and men.

We employed a utility framework as a means to conceptualize the range of alternative and competing rewards available (and potential costs) to wives. Such an approach aids our understanding in numerous ways but it is especially helpful in resolving the kind of issue that Blake poses. She claims that a major thrust of the modern neofeminist movement has been to seek to bring about equality of responsibility for child care on the part of husbands and wives (1972). At the same time, however, she insists that there has not been a corresponding stress on antinatalism. Instead of bringing husbands into the child-rearing process (as many feminists say we should), she argues that we should instead create an atmosphere in which the question becomes, "Why have children at all?" or "Why not simply one child?" Her claim is that currently such questions are rarely (if ever) raised on either a societal or familial level.

In the light of our findings, however, such a claim seems exaggerated (see also Veevers, 1974). A major structural and policy issue indeed emerges if one seriously expects many men soon significantly to deemphasize universalistic achievement rewards to seek the particularistic benefits of child rearing (though also see our later discussion). But this situation does not necessitate a static impasse. If one thinks in terms of a model of marriage that includes reward-seeking, bargaining, exchange, negotiation, conflict, and so forth (see following sections, "Problems for Future Research"), it is apparent how wives can gain relatively greater access to individualistic benefits without necessarily being able to involve husbands as fully as they might wish in traditional patterns of child care and domestic duties. The impasse can be resolved (whether consciously or otherwise has not yet been of paramount importance) through having fewer utilities of one sort (children) which then permits wives more utilities of another sort (greater individualistic occupational access). However, as we have seen, this type of resolution does not mean that husbands have not been moving in the direction of greater egalitarianism.

The strategy employed here to operationalize these utility notions and to link them to fertility control was first to attempt a valid analysis of marital role structure. The sex role differentiation just described is, as Holter (1970) puts it, a "distributive system of society." Certain rewards and responsibilities are meted out chiefly on the basis of the ascribed characteristic of gender. Our objective was to try to analyze this distributive system in terms of the various dimensions of marital role structure. By so doing we get some idea of preferred utilities. In short, variation in role structure indicates differences in preferred rewards and costs. Our approach was first to distinguish among wife, husband, and maternal positions and second to distinguish between dimensions that represent different aspects of these positions or statuses.

ANALYSIS OF MARITAL ROLES

The literature has lacked a detailed analysis of marital roles, and what immediately became apparent was the multidimensional nature of these social positions. First of all, for example, we found two aspects to the status of wife. One is the TW (traditional wife) role, which represents or emphasizes more traditional gratifications of wife behaviors, and the other is the SA (self-actualization) role, which emphasizes more contemporary orientations. Similarly, the position of husband was differentiated into three sets of roles—the first, PHA (problematic husband alterations), representing a willingness for problematic (in the sense of noninstitutionalized) costs to husbands which aid wife reward-seeking. The second, IE (institutionalized equality), emphasizes institutionalized equality of responsibility between spouses for domestic and child-care duties—again a "cost" to husbands relative to their traditional prerogatives. The third, TH (traditional husband), indicates ideological preferences for traditional male authority; the greater the rejection of this authority, the more rewarding or beneficial the situation is for wives.

Finally, the position of mother can be delineated into two dimensions, the first of which, RLM (religious legitimation of motherhood), indicates the sacredness with which maternal behaviors are viewed. This dimension applies equally to non-Catholics as well as to Catholics and thus gives us an indicator of "religiosity" on which both groups can be validly compared. The second aspect of the maternal position, TM (traditional mother), emphasizes the kinds of orientations and gratifications that women have traditionally associated with child care. In addition to these three structural positions and their seven sets of role norms, we utilized an index of wife capabilities, AE (abilities evaluation), and measures of instrumental (ISC) and expressive (ESC) self-concepts.

Theoretically, we would expect at least some of the seven role dimensions to be correlated with each other; this expectation held to some degree for both sexes, though it tends to vary by wife employment, age, and so forth. There were also relationships between certain aspects of role modernity and the AE, ESC, and ISC dimensions. Hence, while it is exceedingly useful to make analytic distinctions among and thus be aware of the sometimes subtle emphases represented by these various aspects of marital role structure, in actuality they often operate concurrently and in conjunction with one another. This was our basic rationale for considering potential correlations between any of these ten dimensions and say, birth intentions or age at marriage. Although this may have been a somewhat cumbersome technical procedure, it was faithful to the complexities of actual marital situations. In the "real world" the influence on any given aspect of fertility control, of say, orientations toward problematic alterations in husbands' behaviors (PHA) occurs simultaneously with norms pertaining to traditional emphases in the wife position or degree of secularity toward the maternal position, and so forth. Moreover, since the study was exploring links between sex role norms and fertility control, there was no easy way to know beforehand what particular dimensions would be correlated with what fertility variables. It was essential to allow any and all possibilities to emerge.

In an effort to better familiarize ourselves with these roles and self-concept dimensions we made initial comparisons based on sex, age, race, education, and religion. Perhaps more than any other of these five variables, education seemed to emerge as the most consistent discriminator. Those with most education tended to be most role-modern, most instrumental, and report the highest AE rankings. On certain dimensions, younger persons tended to be more role-modern than older persons, as we had predicted. These age differences were not consistently significant, though older persons were never more sex role-modern than younger persons. Yet men were sometimes more modern than women and women than men; blacks were generally more modern or egalitarian than whites, though not consistently so. Religion tends to be the least consistent discriminator of all, although over some dimensions Catholics tend to be more traditional than non-Catholics. In terms of a summary generalization we might conclude that young men and women of both races who are better-educated (and perhaps non-Catholic) tend to be the most modern or egalitarian or individualistic with regard to sex role norms. Therefore, in terms of ongoing social change we may expect the young and the better-educated to be in the vanguard of movement away from marital role structures based on specialization and toward structures based instead on interchangeability (Scanzoni, 1972).

Towards a Model of Fertility Control

Projecting this movement leads to a discussion of just how the foregoing enables us to work towards a model of fertility control. It is worthwhile noting that theoretical predictions regarding expected findings were made prior to data collection, i.e., that sex role norms would be expected to influence particular aspects of fertility control in certain ways. Actual findings, have of course, refined, specified, and elaborated these original expectations, but basically they have been confirmed. The fact that the findings were theoretically accounted for beforehand should enhance our confidence in their validity. Moreover, given Yaukey's (1969) observations regarding the lack of recent theoretical development in the realm of fertility control, it would appear that this particular theoretical approach may, in the future, be a most fruitful one to explore still further.

Recall that we used three flow charts to represent visually the processes that were assumed to be operative in terms of the particular issues being explored. Although it would require a longitudinal design to combine the several processes involved, we shall nonetheless attempt to incorporate them theoretically in a fashion such that they could be tested within the scope of such a design. We shall present major findings of the study in a propositional form—a set of interrelated statements that could serve as hypotheses for further investigation.

To take into account the effects of situational constraints on norms, we subdivided respondents by employment and education, and where that is particularly significant we note that as well. Detailed findings too specific to be presented in propositional form can of course be located in appropriate chapters. Finally, for reasons discussed in Chapter Three, the model developed here is only indirectly applicable to men, and it does not appear appropriate for older women (except in the case of proposition 17a). How future research might profitably incorporate men into the model is discussed later in this chapter.

The Propositions

The 18 propositions apply to younger black and white Catholic and non-Catholic wives in general, except where it is observed that a particular statement has greater pertinence for one or another category of wives.

1. The higher the background status, the greater the sex role modernity.
2. The higher the education, the greater the sex role modernity.
3. The greater the sex role modernity and the higher the education, the higher the age at marriage.

The model begins with that period of time prior to marriage, the period of childhood and adolescent socialization. During this time sex roles are being learned and preferences for individualistic gratifications are being formed. Although we did not collect information on premarital sexual activity, recent national surveys strongly confirm what has been emerging for some time, that women of lower status tend to be more sexually active and more contraceptively naive (Kantner and Zelnik, 1972, 1973). They also tend to marry sooner, a decision often complicated and precipitated by premarital pregnancy. It may be that single women from higher-status homes learn to structure their sex roles in more individualistic terms and that this tends to be one type of influence on their sexual activity. It could be one reason that they are more circumspect in sexual behavior and contraception, because pregnancy and childbirth would complicate their aspirations for individualistic gratifications. Their aspirations also tend to motivate them to pursue additional education, and both the education and the individualism motivate them to postpone or defer the gratifications of marriage. Furthermore, avoiding premarital pregnancy enables single women to work prior to marriage, and this type of work behavior also has a delaying effect on marriage.

We do not mean to imply that sex role is the cause of education, but neither is the reverse valid. Greater socioeconomic rewards through parents appear to cause aspirations for both individualistic and status (educational) rewards, and each of the latter in turn over time probably generates increments in the other in a mutually reinforcing pattern. Moreover, persons from higher-status homes learn not only to aspire to greater socioeconomic rewards, they also learn to expect that the probability is good that they can realistically obtain these benefits. Thus, they are more motivated to defer certain kinds of sexual and familistic gratifications than are persons of relatively lesser status whose socioeconomic expectations are considerably lower. In this way status expectations (as well as aspirations) are linked with and help reinforce individualistic aspirations and expectations.

4. The greater the sex role modernity, the lower the total number of births intended by never-married white university students.
5. The greater the sex role modernity, the more likely married women are to be currently employed full time.
   a. This holds mostly for white non-Catholics and blacks.
6. The greater the sex role modernity and the fact of full-time employ-

ment and the greater the education and the later the age at marriage, the lower the total number of births intended by younger married women.

The literature indicates that single persons (even children; Gustavas and Nam, 1970) can verbalize family ideals and expectations; that these intentions tend to increase with length of marriage, indicating some rationalization to account for contraceptive failures; but that nevertheless completed family size is strongly predicted by these sorts of birth orientations. Pushing the process back one step, we have sought to account for these intentions by conceptualizing children as familistic kinds of rewards, the quantity of which is contingent on preferences for alternative individualistic gratifications. Our assumption is that as persons grow up they very early develop a sense of themselves in terms of desired and actual degree of autonomy, independence, and achievement. Kohn and others have shown that this sense of autonomy varies positively with social class (Kohn, 1969; Pearlin, 1972).

This development is obvious in the case of boys, but it is equally significant for girls in connection with such phenomena as "the motive to avoid success" (Horner, 1970). Both boys and girls grow up with differing degrees of preferred autonomy and independence, or aspirations for individualistic achievement. These differences exist within and between the sexes. In an achievement-oriented society these kinds of orientations are probably at the core of the individual's socialization and development of identity. At the same time that these preferences for individualistic, universalistic rewards are developing, other types of potential particularistic gratifications also come into focus. In the immediate picture these might include peer benefits, while over the long term the image might encompass the rewards of marriage and children.

Presumably, the choice (conscious or otherwise) between individualism and familism becomes most salient or meaningful at marriage. However, it may be almost as salient for single persons completing or beyond high school who are part of the marriage market—obviously so if they engage in coitus. Proposition 4 indicates that among persons still in the marriage market, as well as among married women (Proposition 6), preferences for individualistic benefits tend to depress preferences for alternative familistic rewards. When women who have grown up becoming oriented to individualism are faced with familism they tend to make choices favoring the former.

Proposition 5 seeks to help resolve the thorny question of the causal sequence between wife employment and birth intentions. The assumption is that current wife employment and birth intentions are both explained by sex role modernity. Thus, preferences for individualistic gratifications are prior in significance to the dynamics of the employment–fertility relationship.

7. The higher the education and the greater the sex role modernity and the later the age of marriage, the more likely wives are to work full time prior to any children.

8. The more operative are all the elements in Proposition 7 including wife employment prior to children, the greater the number of months between marriage and the first child.

We assume a causal sequence in which wives who are more individualistically oriented tend to be more motivated to seek occupational gratifications at the earliest stage of their marriage, as well as motivated to defer for a greater length of time the birth of the first child. Relative freedom and flexibility to pursue occupational interests and to delay the first child suggests a reduced likelihood that there has been premarital pregnancy. Such pregnancy would often tend to lower marriage age and obviously shorten the interval to the first child. It would also tend to limit the flexibility of the wife's job decisions at that time. Therefore, what is likely operating among women who are more role-modern is a kind of "deferral syndrome" in which marital and familistic gratifications tend to be deferred for longer periods owing in large measure to preferences for individualistic and status gratifications.

9. The greater the sex role modernity and the higher the education and the later the age at marriage and the fact of working prior to children as well as the fact of current employment and the longer the interval between marriage and the first child, the lower the current parity.
   a. Among working wives, the greater the job status and income the lower the current parity.

Among younger couples at any given time their current family size, or actual level of familistic rewards, is the result of this complex chain of influences. Deferral of marriage, early and current employment, deferral of the first child, increased education—all these behaviors can be taken to indicate preferences for individualistic gratifications, as can the sex role norms themselves. Taken together, the more strongly these indicators are operative, the less desirable and more costly are alternative familistic events. Furthermore, among that subset of currently employed wives, the tangible and intangible gratifications of higher status and of income also operate to make familism (children) less desirable and more costly.

10. Among white non-Catholic wives who work or who are well educated, the greater the sex role modernity, the less the likelihood of past contraceptive timing failures.

11. Among white non-Catholic wives who do not work or who are less well educated, the lower their birth intentions, the less the likelihood of past timing failures. This also holds to some degree for Catholics and blacks.

12. Among Catholics and blacks, there is a tendency for sex role modernity and past timing failures to be positively related. However, educated blacks show certain dimensions of sex role modernity to be associated positively with timing success.
13. Among all groupings, timing failures and parity tend to be positively related.

An important element in pre-research theorizing was that modern sex role norms would motivate wives to be more careful contraceptors. Acknowledging the uncertain reliability of retrospective assessments of contraceptive behaviors, we nonetheless discovered that two subsets of non-Catholic wives verified our expectations that individualism would operate in this significant fashion to minimize unintended familism. Among other non-Catholics and blacks, intending fewer children (explained in part by sex role modernity) seemed to influence careful contraception. However, causality is unclear here because rigor could affect birth intentions. Concomitantly among Catholics and some blacks it is not certain whether timing failures stimulate greater egalitarianism or whether individualism prompts certain wives to accept familistic costs early in marriage so as to permit greater access to individualistic gratifications later on. In any case it is apparent that sex role norms and the whole issue of contraceptive rigor are intimately interconnected, and we pursue the matter again in Propositions 17, 18.

14. The greater the parity, the less the perceived satisfactions with economic gratifications and with marital (husband-wife) gratifications.
    a. This holds most strongly where wives work.

While there are complex feedback loops operating, we may say that husband's actual economic position (SES) affects wife's economic satisfaction positively and their parity negatively. But parity also seems to decrease economic satisfactions and also marital satisfactions; and economic and marital satisfactions are positively related. These links are clearest where wives work, and as Proposition 5 indicates sex role norms influence that decision. More generally, we may say that not only are there inverse links between individualistic and familistic rewards; in addition the latter exist inversely with socioeconomic benefits (actual and perceived) and with marital satisfactions. Again causality is uncertain because sometimes wives who feel economically and maritally disadvantaged or dissatisfied may seek children as compensatory mechanisms.

15. Except for those who are employed full time, Catholic wives tend to show positive relationships between husband's income and both birth intentions and parity. These particular Catholic wives tend to reveal similar positive relationships between economic satisfactions and both birth intentions and parity.

Some subsets of Catholics represent an exception to the generalization that familistic and economic gratifications exist inversely. Instead, the presence of the latter tended to stimulate familistic benefits (or perhaps make their costs less onerous). Evidently Catholics more than non-Catholics accept the pronatalist norm that "good persons should have as many children as they can afford." This attitude is probably linked with their conceptions of "proper" and "rewarding" religious behavior. It may be that in the future Catholics will come to reinterpret those aspects of doctrine and morality that relate children to economic resources in a fashion similar to that now held by non-Catholics. In any case, we may expect those Catholics who are most individualistic to be least likely to allow their family sizes to be significantly influenced by either economic rewards or else traditional religious interpretations. This last conclusion can be elaborated by considering the following proposition unique to Catholics.

16. The less their religious devoutness, the greater the fertility control patterns of Catholics resembled those of white non-Catholics in comparable situational contexts.
   a. The greater the sex role modernity, the less the religious devoutness of Catholics.

Devoutness (frequency of receiving communion) can be explained as positive valuation of certain religious rewards. Those religious rewards stimulate familistic rewards because in order to obtain the former, couples have to be obedient in not thwarting accumulation of the latter. Significantly, we found that sex role modernity and devoutness are inversely related, suggesting that those Catholics who follow dominant societal trends and become more individualistic will also become less devout. Less devoutness along with increased individualism should thereby enhance their fertility control. It may be, of course, that some younger Catholics will continue to participate in the Mass frequently but "reinterpret" the content of religious rewards contained in their devoutness. That is, just as frequency of church attendance among Protestants seems to make no difference in their fertility control, so participation in the Mass may among Catholics eventually come to have the same lack of effect on family size.

17. The greater the sex role modernity, the more likely it is that wives will currently be using more efficient and effective techniques to prevent unintended conceptions.
   a. This holds most strongly among non-Catholics (older as well as younger aged cohorts) and blacks.
   b. Catholic wives tend to reveal negative associations between sex role modernity and contraceptive efficiency.

When we seek to account for motivations underlying current contraceptive behavior we may draw on the same theoretical model just discussed. Current behavior involves two major issues: one is use or non-use of any method to prevent pregnancy; the other is relative efficiency (effectiveness) of the method chosen. Use of some method and use of more efficient techniques indicate preferences for fewer familistic gratifications (and costs), whereas their opposites suggest, at the least, indifference to additional costs and perhaps even preferences for additional such benefits. The method-efficiency issue tended to be explained by sex role modernity, as well as by other kinds of related variables. That is, the more persons were oriented towards rewards that function as alternatives to childbearing and caring, the more motivated they were not merely to practice some form of contraception but also to utilize more efficient technologies. Catholic wives, as they had done in connection with past timing failures, revealed relationships precisely opposite to those for non-Catholics, and this time opposite to blacks too. Do younger, more modern Catholic wives prefer to experience familistic costs earlier rather than later; or does reduced contraceptive rigor somehow stimulate egalitarianism?

18. The greater the sex role modernity, the stronger the motivation and the greater the confidence of younger wives that they shall be able to prevent unwanted children or "number failures."
    a. Lowered birth orientations and increased method-efficiency also tended to increase expected contraceptive efficacy.

Finally, when we focused on a very critical dimension of contraceptive behavior—expectations for future efficacy based on experience—we found that here too the same type of reward-alternative model (individualism versus familism) strongly predicted positive efficacy. Interestingly, the level of method efficiency (the pill and other efficient techniques) was not as powerful an influence on expectations that unwanted pregnancies could be avoided as were sex role norms. This point raises the critical issue of motivation versus technology in contraceptive behavior which was discussed at length in Chapter Five. Our conclusion was that neither element by itself is sufficient for optimum fertility control. What is necessary and sufficient for such control is keen motivation to restrict familism prompted by individualistic and status rewards, combined with sophisticated, safe, and available technologies. Bumpass (1973) maintains that the era is already upon us in which these factors are strongly present and that, as a result, birth rates in America should continue to remain low. We shall return later to the question of fluctuations in birth rates, but the point is that technology does not overwhelm motivation when it comes to fertility control. Instead, sophisticated technology is the adjunct (albeit essential) of motivation and the rewards that stimulate it.

Before we move to a summary proposition, two further matters pertaining to our findings require brief attention. The first is that in spite of unique historic pressures resulting in greater marital egalitarianism in black society, blacks sometimes tended to exhibit patterns of fertility control less rigorous than those of white non-Catholics. These divergences are probably due to the fact that blacks (males especially) have been systematically denied equal access to educational and occupational opportunity structures in which, after all, individualistic aspirations are most generally carried out. To the degree such discrimination diminishes (Recent census data suggest that to some degree it has, at least for well-educated, younger persons. See *Current Population Reports*, P-23, No. 46.), blacks will realistically come to expect greater levels of socioeconomic gratifications. Consequently, perceptions of these kinds of benefits should, in combination with their already pervasive individualism, enhance the motivations of black couples at all status levels to practice more rigorous and effective fertility control. Meaningful access to socioeconomic alternatives to familism should result in decreases of the latter. This gradual black-white convergence does not mean that blacks are "imitating middle-class whites" or encouraging "genocide." But as Blake (1972) implies, it is couples that have children, not races. As long as modern societies are structured as they are now in terms of prevailing stratification systems and achievement possibilities, then a reward-alternative model of fertility control has considerable relevance irrespective of skin color.

A second matter has to do with relationships between fertility control variables and our three indicators of social mobility. Operating on Featherman's suggestion (1970) that we look for such associations within "select subgroups" of our sample, we found that among non-Catholics mobility was generally linked with more rigorous fertility control patterns. Among Catholics and blacks, that type of positive link sometimes appeared as well, but at other times mobility was related to less rigorous fertility control patterns. We had neither the proper design (longitudinal) nor the range of additional measures required to adequately fit these several types of associations into our overall model. However, as we observe later, it seems reasonable for future studies of fertility control to conceptualize mobility variables within a reward-alternative framework, and to take into account both the causes and consequences of mobility aspirations and behaviors within the context of particular situational constraints.

A Summary Proposition

To try to subsume all the foregoing propositions under one more abstract statement will of necessity result in obscuring much important detail. Indeed even those 18 propositions were themselves summaries of a vast array of detailed findings. But to the degree that sociology is a "gen-

eralizing science" the objective is to develop statements that are as suc-
cinct and parsimonious as possible and yet broad enough to subsume the
widest possible range of verified empirical phenomena. We have cited this
statement throughout the book in the form of an hypothesis of prediction
about what we expected to find. We have moved from that general level
down to the less abstract level of Propositions 1 through 18, and now go
back again. Simply stated: *The greater the individualism, the less the
familism.* Those concepts and the indicators that represent the constructs
of individualism and familism have already been described in great detail.
The basic notion underlying these constructs and their linkage is that they
represent sets of rewards that at this time exist inversely to each other. To
have one set tends to exclude the other.

Whether in the future intensive male involvement in child care, or else
extensive day-care centers will render the two sets of rewards no longer
incompatible remains to be seen. Either or both possibilities would represent a significant structural alteration in patterns of child care arrangements, and we shall have more to say about them. However, we would
expect that societal evolution towards either of those possibilities would
not occur without passage first through the evolutionary stage described
in these pages. That is, it is likely that for the great majority of persons the
major thrust will be in the direction of changes in sex roles identified in
earlier chapters. Only after that would, perhaps, an increasing number of
persons move seriously in the direction of having both additional children
and female achievement as a result of either or both of the two potential
arrangements in question.

CONNECTIONS WITH GENERAL SOCIAL THEORY

The stated relationship between individualism and familism applies
not just to women's new interests contrasted to traditional interests. It is,
in addition, broad enough to subsume and explain relationships between
extended kinship networks and particular conjugal units. Historically in
Western societies, and currently in developing societies, parts of larger
family structures may be confronted with alternative and competing sets
of rewards (Anderson, 1971). For example, conjugal units may have to
choose between obligations to and rewards from the kin, or else gratifications from non-kin sources. It could be hypothesized that the greater the
familism (participation in kin-oriented rewards and costs), the less the
individualism (participation in behaviors that bring direct costs and benefits and advantages to the conjugal unit itself). Duty, loyalty, obligation to
kin, traditionalism, familism—all these constructs represent the same basic
notions. And these notions are inverse to those of individualism or moder-

nity or "rationality" (in the Weberian sense), which imply seeking to place the interests of one's own particular significant membership group ahead of the interests of the larger whole.

Therefore, familism can subsume: (1) the primacy of kin obligations over nuclear unit obligations and (2) the primacy of traditional female behaviors in childbearing and caring over alternative potential behaviors. Individualism can subsume: (1) the primacy of nuclear unit over extended kin and (2) the primacy or at least equality in significance of achievement behaviors vis-à-vis nurturant behaviors towards husband and (any) children. The phenomenon of divorce can likewise be subsumed under these two constructs. Familism implies that obligations and duties to the larger groups (nuclear unit) take precedence (especially for the woman) over concerns about individualistic costs and rewards. That traditional posture can be contrasted with a modern, or "rational," or individualistic position in which one's own interests must be at least equal to or perhaps even greater in significance than group interests (Scanzoni, 1972).

Thus, Weber's concept of the movement of modern societies from traditional to rational implies within family structures a movement from the familistic to the individualistic (Goode, 1963). This movement can be observed in shifts from the predominance of extended families to the predominance of conjugal family patterns; from the relative absence of divorce to its increasing frequency; and from conjugal family structure based on role differentiation to structure based on role interchangeability, in which the woman no longer gains social status and major life satisfactions from husband and child care but through her own participation within the opportunity structure (see Goldscheider, 1971:135–181).

Recent years have witnessed the convergence of a variety of theoretical perspectives in which the common emphasis or integrating thread is on change or process or movement (Buckley, 1967). At the macro and micro levels theorists who focus on conflict refer to competing *interests* and interest-groups (Dahrendorf, 1959; Deutsch, 1971). At the micro level, other theorists interested in utilitarianism and exchange refer to *reward-seeking* (Homans, 1961; Blau, 1964). Conceptually "interests" and "reward-seeking" appear to fall into the same genre. The point is that in striving to explain many forms of social behaviors modern sociology is increasingly moving in the direction of a convergence of these (and related) notions, set within the still more abstract notion of "systems theory."

Therefore, conceptualizing fertility control in terms of female "interests" or "reward-seeking" and arguing that a systems approach is requisite for further valid knowledge place this whole question squarely in the mainstream of theory development in modern sociology (in addition to the substantive and policy significance of changes in women's roles discussed later). Thus propositions developed from studies such as this one can contribute towards refinement and elaboration of more general social theory and be subsequently applied to other substantive areas as well as to later fertility studies. At the more general level we shall be developing propositions in which notions about reward-seeking and competing interest-groups are central. At the more substantive level of the sociology of fertility those propositions can illuminate reward-seeking by males and females, as well as illuminate relationships between the sexes as competing interest groups in relation to family structure and fertility control.

Problems for Future Research

Throughout the book we have noted the exploratory nature of our efforts to link sex role and fertility both theoretically and empirically. Numerous shortcomings emerge in any piece of research, inevitably in an initial effort such as this. What we want to do now is to pinpoint the most significant of these problems in order to manage them more effectively in subsequent investigations, and also to help us better assess our own conclusions.

PROCESS

The most pressing of these problems centers around the need for a design in which respondents are followed from, say, the time of marriage and interviewed repeatedly over a number of years. Such a procedure introduces its own complications, such as attrition due to death or subsequent refusals, or divorce and possible remarriage. Nevertheless, as by definition fertility control is a series of ongoing processes, it needs to be studied in an ongoing fashion. At marriage, for example, one would measure for both sexes the degree of sex role modernity, birth intentions, actual and anticipated employment behaviors, actual and anticipated contraceptive behaviors, and aspirations for social mobility. Valid information could then also be collected retrospectively on socialization experiences in home, school, and community. As this would be the only time such information was gathered, great depth could be achieved in examining specific varieties of parent–child interaction to determine how parental norms and behaviors influence the development of sex roles and self-perceptions. The formation of sex role norms could be investigated with regard to respondent's own and the opposite sex. As the couple was followed over time, changes could be observed in role and marital structure, primary relations, and empathy, in fertility behaviors, and in status and income of both partners. The result would be a much clearer picture than we presently have of the complex causal influences described earlier. One would then be better able to determine the actual degree of significance of role orientations as influences on movement of wives in and out of the labor force, on birth intentions, on contraceptive efficacy, and so forth.

Negotiation and Change

It is especially important to focus on changes in role norms and on the forces that account for them. Being able to analyze changes would be especially useful in the case of persons from working-class (or lower-class) homes who had learned rather traditional sex roles but began to shift them in a more modern direction. Whatever the class background, such a study would provide a unique opportunity to investigate the dynamics of the bargaining processes whereby husbands and wives translate their learned normative sex role structures (for both self and spouse) into actual behavioral outcomes. These kinds of processes are assumed to exist in the findings reported in earlier chapters, but they were not specifically measured. This issue became especially evident in Chapters Four and Five when we examined contraceptive behavior, both past and current. Moreover, the question of power within marriage is endemic to these matters of bargaining, potential for conflict, and change and/or maintenance of particular behaviors.

Thus in seeking to understand behaviors that are strongly linked with family size such as, for example, wife employment or birth planning more study is needed of the kinds of "negotiations" that go on between husbands and wives. One of the (needed) benefits from such an investigation would be a more systematic integration of utility theory with social exchange theory. The basic explanatory framework used throughout this book to explain fertility control has been the former, while exchange theory has been used elsewhere to explain marital structure and process (Scanzoni: 1970, 1971, 1972). As both perspectives are based on notions of reward-seeking and maximization of a wide range of resources, they intrinsically overlap. Future work therefore should focus on the general process of reward-seeking throughout marriage.

Such investigations might discover that the less individualistic wives are, the less likely they are to seek to bargain with or to challenge their husbands over issues related to employment, contraception, household chores, or children. Conversely, wives who are more individualistic are more likely to raise questions and issues in connection with each of these behavioral areas—questions as to the equity and justice of particular marital and familial arrangements. On the other hand, wives who are more role-traditional are probably less likely to raise these kinds of questions and simply more willing to conform to traditional behaviors with regard to their own (wife, mother) and their spouse's (husband) positions.

Norms and Behavior

At several points in the book reference was made to the issue of links between norms and behavior. One reason these links may have been difficult to trace was that, until recently, sociologists gave relatively little notice to process and change. Within marriage the links between structure (sex role norms) and ongoing behavioral outcomes (fertility control) can be more thoroughly investigated by focusing on social processes of exchange and authority and on conflict and its resolution. We were able to show, for instance, that sex role norms are related to contraceptive behaviors, as well as to behaviors pertinent to age at marriage, employment, child-spacing, and actual parity. But only a longitudinal design could identify the feedback that norms and behaviors incrementally exercise on each other over time.

Rationality

A related and crucial matter is the issue of the degree of purposive rationality that persons apply to their fertility control. Throughout the book we have assumed that this varied on a continuum from almost none to extremely great. For example in the past, the 18-year-old newlywed working-class girl was probably often found at the "almost none" end of the rationality continuum. Other men and women may have been found at different points on the continuum depending on age, parity, religion, and so forth (Kammeyer, 1973). However, our underlying assumption was that the more keenly persons are aware of and desirous for alternatives to familism, the more purposive-rational they tend to become in their birth-planning and contraceptive behavior, whether they are conscious of it or not. Therefore, one of the vital questions to explore in the future is this whole issue of rationality in contraception and how it is related to husband–wife bargaining and exchange in general. How conscious are couples of behaving rigorously in their contraception in order to achieve certain alternative gratifications or avoid unwanted costs? Does sophisticated technology make them more conscious of the potential for increased rationality, as Bumpass (1973) suggests?

Alternate Life Styles

Based on Chapters Four and Five, the kinds of hypotheses that we might carry into such research center around the issue of preferred marital role structures or life styles. For the more strongly traditional structures are preferred, the less salient is the matter of rationality in birth planning or in alternative female life style. The woman simply conforms to what have for so long been traditional female behaviors. Conversely, the more innovative structures or life styles are preferred, the more rationality is automatically imposed. For if these "different" or "modern" arrangements are to be achieved, then husbands and wives must begin to negotiate (rather consciously) about number of children, timing, contraceptives, and actual husband and wife behavior in the spheres both of home and occupation.

BIRTH PLANNING

Our findings on Catholics, and to some extent on blacks, underscore the need for sophisticated measures of birth planning that identify the point or points in time at which women (and men) feel most "prepared" to cope with the costs (both individualistic and economic) of a child or children. Assuming that voluntary childlessness or "child-free" marriages will exist for only a very small minority of couples, the question of when is the most propitious time for individualistic women to bear familistic costs becomes exceedingly significant. Should they be borne early or later in marriage? Which options are least punishing to their own interests? to family consumption interests? What strategies, if any, exist for coping with a child so as to reduce those punishments? Should we not reconceptualize the notion of timing failure for persons still short of their target number who, though they may "accidentally" ease into pregnancy, have or develop a strategy to minimize its costs?

MARITAL STATUSES

Once in-depth information on these kinds of dynamic processes is systematically interrelated with the several normative dimensions of wife, mother, and husband positions, it would then be possible to begin to classify marriages empirically on a continuum in which the wife holds the position of equal partner, junior partner, or complement (Scanzoni, 1972). As discussed in Chapter Two, analysis of the normative dimensions of marital positions brings us closer to such an objective, but the intervening chapters make it quite clear that until we know much more about the ongoing processes of exchange, conflict-resolution, and authority, we are not in a position to identify marriages on a continuum of egalitarianism, or of traditional to modern. It thus becomes apparent that a longitudinal study is requisite not only to understand and explain dependent variables such as fertility control, but it is equally critical if we are to grasp independent elements such as marital structure, process, and interaction. Of course, from a "systems" perspective the "dependent" variables then act on formerly "independent" elements.

BENEFITS TO HUSBANDS

In this same vein a most crucial question is investigation into the kinds of compensations that husbands receive in lieu of relinquishing traditional male prerogatives in the interests of wife reward-seeking. In a very real sense husbands who operate in a situation of greater role modernity tend to avoid the material costs of additional numbers of children. This type of cost-avoidance, however, is part of a larger pattern in which socioeconomic position, sex role modernity, and both types of marital gratifications (empathy and primary relations) generally tend to be positively related. Thus, within the processes of ongoing marital exchange men with higher status who receive greater marital satisfaction may feel more "obligated" to concur in their wives' individualistic reward-seeking. Male concurrence is probably part of a process of ongoing marital reinforcement in which the more husbands concur with wives' individualism, the more positively do wives tend to respond in terms of marital gratifications. In addition to having learned prior to marriage to be more amenable to female individualism, higher-status men may be more motivated to concur with that individualism because it involves fewer material costs and also because their concurrence may also stimulate still greater marital gratifications.

STRATIFICATION

But perhaps there remains a more profound benefit that men receive from modern-oriented wives—profound in terms of what it might portend for future analyses of stratification and family systems. Traditionally, the location of a family in the stratification system was determined by the husband's job status, and that status had major consequences for all varieties of marital and familial interaction. It may be that among younger, more modern-oriented couples wives can offer to their husbands similar (though in most instances, not yet equal) benefits in terms of job prestige and income to those that husbands have traditionally offered wives. To some degree at least—and perhaps increasingly over time— husbands in such couples can identify with their wives' achievements and even participate in their tangible benefits, just as wives have done and will continue to do with regard to their husbands' achievements and benefits (Fogarty *et al.*, 1971). To the extent that these sorts of wife inputs become more institutionalized within marital structure among the better educated, it will then become necessary to devise measures of family social status that include more than merely the husbands' job position. Such measures might include, for example, work histories indicating career commitment as well as job positions of both spouses (Haug, 1973).

In any event, the point is that husbands who are oriented toward individualistic gratifications for wives and thus concur in their reward-seeking may in exchange experience certain kinds of status and economic benefits (intangible and tangible) that may motivate them to continue to reinforce their wives in their individualism. It is for this reason, therefore, as well as for the others discussed, that modern-oriented men are apparently more willing to relinquish traditional male prerogatives and, in so doing, experience lowered family fertility. Moreover, in this same regard, we discovered that higher-status men react more positively to the employment of their own wives (employment which is not so much out of necessity as out of desire) than do lower-status men. Being less threatened by their working, higher-status men are less likely to consider their wives as "rivals" in Parsons' (1955) sense, and thus from this standpoint less threat is posed to marital stability than in less-advantaged homes where wives work more out of necessity than desire.

Socialization

A final question pertains to the socialization of any children born to couples being followed over time. How old do children have to be before parents begin to behave in ways toward them that will shape their own sex role definitions? Is there indication that these children are being socialized in ways that will result in their becoming even more sex role modern than their parents? If so, what is the magnitude of these differences? In sum, a full understanding of the processes of fertility control requires information covering a wide range of variables which is intergenerational as well as intragenerational in nature. Data are required at the time of marriage on background experiences, on how they regulate their own fertility over the years, and on how they influence children to adopt certain roles which will in turn affect the children's subsequent fertility behavior.

Practical and Policy Implications

What are the immediate applications of a theoretical approach to fertility control based on notions of alternative rewards, individualism, and marital egalitarianism? "Immediate" must be approached in its several senses because the capability to respond immediately varies depending on the type of social situation: a single person, a young married person, an older married person, officials of nongovernmental organizations seeking to achieve certain fertility and population goals, officials responsible for school curricula, legislators and governmental policy planners, and so forth, for a variety of situations. Furthermore, a question that must be considered when discussing applications pertains to the relative importance to or significance of sex roles for fertility control, given declining birth rates of the early 70's, the 1973 Supreme Court ruling permitting abortions, increasing use of sterilization and sophisticated contraceptives, as well as possible constriction of labor force opportunities among jobs that women have traditionally entered.

To take the matter of job opportunity first, recall that throughout the book the assumption has been made that sex role orientations precede in significance both fertility and employment. Women who are individualistically oriented, finding that "traditional" women's jobs are limited can, for instance, turn to medicine (including paramedical work) or to many additional kinds of technical or vocational occupations that are rapidly expanding and currently have many unfilled vacancies. Likewise, they can enter those segments of industry, business, and management that are expanding both nationally and internationally. Willingness of a woman to travel in connection with her occupation or to work anywhere in the world are variables that are probably strongly predicted by sex role modernity.

By the same token, in contrast to those strongly individualistic women who will not be deterred by restricted traditional opportunities, other more sex role moderate women may be so deterred. That is, some of these women who in the past might have limited fertility and sought gratifications from traditional female occupations, once they find these opportunities narrowed may be unwilling for the kinds of costs (e.g., competitiveness) and responsibilities attached to "male" occupations. Consequently they may turn to children for gratifications not obtainable elsewhere. This possibility also speaks to the recent decline in birthrates. What went down can go up (Campbell, 1973), and if traditional female labor markets contract, it is possible that certain segments of the population who up to now have had access to these markets may consequently turn back to familistic compensations in significant numbers. Whether this would retard or reverse current birth declines depends, of course, on degree of job contraction and of sex role traditionalism. Thus while our assumption has been that increased sex role modernity has been one factor accounting for recent birth declines, there is no certainty as to the extent to which sex role modernity will continue to permeate working-class and lower-middle class segments of society, or no certainty regarding job opportunities to translate that modernity into behavior.

Recent events in which strong opposition has been mounted to passage of the Equal Rights Amendment, to abortion reforms, and to the whole concept of women's liberation of neofeminism indicate the possibility of some degree of societal reaction to individualistic gratifications for women. How many persons agree now or will come to agree with Pope Paul VI when in attacking the Women's Liberation Movement for its pro-abortion stand, he stated (UPI, December 10, 1972, as reported in *The National Observer*):

True women's liberation does not lie in formalistic or materialistic equality with the other sex, but in the recognition of that specific thing in the feminine personality—the vocation of a woman to become a mother.

Nonetheless, as discussed earlier, trends in Western society are moving in a direction opposite to that statement. But if among certain groups of whatever religious or humanist persuasion reaction occurs—for ideological or pragmatic reasons—then certain behavioral consequences may follow. Some of these consequences may include increases in family size alongside greater indifference to contraceptive rigor.

This matter of contraceptive indifference also speaks to the point of the significance of sex role orientations. For no matter how sophisticated the technology, motivation and its determinants underly its effective use. Likewise, even the strongest proponents of abortion agree that it is a "final solution." If effective contraception based on determined motivation becomes more widespread, the necessity to terminate unwanted pregnancies should diminish. If the reason for sterilization is that family size is already "too large," this type of situation too could diminish if contraception were employed with more determined rigor. At the same time, we could predict that future research will reveal that if sterilization is employed early in marriage (vasectomy, perhaps) while family size is still quite small, the motivation may have been strongly stimulated by sex role modernity or preferences for other than traditional gratifications.

In brief, the argument can be made that variations in sex role structures are at the very core of fertility control not only for the present, but as far into the future as anyone alive can realistically project. Segments of reaction to female individualism or segments of extreme feminism in which total antinatalism is espoused can be contrasted with a broad middle spectrum of gradual movement toward reduced role traditionalism. Being able to identify men and women (single or married) in terms of their varying sex role orientations will enable us to explain and understand birth patterns in a more complete and detailed way than has heretofore been possible.

Furthermore, it will supply, as Rainwater (1965) has already suggested, an additional and needed dimension and depth to demographic macroprojection of future birth trends. Predictions of birth trends has often been frustrating, and recent efforts are based on the principle of an array of estimates in which population growth may range from high to low depending on a variety of traditional demographic variables (*Current Population Reports*, P–25, No. 480). What is needed to increase the reliability of such predictions is a more systematic investigation of sex role structures (and husband–wife processes) and the inclusion of these kinds of variables in such long-range predictions.

Bumpass (1973:69) describes his projection of future population growth in the following terms:

I see a future of fertility below replacement, not as a fad, not as a response to environmental concern, but simply as an intrinsic characteristic of a modern fertility control society.

His contention is based on the one hand on sophisticated technology, such as the pill, but on the other on the same kinds of notions pursued throughout these pages. He argues that "succeeding cohorts of young women may be expected to hold progressively less to ascriptive values of motherhood . . . motherhood is fully a matter for rational evaluation . . . costs as well as virtues must be weighed . . . motherhood has been the last major vestige of ascribed status in a modern industrial society" (p. 68).

A different position is taken by Campbell (1973) when he argues that recent birth rate declines can in large part be attributed "to delays in childbearing that will be made up later . . . it is quite possible that fertility could rise again to the high levels experienced by the parents of this generation" (p. 112). (See Blake, 1974, for a similar argument.) It may be that a view somewhere between those of Bumpass and Campbell is most plausible. That is, certain segments of the population may indeed return to having larger numbers of children, while other segments may replace at fertility or below. As indicated before, the latter segments are likely to be composed of persons who are most individualistic. Even if traditional female labor markets contract or if there are sharp increases in family size among more traditional women, those persons who strongly seek individualistic rewards will be the ones maintaining minimal family sizes.

Recall those reports that because of alarm over below-replacement fertility, various governments banned techniques such as the pill or abortion. No one can say for certain that such events could not occur in any modern society, including the United States. Alleged reasons for such drastic action could be manifold, including the health hazard issue. If government support is withdrawn from the use of certain sophisticated technologies, what persons would be most likely to maintain the smallest families? Evidence from Chapters Four and Five indicate that it would be those who are most role-modern or individualistic. They are the ones most strongly motivated to avoid familistic costs because they instead perceive and prefer viable and more compelling alternatives.

In short, the future of fertility control in the United States and other western societies may present quite a mixed picture. For a variety of reasons certain subgroups may begin or else continue to reproduce themselves well above the replacement level. Baumann (1972), for example, maintains that even if the poor cease to have any "unwanted births," they will continue to reproduce themselves beyond what is necessary for zero population growth. More advantaged groups may behave in the same fashion. Conversely, other subsets of the population may, in response to individualistic aspirations, reproduce far below replacement. One task of ongoing future research will be to identify these contrasting subsets and explain the reasons for variations in their behavior.

VALUE JUDGMENTS AND FERTILITY CONTROL

Besides its central substantive significance in fertility control, there are certain value judgments that need to be made quite explicit with regard to practical applications of a sex role perspective. Presumably few would disagree that for now reduced population growth is indeed a desirable goal, not simply in most modern societies but unequivocally so in virtually every developing land. But the question of a woman's central function in life is more debatable, as witnessed by the Pope's statement and by the nonreligious but similar expressions of certain behavioral scientists and therapists "from Freud to Deutsch to Erikson" (Blake, 1972).

If one's values lean toward women pursuing behaviors centered in husband, children, and home, then little need be done on a societal or individual level except vigorous affirmation of these traditional patterns. On the other side, if one's values lean more toward increasing individualism for women—equal in scope to that of all persons—then certain steps must consciously be taken to achieve that goal. And as Blake (1972) argues, if these kinds of steps are taken this will ensure that measures are simultaneously being instituted that will aid in the reduction of population growth.

Such steps include single men and women consciously facing what type of *life style* they prefer for themselves in the context of women's individualistic aspirations. For some persons (women in particular) this may result in not marrying at all. If the decision is made to marry, the next decision is whether or not to support in practice or at least in principle the slogan about children: "None is fun," of the National Organization for Non-Parents, NON (*National Observer*, December 31, 1972, p. 9). This organization promotes antinatalism as a live option in the sense discussed by Blake (1972). However, if a couple decides to have a child the arrangements (including obviously the practice of contraception) could be such as to permit maximization of the wife's aspirations at whatever level they might exist. Equally important, the socialization of the child could be consciously directed away from traditional sex role stereotypes (just as many parents today seek to avoid racial or ethnic stereotypes) and toward an emphasis on men and women first and primarily as persons, not as "masculine" or "feminine" beings. Such persons would grow up with, among other things, a strong willingness to experience gratifications besides those provided by children, and thus these parents would influence population growth not only in their own but probably in the next generation as well.

From the standpoint of the larger society interested in reducing population growth, all possible steps should be taken to foster the development of individualistic aspirations in women. This obviously means stimulating a growing economy, support of equal opportunity, and anti-discrimination laws and ERA, but it also involves far more. It means that the media as well as the educational system should be used to promote more modern sex roles in the same way that they are currently used to promote "family planning" in general or to warn against the problems of drug abuse, alcoholism, or V.D. The challenge begins during the preschool period and extends on up through the elementary and secondary schools. The mass media should be encouraged to cease fostering sex role stereotypes in the same way that they have substantially ceased to promote racial stereotypes. The same principles also apply to racial and sex role stereotypes that children find in books from the time they are 2 years old. School curricula should be arranged to face children repeatedly with the "sex role question" and to make them think about the variety of possible gratifications that are open to them.

The major objective would be to allow children and adolescents to perceive that they do in fact have options open to them. Girls (especially from working-class and lower-class homes) need to see that they do not have to become pregnant prior to marriage and that they do not have to marry young or at all if they wish. If they marry, they need not have any children or as few as they wish. All of this is predicated on the notion that women learn (and men accept) that alternative gratifications to familism are viable for and open to women. Women need to see that if they want to do so they can achieve independent identities and statuses as persons. They can participate in the kinds of benefits and gratifications that a modern society offers to its members irrespective, presumably, of ascribed criteria such as race and sex. The more this fundamental evolution of sex role definitions permeates more segments of society, the more we may expect reductions in premarital pregnancies and illegitimate births, reductions in unwanted children in marriage, and an overall reduction in sizes of families and birthrates.

Although most of the foregoing has had particular relevance for developed societies, it should not be assumed that the issue of sex roles and female individualism has no application to developing lands. There are studies which reveal that wife employment and fertility are inversely linked in many of these societies, especially if work and home roles are incompatible (Haas, 1972). But more basic than work in both developed and developing lands are sex role definitions, as Haas reports from a study done in Latin America (1972). Indeed, not only are sex role definitions more basic than wife employment, they are perhaps more basic than the mere distribution of contraceptives. Clearly, past programs to control population growth in most parts of the developing third world have not been very encouraging. Population growth there remains rapid and exacts enormous costs individually, economically, and politically.

Virtually everyone agrees something must be done, but as yet scant attention has been paid to appealing to the individualistic interests of women as a factor to begin to stimulate more effective contraceptive behavior and reduced family size intentions. It is now the case that there is often a vicious cycle in which overpopulation wipes out economic gains, undercutting job opportunities, which in turn would be an important element adding to the motivation to exercise individualism and to control fertility. In turn, lack of fertility control results in increased population, and the cycle continues. Nevertheless, some attempt must be made somewhere to cut into and weaken this vicious cycle. One way might be to establish programs such as those just outlined that would self-consciously force children, adolescents, and adults to think about individualistic and familistic alternatives. Perhaps this would be most meaningful to single persons who are not yet involved with marriage and children. Thus it might take some time before the effects could be felt. But in the meantime what other approaches are meeting with greater success?

To be sure, one stumbling block to stimulation of female individualism in developing lands is the paucity of arenas (i.e., occupational opportunities) in which to pursue alternatives to familism. Perhaps this can be partially met by stressing willingness for geographic mobility (including cross-national), but this may be an exceedingly complex matter wherever kin ties are strong. At the same time, there may be some societies in which a significant minority of women become relatively well educated and certain kinds of job opportunities are available to them. Nevertheless, such strong sex role traditionalism prevails that the potential individualistic gratifications presented by these situations are apparently not preferred and thus not greatly exploited, especially after marriage. Programs designed to increase effective fertility control through greater sex role modernity would need to focus first on those societies that present the greatest level of actual alternative possibilities to women. In these situations, alternative gratifications to familism at least become more practicable and viable. What is more, wives would then gain resources to aid them in subsequent bargaining with their husbands for greater control of the processes of contraception and fertility in particular, and of their own and their family's destiny in general.

Mainland China represents an example of a non-Western society in which it became explicit government policy to generate sex role equality (Fong, 1970). Stemming, of course, from a basic tenet of Marxist ideology regarding equality of the sexes, this policy has fostered self-consciousness among China's young regarding female individualism (Fong). Although Fong reports that this has caused some tension between older persons who are more sex role traditional and younger persons who are not, the latter are nonetheless apparently moving rapidly in a more modern direction. In both rural and urban settings "the changing conditions of society have provided youth with *alternatives* to following in the footsteps of their parents" (Fong:399, italics supplied). These alternative behaviors involve considerable affinity toward government policies which encourage later age at marriage, use of contraceptives, and fewer children (Fong). While much more systematic investigation is needed to establish trends, it may be that China is beginning to accomplish some sort of check on population growth and if so, it will to a certain extent be owing to the institutionalized and government-sanctioned stress on sex role equality.

Aird (1972) has traced "the development of family limitation policies" in mainland China since 1949, and he corroborates Fong by indicating that governmental policies aimed at restructuring marriage and achieving sex role equality have had a major function in reducing China's estimated crude birth rate from 45.0 in 1953 to 37.3 in 1970. Moreover predicting from the acceleration of such policies he projects a possible low figure of 22.4 by 1990. The policy implication for other developing countries is his conclusion that "the greatest single deterrent to family limitation in China has been the powerful and persistent values surrounding early marriage and abundant progency . . . they are . . . closely linked to traditional concepts of family roles . . ." (p. 322). Significantly, he argues that it is not Maoist propaganda in the abstract that has altered or that will alter marital roles. Instead "traditional values will not easily be changed by propaganda except in directions which *they perceive as offering personal advantage*" (p. 323; italics supplied).

Using the concepts employed in these pages, "personal advantage" can be translated into reward-alternatives. Persons in developing (as well as developed) lands will not likely forego the enormous benefits of children (familism) unless they perceive that they can enjoy viable compensatory alternatives. These include individualistic gratifications and socioeconomic benefits, and the evidence indicates that they tend to be correlated.[1]

Does the example of China suggest that unless third-world governments move toward an unequivocal policy promoting sex role equality and take practical steps (including more active control of the means of economic production) to institutionalize its behavioral implications, that programs of population control will continue to meet with only limited success? Perhaps what is required are investigations comparing nations with strong central governments that move in that egalitarian direction with others that do not. The picture is not totally bleak if what Sinha (1970) concludes regarding Indian family structure is generalizable to other third-world settings. In the statement which follows he suggests that there is considerable fluidity in Indian and perhaps in most other family systems in the third world (p. 332). (See also Pescatello, 1973). What seems necessary (and possible) therefore is for governments presently committed to checking population growth to go one step deeper and commit themselves as well to do whatever is necessary to exploit this apparent flexibility and to seek to institutionalize sex role equality. In this fashion when increasing numbers of women have the live option to choose between or to achieve some meaningful balance of individualistic and familistic gratifications, we can reasonably expect family size and population growth in the third world to diminish.[2]

> The roles found in the Indian family system are not static. Indians are willing to give up, although reluctantly, some of their older family patterns because of their own failure to provide viable alternatives and creative opportunities for the growth and actualization of the individual's potentialities. The real freedom to formulate educational plans, choose genuine work careers, and select intimate and preferred marriage partners would eventually rest on the dissolution of sex stereotyping and radical changes in role definition.

Notes

1. Aird (1972) contrasts mainland China with Taiwan, where the estimated crude birth rate has gone from 46.6 in 1952 to 28.1 in 1970 (p. 326). He attributes the lower Taiwanese rates to greater economic development, urbanization, and literacy. It may thus be argued that the larger economic benefits available on Taiwan have begun to function as alternatives to familism. However, before Taiwan's birth rate and population growth can be lowered to approach anywhere near those of Western societies, it is likely that greater stress on female individualism and on sex role equality would be requisite. One might wish that the mainland stress on sex role modernity could somehow be combined with the achievement opportunities on Taiwan. Such a subset of Chinese might indeed reproduce at levels far below that currently observed in either setting.

2. Recently some Third World governments have begun to wonder aloud whether "population growth is positively good" (Population Council, 1973:24). Were such a belief widely accepted and disseminated it would likely have negative consequences for significant changes in women's roles throughout the Third World.

Appendix of Tables

TABLE 2-1. Differences in Role Orientations by Sex, Age, Race, and Religion (Mean Scores)

	TW			SA			PHA			IE			TH		
	Men		Women	M		W	M		W	M		W	M		W
Non-Catholic College Students	18.88	+	19.29	6.51	*	5.88	6.99	**	8.03	2.71	+	2.99	4.31	+	4.16
	*			*		**	**		*	+		*	+		+
Catholic College Students	17.03	+	16.93	7.07	+	7.06	8.46	*	9.71	3.08	+	3.59	3.97	+	3.82
	**			**		**				*			+		+
Young Non-Catholics	15.08	*	14.32	7.50	**	6.94	9.32	**	10.29	2.67	**	2.96	3.45	**	3.05
	**			**		**	+		+	+		+	**		**
Older Non-Catholics	13.65	+	13.60	8.08	+	7.79	9.59	**	10.51	2.68	*	2.88	3.06	*	2.73
Young Catholics	14.88	*	13.78	7.71	*	7.08	9.85	+	10.34	2.72	+	2.62	3.34	*	3.00
	**			**		**	+		+	+		+	*		+
Older Catholics	13.07	+	13.57	8.44	*	7.93	10.18	+	10.74	2.86	+	2.75	2.97	+	2.77
Young Blacks	13.00	+	13.82	6.39	+	6.00	9.12	+	8.81	2.76	+	2.46	2.53	+	2.80
	+			+		+	+		+	+		+	+		+
Older Blacks	12.67	+	13.04	6.57	*	6.08	8.82	+	8.81	2.68	*	2.40	2.40	*	2.68
Young Couples	14.53	+	14.08	7.65	**	6.92	9.63	*	10.19	2.82	+	2.74	3.24	+	3.02
	**			+		**	*		+	+		+	+		+
Older Couples	13.52	+	14.00	8.05	+	7.64	10.38	+	10.42	2.96	+	2.87	2.97	+	2.84

Symbols between columns and between rows indicate level of significance of differences between scores.
Symbols: * means P < .05, ** means P < .01, + means N.S.
Low mean scores indicate modernity for SA, PHA, and IE; high mean scores indicate modernity for TW and TH. All n's appear in end-of-chapter notes to Chapter Two.

TABLE 2-2. Differences in Role Orientations by Education, Sex, Race, and Religion (Mean Scores)

	Level of Education	TW Men	TW Women	SA M	SA W	PHA M	PHA W	IE M	IE W	TH M	TH W
Young Non-Catholics	High	17.11	17.36	6.69	6.25	8.82	9.34	2.67	2.95	3.78	3.49
		**	**	**	**	**	**	+	+	**	**
	Low	13.26	13.37	8.22	7.17	9.77	10.58	2.68	2.97	3.15	2.91
Older Non-Catholics	High	15.48	16.82	7.60	6.89	9.01	9.59	2.87	3.04	3.42	3.17
		**	**	**	**	**	**	*	+	**	**
	Low	12.76	12.68	8.31	8.04	9.87	10.77	2.58	2.84	2.88	2.61
Young Catholics	High	16.55	15.98	7.15	6.42	9.35	9.54	2.71	2.46	3.63	3.40
		**	**	**	*	+	*	+	+	*	*
	Low	13.74	13.12	8.10	7.27	10.19	10.58	2.72	2.67	3.14	2.87
Older Catholics	High	13.53	14.39	8.29	7.85	10.25	9.80	3.10	2.83	3.07	3.04
		+	+	+	+	+	**	+	+	+	+
	Low	12.84	13.31	8.52	7.96	10.15	11.04	2.73	2.72	2.91	2.68
Young Blacks	High	14.92	15.93	6.45	6.56	9.00	9.11	2.73	3.15	3.11	2.63
		**	**	+	+	+	+	+	*	**	+
	Low	12.26	13.30	6.37	5.87	9.16	8.73	2.78	2.29	2.30	2.85
Older Blacks	High	13.92	13.86	6.59	6.31	9.03	8.98	2.98	2.67	2.85	2.89
		**	+	+	+	+	+	+	+	*	+
	Low	12.38	12.91	6.57	6.05	8.76	8.80	2.62	2.36	2.30	2.65

Symbols between rows indicate level of significance of differences between scores.
Symbols: * means P <.05, ** means P <.01, + means N.S.
Low mean scores indicate modernity for SA, PHA, and IE; high mean scores indicate modernity for TW and TH.
All n's appear in end-of-chapter notes to Chapter Two.

TABLE 2-3. Differences in Role Orientations by Sex, Age, Race, and Religion (Mean Scores)

	RLM		TM		ISC		ESC		AE	
	Men	*Women*	*M*	*W*	*M*	*W*	*M*	*W*	*M*	*W*
Non-Catholic College Students	1.37	+ 1.21	3.07	+ 3.01	4.18	+ 4.30	3.24	+ 2.97	—	—
	*	**	**	+	+	+	+	+	—	—
Catholic College Students	1.04	** 0.54	2.39	* 2.95	4.27	+ 4.73	3.13	+ 3.18	—	—
	**	+	*	+	+	+	+	+	+	+
Young Non-Catholics	0.63	** 0.37	2.07	+ 2.12	3.20	** 4.97	3.49	+ 3.58	3.96	** 5.76
	**		*		+		**	**	+	+
Older Non-Catholics	0.36	+ 0.34	1.85	** 2.07	3.46	** 4.80	2.86	+ 2.97	3.62	** 5.80
	**		*		+		+	**	+	+
Young Catholics	0.48	* 0.32	2.20	+ 2.14	3.06	** 4.82	3.15	+ 3.37	3.72	** 5.48
	**		*		+		+	**	+	+
Older Catholics	0.25	+ 0.18	1.87	* 2.11	3.30	** 4.69	3.12	+ 2.85	3.34	** 5.38
	**		*		+		*		*	+
Young Blacks	0.41	* 0.26	2.25	* 2.58	2.56	** 3.46	3.08	+ 3.24	3.88	* 4.63
	**		*	**	+		*	**	*	+
Older Blacks	0.21	* 0.14	1.96	* 2.20	2.88	** 3.73	2.67	+ 2.44	3.31	** 4.78
	**		*		+		*		*	+
Young Couples	0.60	** 0.39	2.03	+ 2.05	2.87	** 4.91	3.36	* 3.71	3.93	** 5.53
	**		+		+		*	**	+	+
Older Couples	0.37	+ 0.30	1.86	** 2.25	3.01	** 4.44	2.91	+ 3.00	3.55	** 5.28

Symbols between columns and between rows indicate level of significance of differences between scores.
Symbol: * means P <.05, ** means P <.01, and + means N.S.
High mean scores indicate modernity for RLM and TM; low scores on ISC, ESC, and AE indicate positive perceptions.
All *n*'s appear in end-of-chapter notes to Chapter Two.

TABLE 2–4. Differences in Role Orientations by Education, Sex, Race, and Religion (Mean Scores)

Level of Education	RLM Men	RLM Women	TM M	TM W	ISC M	ISC W	ESC M	ESC W	AE M	AE W
Young Non-Catholics High	0.88	0.80	2.33	2.53	2.90	4.53	3.44	3.75	3.29	4.42
	**	**	**	**	*	+	+	+	**	**
Low	0.40	0.23	1.84	2.00	3.46	5.10	3.54	3.53	4.56	6.17
Older Non-Catholics High	0.60	0.70	2.07	2.44	3.09	4.42	2.64	3.30	2.70	4.25
	**	**	*	**	*	+	+	+	**	**
Low	0.25	0.24	1.74	1.97	3.64	4.91	2.97	2.87	4.07	6.32
Young Catholics High	0.66	0.45	2.41	2.48	2.86	4.48	3.03	3.26	3.47	3.92
	**	+	+	*	+	+	+	+	+	**
Low	0.37	0.28	2.05	2.04	3.19	4.92	3.23	3.40	3.89	5.94
Older Catholics High	0.46	0.29	2.11	2.30	3.17	4.28	3.33	2.57	2.94	4.02
	**	*	*	+	+	+	+	+	+	**
Low	0.15	0.15	1.74	2.05	3.37	4.81	3.01	2.95	3.54	5.82
Young Blacks High	0.88	0.61	2.82	3.27	2.29	2.19	3.66	3.33	3.98	3.67
	**	**	**	**	+	**	**	+	+	*
Low	0.22	0.18	2.03	2.42	2.65	3.77	2.86	3.22	3.85	4.87
Older Blacks High	0.25	0.29	2.39	2.52	2.51	3.00	2.88	2.64	2.69	3.39
	+	**	*	*	+	**	+	+	+	**
Low	0.20	0.12	1.87	2.15	2.96	3.86	2.62	2.41	3.45	5.00

Symbols between rows indicate level of significance of differences between scores.
Symbols: * means P <.05, ** means P <.01, and + means N.S.
High mean scores indicate modernity for RLM and TM; low scores on ISC, ESC, and AE indicate positive perceptions.
All *n*'s appear in end-of-chapter notes to Chapter Two.

TABLE 2-5. Correlations for Wives Among Role Modernity, Positive Self-Perceptions, and Background Variables (n=1590)

	Race	Father's Occ.	Mother's Educ.	Father's Educ.	Wife's Age	Religion (Catholic)	Educ.	TW	SA	PHA	IE	TH	RLM	TM	ISC	ESC	AE
Race (black)		-.37	-.17	-.23	.15	.00	-.14	.06	.22	.24	.12	.06	.11	.07	.20	.15	.15
Father's Occupation			.30	.39	-.14	.02	.32	.19	.00	.05	.06	.08	.15	.07	.03	.09	.13
Mother's Education				.52	.25	.03	.39	.17	.04	.01	.06	.12	.20	.12	.02	.08	.09
Father's Education					.21	.00	.36	.18	.00	.05	.08	.11	.18	.09	.05	.10	.11
Wife's Age						.02	-.07	-.07	-.06	-.03	-.02	-.10	-.06	-.04	-.02	+.23	-.04
Religion (Catholic)							.00	.00	.02	.05	.03	.00	-.12	.00	.02	-.07	.04
Education								.29	.29	.28	.07	.15	.28	.16	.08	-.13	.23
TW									.29	.28	.06	.36	.39	.37	.12	-.13	.10
SA										.46	.21	.04	.17	.30	.19	.00	.20
PHA											.28	.04	.16	.23	.13	.07	.13
IE												.01	.01	.04	.06	.00	.02
TH													.18	.16	.00	-.17	.02
RLM														.21	.02	-.11	.10
TM															.13	.06	.11
ISC																-.10	.46
ESC																	.05
AE																	

TABLE 2-6. Correlations for Husbands Among Role Modernity, Positive Self-Perceptions, and Background Variables (n=1506)

	Race	Father Occ.	Mother Educ.[1]	Father Educ.[1]	Wife Age	Religion (Catholic)	Education	TW	SA	PHA	IE	TH	RLM	TM	ISC	ESC	AE
Race (black)		-.37	—	—	.12	.02	-.19	-.14	.22	.10	.00	-.22	-.11	.02	.10	.09	.03
Father's Occupation			—	—	-.17	-.03	.38	.23	.03	.02	.03	.18	.19	.09	.07	.09	.11
Mother's Education[1]				—	—	—	—	—	—	—	—	—	—	—	—	—	—
Father's Education[1]					—	—	—	—	—	—	—	—	—	—	—	—	—
Wife's Age						.06	-.17	-.13	-.05	.00	.00	-.11	-.17	-.08	.05	.14	.10
Religion (Catholic)							.01	.00	-.03	-.02	-.02	.00	-.06	.00	.03	.01	.01
Education								.35	.07	.05	.06	.25	.27	.14	.10	.04	.14
TW									.22	.24	.06	.39	.35	.37	.01	.04	.07
SA										.47	.13	.02	.14	.31	.06	.04	.12
PHA											.30	.07	.12	.33	.03	.06	.15
IE												.05	.06	.09	.04	.08	.11
TH													.18	.16	.08	.06	.11
RLM														.15	.03	-.14	.00
TM															.05	.04	.13
ISC																-.19	.14
ESC																	.07
AE																	

[1]Questions not asked of men

TABLE 3-1. Births Intended, Wanted, and Desired by Age, Sex, Race, and Religion

| | WHITES | | | | | | BLACKS | |
| | All | | Non-Catholics | | Catholics | | | |
Age	Women (n)	Men (n)	Women (n)	Men (n)	Women (n)	Men (n)	Women (n)	Men (n)
				Mean Number Intended				
18–24	2.61(374)	2.65(321)	2.48(231)	2.54(225)	2.81(143)	2.94(96)	2.58(76)	2.69(58)
25–29	2.69(216)	2.70(223)	2.59(140)	2.65(155)	2.88(76)	2.79(68)	2.61(62)	2.95(68)
30–44	3.42(533)	3.22(603)	3.14(342)	2.94(397)	3.91(191)	3.74(206)	3.67(329)	3.55(233)
				Mean Number Wanted				
18–24	2.59	2.59	2.46	2.48	2.79	2.89	2.44	2.62
25–29	2.54	2.61	2.43	2.55	2.76	2.75	2.40	2.69
30–44	3.08	2.97	2.84	2.74	3.52	3.41	3.06	3.08
				Mean Number Desired				
18–24	2.81	2.71	2.59	2.64	3.16	2.89	2.68	2.74
25–29	3.16	2.72	3.30	2.69	2.93	2.78	2.81	2.59
30–44	3.28	3.10	3.02	2.88	3.75	3.54	3.14	2.95

TABLE 3-2. Mean Differences Among Key Variables by Full-Time Employment for 18–29-Year-Old Wvies, by Race and Religion

	Whites						Blacks		
	Non-Catholics			Catholics					
	Employed			Employed			Employed		
Role Dimensions, Social Status, and Fertility Control Variables	Yes		No	Yes		No	Yes		No
TW[1]	15.3	*	13.6	13.7	*	13.9	14.4		13.2
SA	6.1		7.5	6.7		7.4	5.4	*	6.7
PHA	10.1	*	10.4	10.3	*	10.4	8.9		8.8
IE	2.7		3.1	2.9		2.4	2.2		2.7
TH	3.2		3.0	2.9		3.0	2.9		2.7
ISC	4.3	*	5.4	4.6		5.0	3.2		3.8
ESC	3.6		3.5	3.3		3.4	3.0		3.4
RLM	0.50	*	0.30	0.42	*	0.24	0.40	*	0.16
TM	2.4	*	1.9	2.3		2.0	2.7		2.4
AE	5.0	*	6.2	5.1	*	5.7	4.5		4.8
Husband Education (years)	13.1	*	12.2	12.7		12.8	12.1		12.0
Wife Education (years)	12.7	*	11.7	12.3		12.2	12.0		11.6
Husband Income[2]	8.1	*	8.6	8.0	*	9.4	7.5		6.9
Wife Marriage Age	20.0	*	18.6	20.1		20.0	20.0		19.3
Husband Marriage Age	21.8	*	21.0	22.4		22.1	22.8		22.4
Husband SES Score[3]	65.0	*	59.2	64.5		67.8	59.0		54.1
Months Before First Child	26.1	*	18.2	21.7		17.3	16.0		12.8
Birth Intentions	2.3	*	2.7	2.7	*	3.0	2.4	*	2.8
Birth Desires	2.4	*	2.7	3.0		3.2	2.4	*	3.2
Births Wanted	2.3	*	2.6	2.6	*	3.0	2.3		2.6
Parity	0.9	*	1.9	0.76	*	1.82	1.7		2.0
(n)	(145)		(225)	(95)		(122)	(71)		(67)

* means differences significant at .05 or beyond between columns.
[1] Coding follows Chapter Two. Modern = high score on TW, TH, RLM, and TM but a low score on SA, IE, PHA. Low score on AE, ISC, and ESC means
more positive self-evaluation

[2] In thousands of dollars (mean figures)
[3] Census Bureau SES Scale

TABLE 3-3. Influences on Birth Intentions for White, Noncatholic Wives Aged 18–29, by Full-Time Employment and by Education

Full-Time Employment

Yes (n=145)

	r	beta
Age at Marriage	−.27	−.26*
TM Modernity	−.34	−.23*
SA Modernity	−.24	−.10
PHA Modernity	−.25	−.10
Education	−.18	−.06
TW Modernity	−.28	−.05

Mult. R = .44 R² = .20

No (n=225)

	r	beta
Instrumental Self-Concept	−.20	−.18*
Age at Marriage	−.25	−.14*
RLM Modernity	−.18	−.10
TW Modernity	−.20	−.09
Education	−.25	−.08

Mult. R = .36 R² = .13

Education

Low to Average (n=278)

	r	beta
Age at Marriage	−.25	−.22*
First-Child Spacing	−.21	−.18*
TM Modernity	−.16	−.13*
Pre-Child Employment	−.16	−.01

Mult. R = .33 R² = .11

High (n=88)

	r	beta
Primary Relations	+.29	+.34*
TW Modernity	−.47	−.29*
Age at Marriage	−.29	−.22*
Husband's Education	−.23	−.19*
Intergenerational Mobility	−.22	−.12
IE Modernity	−.23	−.11
Full-Time Employment	−.22	−.11
SA Modernity	−.36	−.07
TM Modernity	−.37	−.06
PHA Modernity	−.29	−.03

Mult. R = .63 R² = .39

*Significant at .05 or beyond

TABLE 3–4. Influences on Age at (First) Marriage for White Non-Catholic Wives Aged 18–29, by Full-Time Employment and by Education

Full-Time Employment

	Yes (n=145)		No (n=225)	
	r	beta	r	beta
Education	.57	.48*	.66	.58*
Premarital Job	.33	.28*	.41	.25*
AE Rank	.28	.11*		
TW Modernity	.23	.07	.27	.10*
TH Modernity	.19	.07		
Mother's Education	.34	.06		
Father's SES	.27	.01		
RLM Modernity	.20	.01	.21	.04
	Mult. R = .65		Mult. R = .71	
	R^2 = .42		R^2 = .50	

Education

	Low to Average (n=278)		High (n=88)	
	r	beta	r	beta
Premarital Job	.44	.40*	.19	.18*
Husband's Education	.31	.25*	.21	.22*
AE Rank	.19	.13*		
TM Modernity			.31	.29*
TW Modernity			.20	.02
SA Modernity			.19	.01
	Mult. R = .53		Mult. R = .41	
	R^2 = .28		R^2 = .17	

*Significant at .05 or beyond

TABLE 3–5. Variables Correlated with Birth Intentions for White Never-Married University Undergraduates, by Sex, for 1971 and 1974

	1971		1974	
	Women	*Men*	*Women*	*Men*
Religion (Catholic)	+.21	+.19	+.24	+.10
Father's Job Status	−.04	+.06	−.06	−.03
Year in School	−.12	−.05	−.15	−.02
TW Modernity	−.37	−.22	−.37	−.30
SA Modernity	−.26	−.23	−.29	−.22
PHA Modernity	−.24	−.19	−.42	−.20
IE Modernity	−.26	−.11	−.24	−.16
TH Modernity	−.31	−.09	−.29	−.21
RLM Modernity	−.25	−.21	−.33	−.15
TM Modernity	−.25	−.21	−.31	−.21
Age	−.11	−.02	−.15	−.11
Instrumental Self-Concept	−.05	+.13	x	x
Expressive Self-Concept	+.10	+.03	x	x
Mean Number of Children Intended	2.1	2.2	2.2	2.1
n	(199)	(167)	(197)	(191)

x = not measured in 1974

TABLE 3-6. Influences on Birth Intentions for White Catholic Wives, Aged 18-29, by Full-Time Employment and by Education

Employed Full-Time

Yes (n=92)	r	beta
TM Modernity	-.27	-.23*
First-Child Spacing	-.22	-.19*
RLM Modernity	-.28	-.16*
Work for Enjoyment	-.24	-.14
Husband's Age At Marriage	-.21	-.13
Husband's Income	-.17	-.12
SA Modernity	-.16	-.01
Mult. R = .48		
R² = .23		

No (n=122)	r	beta
Husband's Income	+.28	+.23*
Husband's Age at Marriage	-.19	-.18*
First-Child Spacing	-.19	-.15*
PHA Modernity	-.24	-.14*
Economic Satisfaction	+.18	+.14*
RLM Modernity	-.18	-.12
TM Modernity	-.16	-.06
Mult. R = .46		
R² = .23		

Education

Low to Average (n=163)	r	beta
First-Child Spacing	-.19	-.19*
RLM Modernity	-.22	-.17*
TM Modernity	-.19	-.15*
Husband's Age at Marriage	-.15	-.09
PHA Modernity	-.16	-.06
Mult. R = .48		
R² = .12		

High (n=50)	r
Husband's Age at Marriage	-.47
AE Rank	-.41
Wife's Age at Marriage	-.38
PHA Modernity	-.33
SA Modernity	-.32
TM Modernity	-.29
First-Child Spacing	-.29
Husband's Education	+.23
Economic Satisfaction	+.23
RLM Modernity	-.22
Full-Time Job	-.22
Devoutness	+.19

*Significant at .05 or beyond

TABLE 3-7. Influences on Age at Marriage for White Catholic Wives, Aged 18-29, by Full-Time Employment and by Education

Employed Full-Time

	Yes (n=92)		No (n=122)	
	r	beta	r	beta
Education	.38	.32*	.43	.29*
Premarital Job	.27	.30*	.27	.27*
Mother's Education	.24	.15*		
Mother Worked			-.21	-.15*
AE Rank	.19	.07	.23	.14*
Father's Education	.21	.03	.23	.12
Mult. R =	.51		.54	
R^2 =	.26		.29	

Education

	Low to Average (n=163)		High (n=50)	
	r	beta	r	beta
Premarital Job	.31	.27*		
Husband's Education	.26	.22*		
Instrumental Self-Concept	-.21	-.21*		
Father's Education	.21	.20*		
PHA Modernity			.28	
RLM Modernity			.25	
Instrumental Self-Concept			.24	
Father's SES			.21	
Premarital Job			.21	
Mother Worked			-.19	
AE Rank			.18	
Mult. R =	.48			
R^2 =	.23			

*Significant at .05 or beyond

TABLE 3-8. Correlates of Proportion of Married Life Spent in Full-Time Employment for Wives Aged 18-29, by Religion and Race

White Non-Catholics (n=371)	r	White Catholics (n=217)	r	Blacks (n=136)	r
Current Parity	-.48	Current Parity	-.39	TH Modernity	.23
Education	.36	Education	.16	Husband's Job Status	.22
AE Ranking	.25			SA Modernity	.18
TM Modernity	.21			RLM Modernity	.18
TW Modernity	.21			TM Modernity	.18
RLM Modernity	.20			Current Parity	-.17
Instrumental Self-Concept	.20			IE Modernity	.16
SA Modernity	.18			Education	.06

TABLE 3-9. Factors Related to Birth Intentions for Black Wives, Aged 18-29, by Full-Time Employment and by Education

Employed Full-Time

Yes (n=71)	r		No (n=67)	r
TW Modernity	-.29		Wife's Age at Marriage	-.39
Husband's Job Status	-.24		Education	-.37
Work for Enjoyment	-.23		PHA Modernity	-.28
Education	-.21		TM Modernity	-.22
Wife's Age at Marriage	-.20		Premarital Job	-.20
Wife's Income	-.18		TW Modernity	-.19
Wife's Job Status	-.17		AE Rank	-.19

Education

Low to Average (n=111)	r	beta	High (n=27)	r
Age at Marriage	-.24	-.26*	Age at Marriage	-.39
TM Modernity	-.23	-.19*	Expressive Self-Concept	-.34
TW Modernity	-.23	-.15*	First-Child Spacing	-.27
AE Rank	-.15	-.13	Pre-Child Job	-.27
Full-Time Job	-.18	-.13	TW Modernity	-.26
Husband's Education	-.15	-.11	IE Modernity	+.25
Mult. R = .44			TH Modernity	+.19
R^2 = .20			Economic Satisfaction	-.18

* Significant at .05 or beyond

TABLE 3-10. Factors Related to Age at Marriage for Black Wives, Aged 18-29, by Full-Time Employment and by Education

Employed Full-Time

Yes (n=71)	r	No (n=67)	r
Premarital Job	.51	Education	.54
Education	.42	Premarital Job	.43
Mother Worked	−.37	Father's Education	.28
RLM Modernity	.29	TW Modernity	.16

Education

Low to Average (n=111)	r	beta	High (n=27)	r
Premarital Job	.45	.42*	Premarital Job	+.46
Husband's Education	.15	.19*	PHA Modernity	−.36
Mother Worked	−.20	−.16*	SA Modernity	−.25
Father's Education	.15	.09	IE Modernity	−.22
RLM Modernity	.14	.04	TW Modernity	+.18

Mult. R = .52
R^2 = .27

*Significant at .05 or beyond

TABLE 3-11. Correlates of Birth Orientations by Full-Time Employment and by Education

| | Births Wanted by Wives Aged 30-44 | | | | Births Intended by Husbands (Wives Aged 18-29) | | | |
| | Employed Full-Time | | Education | | Wife Employed Full-Time | | Husband's Educ. | |
	Yes	No	Low to Average	High	Yes	No	Low to Average	High
TW Modernity	+.04	-.04	-.04	+.21	-.14	-.08	-.07	-.15
SA Modernity	+.16	-.10	.00	-.03	-.16	-.15	-.18	-.12
PHA Modernity	+.07	+.07	+.08	+.12	-.23	-.05	-.15	-.11
IE Modernity	+.02	+.04	+.01	-.06	+.02	-.04	+.01	-.06
TH Modernity	+.01	-.06	-.04	+.15	+.09	.00	+.01	+.10
RLM Modernity	-.14	-.13	-.18	+.05	-.18	-.09	-.13	-.13
TM Modernity	-.05	+.04	+.07	-.16	-.16	-.14	-.17	-.13
Instrumental Self-Concept	+.14	-.04	+.02	-.02	+.06	+.17	+.17	+.07
Expressive Self-Concept	-.06	+.04	-.02	+.07	-.16	+.17	+.01	.00
Wife's Ability Evaluation	-.04	-.05	-.02	-.13	-.18	+.02	+.03	-.23
Education	-.20	-.22	x	x	-.13	-.14	x	x
Husband's Job Status	-.06	-.22	-.10	-.05	-.10	-.03	-.02	-.08
Husband's Income	+.09	-.12	-.06	+.20	-.07	+.04	-.06	+.07
Own Age at Marriage	-.17	-.29	-.26	.00	-.17	-.16	-.22	-.08
Economic Satisfaction	-.08	-.16	-.12	-.15	.00	+.13	+.11	+.05
Empathy	-.12	+.12	+.07	-.12	.00	+.04	+.19	-.21
Primary Relations	-.02	.00	+.03	-.14	-.03	+.10	+.16	-.05
(n)	(131)	(191)	(72)	(261)	(186)	(194)	(200)	(180)

TABLE 4–1. Births Reported to Date, by Age, Sex, Race, and Religion

Current Mean Family Size

| | WHITES | | | | | | BLACKS | |
| | All | | Non-Catholics | | Catholics | | | |
	Women (n)	Men (n)	Women (n)	Men (n)	Women (n)	Men (n)	Women (n)	Men (n)
18–24	1.16(374)	0.97(321)	1.26(231)	0.99(225)	1.01(143)	0.92(96)	1.78(76)	1.51(58)
25–29	1.92(216)	1.70(223)	1.82(140)	1.65(155)	2.00(76)	1.84(68)	1.89(62)	2.06(68)
30–44	3.25(533)	3.09(603)	3.01(342)	2.83(397)	3.67(191)	3.60(206)	3.48(329)	3.35(233)

TABLE 4–2. Correlates of Pre-Child Employment, First-Child Spacing, and Parity for White Non-Catholic Wives, Aged 18–29, by Full-Time Employment

Currently Employed Full-Time (n=145)

Full-Time Pre-Child Job	r	Length of First-Child Spacing	r	Current Parity	r
Age at Marriage	.42	Pre-Child Job	.37	Age at Marriage	–.49
Education	.35	Education	.22	Pre-Child Job	–.45
AE Ranking	.25	PHA Modernity	.20	Education	–.39
TW Modernity	.22	TW Modernity	.18	Wife's SES	–.36
Premarital Job	.22			Wife's Earnings	–.33
TH Modernity	.20			First-Child Spacing	–.33
				Husband's SES	–.25
				Wife's Job Mobility	–.25
				AE Ranking	–.22

Not Currently Employed (n=225)

Premarital Job	r	Length of First-Child Spacing	r	Current Parity	r
Premarital Job	.47	Pre-Child Job	.47	Age at Marriage	–.36
Age at Marriage	.35	Premarital Job	.20	First-Child Spacing	–.28
Education	.26	Education	.14	Education	–.29
		Age at Marriage	.14	Instrumental Self-Concept	–.23
				AE Ranking	–.20
				Pre-Child Job	–.18
				TW Modernity	–.15

TABLE 4-3. Correlates of Timing Failures for Wives Aged 18-29 with at Least One Child by Race, Religion, Employment

Full-Time Employment

White Non-Catholics (n=78)	r	White Catholics (n=40)	r	Blacks (n=64)	r
Pre-Child Job	−.30	Wife's Earnings	−.46	Parity	+.33
TH Modernity	−.29	Husband's Income	−.42	Birth Intentions	+.30
Wife's Job Status	−.25	Father's SES	−.32	TM Modernity	+.27
Wife's Income	−.25	TH Modernity	+.32	SA Modernity	+.18
Age at Marriage	−.25	Age at Marriage	−.30	Wife's SES	−.17
Parity	+.25	Wife's SES	−.29	Intergenerational Mobility	−.18
TM Modernity	−.19	Intergenerational Mobility	+.28	Wife's Job Mobility	−.18
		First-Child Spacing	−.23		
		Devoutness	−.23		
		SA Modernity	+.22		

Not Employed

White Non-Catholics (n=211)	r	White Catholics (n=105)	r	Blacks (n=61)	r
Parity	+.42	TW Modernity	+.31	Husband's Education	−.29
Birth Intentions	+.23	Parity	+.28	Empathy	−.29
Age at Marriage	−.20	TM Modernity	+.28	TW Modernity	+.21
		SA Modernity	+.24	Parity	+.15
		TH Modernity	+.21		
		Birth Intentions	+.16		
		Husband's Income	+.15		

TABLE 4-4. Correlates of Pre-Child Employment, First-Child Spacing, and Parity for White Non-Catholic Wives, Aged 18–29, by Education

Low to Average Education (n=278)

Full-Time Pre-Child Job	r
Premarital Job	.42
Age at Marriage	.36

Length of First-Child Spacing	r
Pre-Child Job	.44
Premarital Job	.22

Current Parity	r
Age at Marriage	-.42
Pre-Child Job	-.30
Education	-.29
First-Child Spacing	-.28
Premarital Job	-.22
Instrumental Self-Concept	-.18

High Education (n=88)

Full-Time Pre-Child Job	r
Age at Marriage	.36
Premarital Job	.27
Husband's Education	.17

Length of First-Child Spacing	r
Pre-Child Job	.33
AE Ranking	.28
TW Modernity	.22
Instrumental Self-Concept	.21
SA Modernity	.19
PHA Modernity	.18

Current Parity	r
Pre-Child Job	-.42
First-Child Spacing	-.42
AE Ranking	-.38
SA Modernity	-.33
Age at Marriage	-.33
Instrumental Self-Concept	-.32
Education	-.29
Husband's Job Status	-.28
PHA Modernity	
Inter-Generational Mobility	-.22

Parity ≥ 1 (n=48)	r
TM Modernity	-.45
First-Child Spacing	-.42
Instrumental Self-Concept	-.41
TW Modernity	-.40
SA Modernity	-.39
AE Ranking	-.38
Intra-Generational Mobility	-.31
Husband's Job Status	-.30
Age at Marriage	-.29
TH Modernity	-.28
PHA Modernity	-.26
IE Modernity	-.22
RLM Modernity	-.20
Education	-.22

TABLE 4-5. Correlates of Timing Failures for Wives Aged 18-29 with at Least One Chile by Race, Religion, and Education

Low to Average Education

White Non-Catholics (n=242)	r	White Catholics (n=120)	r	Blacks (n=103)	r
Parity	+.37	Parity	+.37	Empathy	-.23
Birth Intentions	+.22	TW Modernity	+.30	Parity	+.17
Age at Marriage	-.19	TH Modernity	+.24		
AE Ranking	-.17	SA Modernity	+.24		
Pre-Child Job	-.16				

High Education

(n=48)	r	(n=50)	r	(n=27)*	r
TH Modernity	-.29	Age at Marriage	-.34	Parity	+.68
First-Child Spacing	-.28	First-Child Spacing	-.30	Age at Marriage	-.55
Instrumental Self-Concept	-.24	Parity	+.29	Birth Intentions	+.54
Parity	+.23	Birth Intentions	+.26	Pre-Child Job	-.43
Husband's Income	-.23	TH Modernity	+.24	Husband's Education	-.30
TM Modernity	-.22			Expressive Self-Concept	-.30
Age at Marriage	-.19			RLM Modernity	-.29
				IE Modernity	+.24
				TW Modernity	-.22

*All cases included

TABLE 4-6. Correlates of Pre-Child Employment, First-Child Spacing, and Parity for White Catholic Wives, Aged 18–29, by Full-Time Employment

Currently Working Full-Time (n=95)

Full-Time Pre-Child Job	r	Length of First-Child Spacing	r	Current Number of Children	r	(Parity ≥ 1: n = 40)	r
Premarital Job	.38	Mother's education	-.23	Age at Marriage	-.55		-.50
Age at Marriage	.33	Pre-Child Job	.20	Husband's Education	-.40		-.43
Husband's SES at Marriage	.23	AE Ranking	.15	Wife's Earnings	-.35		-.27
				First-Child Spacing	-.31		-.39
				Pre-Child Job	-.29		-.07
				Education	-.23		-.27
				Father's Education	-.22		-.03
				Wife's SES	-.20		-.20
				Husband's SES	-.16		-.32
				RLM Modernity	-.02		-.27
				TM Modernity	-.12		-.21
				Intergenerational Mobility	-.03		-.28

Not Currently Employed (n=122)

Full-Time Pre-Child Job	r	Length of First-Child Spacing	r	Current Number of Children	r
Age at Marriage	.30	Premarital Job	.25	Husband's Income	+.42
Premarital Job	.27	Husband's Age at Marriage	.23	First-Child Spacing	-.31
Education	.23	Pre-Child Job	.16	Education	-.29
		Education	.14	Age at Marriage	-.28
				PHA Modernity	-.19
				Devoutness	+.18
				AE Ranking	-.17

TABLE 4-7. Correlates of Pre-Child Employment, First-Child Spacing, and Parity for White Catholic Wives, Aged 18–29, by Education

Full-Time Pre-Child Job

	r
Age at Marriage	.36
Premarital Job	.21

High Education (n=50)

Father's SES	+.36
Premarital Job	+.34
TM Modernity	−.31
Education	−.23

Low to Average Education (n=167)

Length of First-Child Spacing

	r
Husband's age at Marriage	.19
Pre-Child Job	.18
Mother's Education	−.18
Premarital Job	.17
AE Ranking	.13

High Education (n=50)

Age at Marriage	+.40
Mother's Education	−.33
PHA Modernity	+.30
Father's Job Status	+.24
TH Modernity	+.18
TW Modernity	+.18

Current Parity

	r
First-Child Spacing	−.34
Age at Marriage	−.32
Husband's Income	+.30
Pre-Child Job	−.25
Education	−.18

AE Ranking	−.46
Husband's Income	+.45
Age at Marriage	−.40
Education	−.36
First-Child Spacing	−.30
SA Modernity	−.22
PHA Modernity	−.21
TM Modernity	−.18

TABLE 4-8. Correlates of Pre-Child Employment, First-Child Spacing, and Parity for Black Wives, Aged 18–29, by Full-Time Employment.

Full-Time Pre-Child Job	r	Length of First-Child Spacing	r	Current Parity	r
		Currently Working Full-Time (n=71)			
Premarital Job	.38	Pre-Child Job	.29	Age at Marriage	−.38
Age at Marriage	.32	RLM Modernity	.16	Education	−.25
Father's Education	.28			Work for Enjoyment	−.25
RLM Modernity	.21			SA Modernity	−.21
				Pre-Child Job	−.20
				First-Child Spacing	−.20
				Wife's Earnings	−.19
				Husband's Education	−.24
		Not Currently Employed (n=67)			
AE Ranking	.34	Pre-Child Job	.30	Age at Marriage	−.52
Pre-Marital Job	.34	PHA Modernity	.25	Education	−.45
Father's Education	.24	Instrumental Self-Concept	.24	First-Child Spacing	−.42
TM Modernity	.21	AE Ranking	.19	Husband's Education	−.34
TH Modernity	.19	Husband's Education	.19	Premarital Job	−.29
Education	.19			Instrumental Self-Concept	−.22
Husband's Job Status at Marriage	.19			AE Ranking	−.21
				RLM Modernity	−.19

TABLE 4-9. Correlates of Pre-Child Employment, First-Child Spacing, and Parity for Black Wives, Aged 18–29, by Education

Low to Average Education (n=111)

Full-Time Pre-Child Job	r	Length of First-Child Spacing	r	Current Number of Children	r	(Parity ≥ 1) n=103 r
Premarital Job	.34	Pre-Child Job	.29	Age at Marriage	–.37	–.28
Father's Education	.33	IE Modernity	.16	First-Child Spacing	–.30	–.27
AE Ranking	.20	PHA Modernity	.14	Education	–.27	–.26
RLM Modernity				Father's Education	–.22	–.18
Age at Marriage	.19			TW Modernity	–.16	–.24
				PHA Modernity	–.12	–.20

High Education (n=27)

Full-Time Pre-Child Job	r	Length of First-Child Spacing	r	Current Number of Children	r
Premarital Job	.39	RLM Modernity	.36	Age at Marriage	–.57
Expressive Self-Concept	.39	Instrumental Self-Concept	.38	IE Modernity	+.45
Age at Marriage	.37	TW Modernity	.34	SA Modernity	+.41
TH Modernity	.25	PHA Modernity	.34	PHA Modernity	+.37
AE Ranking	–.25	TM Modernity	.37	Pre-Child Job	–.35
		Pre-Child Job	.27	First-Child Spacing	–.37
		Husband's SES at Marriage	.26	Expressive Self-Concept	–.30
		Education	.25	Education	–.28
				Husband's Income	–.21

TABLE 5-1. Variables Correlated with Choice of Efficient Methods for White Non-Catholic Wives (Aged 18-29), at Risk, by Employment and Education

Use of Pill		Group 2 Methods*	
Employed Full-Time			
(n=77)		*(n=35)*	
	r		*r*
TH Modernity	+.25	TH Modernity	+.33
IE Modernity	+.14	Instrumental Self-Concept	−.24
RLM Modernity	+.14	RLM Modernity	+.24
		Husband Education	+.35
Not Employed			
(n=109)		*(n=70)*	
AE Ranking	−.37	AE Ranking	−.41
SA Modernity	+.22	RLM Modernity	+.26
TW Modernity	+.19	Husband Income	+.26
RLM Modernity	+.18	More Children Intended	−.29
More Children Intended	−.18		
Low to Average Education			
(n=145)		*(n=72)*	
AE Ranking	−.25	AE Ranking	−.41
RLM Modernity	+.14	Timing Failures	+.26
TW Modernity	+.14	Full-Time Job	−.26
More Children Intended	−.17	More Children Intended	−.26
		Parity	+.26
		Pre-Child Job	−.23
		Instrumental Self Concept	−.21
		Age at Marriage	−.22
High Education			
(n=42)		*(n=33)*	
TM Modernity	+.40	RLM Modernity	+.36
RLM Modernity	+.31	PHA Modernity	+.33
PHA Modernity	+.29	TH Modernity	+.33
SA Modernity	+.28	TM Modernity	+.27
TH Modernity	+.25	SA Modernity	+.23
Empathy	−.27	Empathy	−.28
Father's Job Status	+.33		

*Condom, IUD, diaphragm with jelly or cream

TABLE 5-2. Variables Correlated with Choice of Efficient Methods for White Non-Catholic Wives (Aged 30–44), at Risk, by Employment and Education

Use of Pill		Group 2 Methods*	
Employed Full-Time			
(n=46)		*(n=47)*	
	r		*r*
TH Modernity	+.38	TW Modernity	+.37
TW Modernity	+.32	TH Modernity	+.36
IE Modernity	+.27	Husband Income	+.33
Expressive Self-Concept	−.26	Husband Education	+.29
PHA Modernity	+.25	IE Modernity	+.27
Husband Education	+.23	Wife Education	+.24
Inter-Generational Mobility	−.26	Husband Job Status	+.24
		Husband Age at Marriage	+.26
Not Employed			
(n=64)		*(n=84)*	
AE Ranking	+.20	AE Ranking	+.26
Instrumental Self-Concept	+.18	Husband Income	+.23
Expressive Self-Concept	+.18	Wife Education	+.16
PHA Modernity	+.14	Timing Failures	−.18
Empathy	+.15		
Timing Failures	−.17		
Low to Average Education			
(n=85)		*(n=95)*	
TH Modernity	+.23	TH Modernity	+.25
SA Modernity	+.15	Husband Income	+.25
More Children Intended	+.13		
High Education			
(n=25)		*(n=36)*	
Instrumental Self-Concept	+.46	Primary Relations	−.43
Primary Relations	−.37	RLM Modernity	+.31
IE Modernity	+.36	TM Modernity	−.28
PHA Modernity	+.35	IE Modernity	+.23
TW Modernity	+.29	Empathy	−.28
Economic Satisfaction	−.26	Economic Satisfaction	−.22
		More Children Intended	−.21
		Husband Job Status	+.21

*Condom, IUD, diaphragm with jelly or cream

TABLE 5-3. Influences on Degree of Expected Future Contraceptive Efficacy for 18-29-Year-Old White Non-Catholic Wives, at Risk, by Employment and Education

Currently Working Full-Time (n=122)

	r	beta
Birth Desires	-.37	-.38*
Birth Intentions	-.19	-.20*
TM Modernity	+.31	+.15*
Method Efficiency	+.21	+.14
PHA Modernity	+.27	+.12
SA Modernity	+.27	+.09
TW Modernity	+.31	+.06
Use of Method	+.17	+.06

Mult. R = .51; R^2 = .26

Not Currently Employed (n=183)

	r	beta
TM Modernity	+.27	+.22*
Birth Desires	-.18	-.15*
Method Efficiency	+.12	+.07
SA Modernity	+.19	+.06

Mult. R = .33; R^2 = .11

Low to Average Education (n=228)

	r	beta
Birth Desires	-.27	-.23*
TM Modernity	+.26	+.18*
Husband's Income	-.13	-.14*
SA Modernity	+.18	+.08
Use of Method	+.10	+.03
Birth Intentions	-.16	-.02
Method Efficiency	+.11	+.08

Mult. R = .39; R^2 = .15

High Education (n=78)

	r	beta
TW Modernity	+.44	+.18*
Timing Failures	-.20	-.18*
TM Modernity	+.36	+.13
PHA Modernity	+.41	+.13
Method Efficiency	+.30	+.11
Birth Desires	-.26	-.11
Use of Method	+.18	+.10
IE Modernity	+.22	+.04
RLM Modernity	+.24	+.02
SA Modernity	+.34	+.03

Mult. R = .55; R^2 = .30

*Significant at .05 or beyond

TABLE 5–4. Variables Correlated with Choice of Efficient Methods for White Catholic Wives (Aged 18–29), at Risk, by Employment and Education

Use of Pill		Group 2 Methods*	
Employed Full-Time			
(n=54)		*(n=17)*	
	r		*r*
Husband Education	−.26	PHA Modernity	−.44
RLM Modernity	−.25	IE Modernity	−.41
SA Modernity	−.24	Parity	+.30
PHA Modernity	−.20	Husband Income	+.23
First-Child Spacing	−.21	Wife Age at Marriage	−.23
Wife Income	−.20	Husband Education	−.22
More Children Intended	−.19	Timing Failures	−.27
Economic Satisfaction	−.19		
Not Currently Employed			
(n=62)		*(n=46)*	
Empathy	−.34	Parity	−.35
SA Modernity	+.31	Empathy	−.31
Parity	−.21	Economic Satisfaction	−.30
Husband Age at Marriage	−.21	Intra-Generational Mobility	−.36
Wife Age at Marriage	−.20	Inter-Generational Mobility	−.21
Devoutness	−.17	SA Modernity	+.17
Low to Average Education			
(n=84)		*(n=46)*	
Empathy	−.23	Intra-Generational Mobility	−.36
SA Modernity	+.21	Inter-Generational Mobility	−.30
Birth Intentions	−.21	Birth Intentions	−.30
Full-Time Job	+.18	Empathy	−.28
Economic Satisfaction	−.18	Husband's Job Status	−.26
		SA Modernity	+.16
High Education			
(n=32)		*(n=17)*	
IE Modernity	−.33	Birth Intentions	−.50
PHA Modernity	−.26	Economic Satisfaction	−.50
TH Modernity	+.19	Education	+.23
AE Ranking	+.22	TH Modernity	+.30
Education	+.26	PHA Modernity	−.30
Husband Authority	+.26	IE Modernity	−.26
Inter-Generational Mobility	+.25	Age at Marriage	+.41

*Condom, IUD, or diaphragm with jelly or cream

TABLE 5-5. Influences on Degree of Expected Future Contraceptive Efficacy for 18-29-Year-Old White Catholic Wives, at Risk, by Employment and Education

Currently Working Full-Time (n=72)

	r	beta
Wife Works for Enjoyment	+.28	+.32*
Wife's Job Mobility	-.25	-.31*
Devoutness	-.26	-.22*
TH Modernity	+.18	+.14
More Children Intended	-.20	-.14
Education	-.17	-.13
Wife's Job Status	-.21	+.12
AE Ranking	+.17	+.11
Total Births Intended	-.15	-.04
Wife's Earnings	-.22	+.04
Mult. R = .52; R^2 = .27		

Not Currently Employed (n=104)

	r	beta
More Children Intended	-.39	-.34*
Economic Satisfaction	-.21	-.18*
Instrumental Self-Concept	-.19	-.13
RLM Modernity	+.18	+.12
First-Child Spacing	-.19	-.12
Total Births Intended	-.16	-.03
Mult. R = .49; R^2 = .24		

Low to Average Education (n=142)

	r	beta
More Children Intended	-.38	-.36*
Use of Group 2 Methods	-.14	-.20*
Economic Satisfaction	-.17	-.15*
Father's Job Status	+.16	+.14*
Total Births Intended	-.18	-.06
TW Modernity	+.12	+.03
Mult. R = .47; R^2 = .22		

High Education (n=43)

	r
TM Modernity	+.33
Devoutness	-.34
Method Efficiency	+.26
Husband's Job Status	+.25
Age At Marriage	+.24
Intergenerational Mobility	+.22
Birth Desires	-.23
TH Modernity	+.21

*Significant at .05 or beyond

TABLE 5-6. Variables Correlated with Choice of Efficient Methods for Black Wives (Aged 18-29) at Risk, by Employment and Education

Use of Pill		Group 2 Methods*	
Employed Full-Time			
(n=45)		*(n=35)*	
	r		*r*
Wife Job Status	−.30	SA Modernity	+.57
Wife Education	−.25	Wife Education	−.45
Wife Works for Enjoyment	+.26	Wife Job Status	−.43
RLM Modernity	+.20	Instrumental Self-Concept	+.41
SA Modernity	+.26	TW Modernity	+.40
Not Currently Employed			
(n=24)		*(n=22)*	
Expressive Self-Concept	−.48	Expressive Self-Concept	−.62
TM Modernity	+.38	TM Modernity	+.37
More Children Intended	−.37	Wife Education	+.33
RLM Modernity	+.31	Husband Income	+.33
Wife Education	+.32	More Children Intended	−.31
Husband Education	+.28	Husband Education	+.30
Husband Income	+.26	Total Births Intended	−.30
Husband Job Status	+.24	Intra-Generational Mobility	−.32
Total Births Intended	−.28	Timing Failures	+.26
Intra-Generational Mobility	−.36		
Low to Average Education			
(n=54)		*(n=28)*	
Full-Time Job	+.35	Expressive Self-Concpet	−.62
TM Modernity	+.32	TM Modernity	+.52
Total Births Intended	−.32	Total Births Intended	−.33
Expressive Self-Concept	−.30	Husband's Income	−.33
More Children Intended	−.29	Intra-Generational Mobility	−.36
Husband Education	+.21	TW Modernity	+.30
RLM Modernity	+.20	RLM Modernity	+.26
		Timing Failures	+.33
High Education			
(n=15)		*(n=7)*	
Instrumental Self-Concept	+.46	†	
RLM Modernity	+.39		
Husband's Income	+.38		
TW Modernity	+.26		
SA Modernity	+.28		
TH Modernity	+.26		
Empathy	+.47		
Age at Marriage	+.35		
Inter-Generational Mobility	−.29		

*Condom, IUD, or diaphragm with jelly or cream
†Cases too few to present correlations

TABLE 5-7. Influences on Degree of Expected Future Contraceptive Efficacy, for 18-29-Year-Old Black Wives, at Risk, by Employment and Education

Currently Working Full-Time (n=55)

	r	beta
Expressive Self-Concept	+.27	+.43*
Age at Marriage	-.27	-.25*
TM Modernity	+.23	+.23*
SA Modernity	+.26	+.17
Positive Husband Reaction to Wife's Job	+.21	+.16
Father's Job Status	+.22	+.14
Intergenerational Mobility	-.27	-.11
Wife's Job Mobility	-.26	+.02

Mult. R = .61; R^2 = .37

Not Currently Employed (n=53)

	r	beta
Father's Job Status	+.34	+.36*
Use of Pill	+.33	+.27*
TM Modernity	+.42	+.23*
Husband's Age at Marriage	+.28	+.19*
AE Ranking	+.26	+.14
Timing Failures	-.21	-.13
Birth Intentions	-.23	-.13
Instrumental Self-Concept	+.29	+.10
PHA Modernity	+.19	+.08
SA Modernity	+.20	+.05

Mult. R = .70; R^2 = .49

Low to Average Education (n=85)

	r	beta
TM Modernity	+.33	+.27*
Intergenerational Mobility	-.23	-.23*
Age at Marriage	-.21	-.22*
AE Ranking	+.21	+.21*
Expressive Self-Concept	+.20	+.20*
PHA Modernity	+.22	+.11
More Children Intended	-.22	-.09
Father's Job Status	+.24	+.04
SA Modernity	+.24	+.01

Mult. R = .57; R^2 = .33

High Education (n=24)

	r
Father's Job Status	+.43
Instrumental Self-Concept	+.40
TM Modernity	+.35
Husband's Income	+.35
Timing Failures	-.32
SA Modernity	+.31
Use of Pill	+.31
Parity	-.30
Intergenerational Mobility	-.25

*Significant at .05 or beyond

References

AIRD, JOHN S.
1972 "Population Policy and Demographic Prospects in the People's Republic of China." Bethesda, Maryland: Center for Population Research, National Institutes for Child Health and Human Development.

ALLINGHAM, JOHN D., T. R. BALAKRISHNAN, and JOHN F. KANTNER
1970 "The End of Rapid Increase in the Use of Oral Anovulants? Some Problems in the Interpretation of Time Series of Oral Use Among Married Women." *Demography* 7:31–41.

ANDERSON, MICHAEL
1971 *Family Structure in Nineteenth Century Lancashire.* London: Cambridge University Press.

BAUMANN, KARL E.
1972 "The Poor as a 'Perfect Contraceptive Population' and Zero Population Growth." *Demography* 9:507–10.

BECKER, GARY
1960 "An Economic Analysis of Fertility." National Bureau of Economic Research, *Demographic and Economic Change in Developed Countries*, pp. 209–40. Princeton, N.J.: Princeton University Press.

BERELSON, BERNARD
1973 "Population Growth Policy in Developed Countries." In C. F. Westoff *et al., Toward the End of Growth: Population in America*, pp. 145–60. Englewood Cliffs, N.J.: Prentice-Hall.

BERTRAND, ALVIN L.
1972 *Social Organization.* Philadelphia: F. A. Davis.

BESHERS, JAMES
1967 *Processes in Social Systems.* New York: The Free Press.

BLAKE, JUDITH
1965 "Demographic Science and the Redirection of Population Policy." *Journal of Chronic Diseases* 18:1181–1200.
1967 "Reproductive Ideals and Educational Attainment Among White Americans." *Population Studies* 21:159–74.
1968 "Are Babies Consumer Durables?" *Population Studies* 22:5–25.

1972   *Coercive Pronatalism and American Population Policy.* Berkeley, Calif.: International Population and Urban Research.

1974   "Can We Believe Recent Data on Birth Expectations in the United States?" *Demography* 11:25–44.

BLAKE, JUDITH, and PRITHWIS DAS GUPTA
1973   "Reply to Cutright and Osborn." *Demography* 10:679–84.

BLAU, PETER M.
1964   *Exchange and Power in Social Life.* New York: Wiley.

BLAU, P. M., and O. D. DUNCAN
1967   *The American Occupational Structure.* New York: Wiley.

BONE, M.
1973   *Family Planning Services in England and Wales.* London: Her Majesty's Stationery Office.

BUMPASS, LARRY L.
1969   "Age at Marriage as a Variable in Socioeconomic Differentials in Fertility." *Demography* 6:45–54.

BUMPASS, LARRY L., and CHARLES F. WESTOFF
1970   *The Later Years of Childbearing.* Princeton, N.J.: Princeton University Press.

BUMPASS, LARRY L., and HARRIET B. PRESSER
1972   "Contraceptive Sterilization in the U.S.: 1965 and 1970." *Demography* 9:531–48.

BUMPASS, LARRY L.
1973   "Is Low Fertility Here to Stay?" *Family Planning Perspectives* 5:67–69.

BUCKLEY, WALTER
1967   *Sociology and Modern Systems Theory.* Englewood Cliffs, N.J.: Prentice-Hall.

CAIN, GLEN C., and ADRIANA WEININGER
1973   "Economic Determinants of Fertility." *Demography* 10:205–24.

CAMPBELL, ARTHUR A.
1973   "Three Generations of Parents." *Family Planning Perspectives* 5:106–13.

COHEN, MALCOLM S.
1969   "Married Women in the Labor Force: An Analysis of Participation Rates." *Monthly Labor Review* 92 (October):31–35.

CLARKSON, F. E., S. R. VOGEL, I. K. BROVERMAN, and D. M. BROVERMAN
1970   "Family Size and Sex Role Stereotypes." *Science* 1970:390–92.

CLAUSEN, JOHN A., and SUZANNE R. CLAUSEN
1973   "The Effects of Family Size on Parents and Children." In J. T. Fawcett, ed., *Psychological Perspectives on Population.* New York: Basic Books.

DAHRENDORF, RALF
1959   *Class and Class Conflict in Industrial Society.* Stanford, Calif.: Stanford University Press.

DAVIS, KINGSLEY
    1967   "Population Policy: Will Current Programs Succeed?" *Science* 158 (November 10):730–39.

DEGLER, C. N.
    1964   "Revolution Without Ideology: The Changing Place of Women in America." In R. J. Lifton, ed., *The Woman in America*. Boston: Beacon Press.

DEJONG, GORDON F.
    1965   "Religious Fundamentalism, Socioeconomic Status, and Fertility Attitudes in the Southern Appalachians." *Demography* 2:540–48.

DEJONG, PETER Y., M. J. BRAWER, and S. S. ROBIN
    1971   "Patterns of Female Inter-generational Occupational Mobility: A Comparison with Male Patterns of Intergenerational Mobility." *American Sociological Review* 36:1033–43.

DEUTSCH, MORTON
    1971   "Conflict and Its Resolution." In C. G. Smith, ed., *Conflict Resolution*, pp. 36–57. Notre Dame, Ind.: Notre Dame University Press.

Dual Careers: A Longitudinal Study of Labor Market Experience of Women.
    1973   Volume 2. Manpower Research Monograph No. 21. Washington D.C.: U.S. Government Printing Office.

DUSENBERRY, JAMES
    1960   "Discussion of Becker." National Bureau of Economic Research; *Demographic and Economic Change in Developed Countries*, pp. 231–34. Princeton, N.J.: Princeton University Press.

EASTERLIN, RICHARD A.
    1969   "Towards a Socioeconomic Theory of Fertility: A Survey of Recent Research on Economic Factors in American Fertility." In S. J. Behrman, L. Corsa, Jr., and Ronald Freedman (eds.), *Fertility and Family Planning: A World View*, pp. 127–56. Ann Arbor: University of Michigan Press.
    1973   "Relative Economic Status and the American Fertility Swing." In Eleanor B. Sheldon, ed., *Family Economic Behavior*. Philadelphia: J. B. Lippincott.

FAWCETT, JAMES (ed.)
    1972   *The Satisfactions and Costs of Children: Theories, Concepts, Methods*. Honolulu: East–West center.
    1973   *Psychological Perspectives on Population*. New York: Basic Books.

FEATHERMAN, DAVID L.
    1970   "Marital Fertility and the Process of Socioeconomic Achievement: An Examination of the Mobility Hypothesis." In L. L. Bumpass and C. F. Westoff, *The Later Years of Childbearing*, pp. 104–131. Princeton, N.J.: Princeton University Press.

FOGARTY, MICHAEL P., R. RAPOPORT and R. N. RAPOPORT
    1971   *Sex, Career and Family*. London: G. Allen & Unwin.

FONG, STANLEY L. M.
    1970   "Sex Roles in the Modern Fabric of China." In G. H. Seward and R. C. Williamson, *Sex Roles in Changing Society*. New York: Random House.

FREEDMAN, R., P. K. WHELPTON, and A. A. CAMPBELL
    1959 *Family Planning, Sterility, and Popualtion Growth.* New York: McGraw-Hill.

GARDNER, BURLEIGH
    1974 "Awakening of the Blue-Collar Woman." *Intellectual Digest* 4:17–19.

GOLDBERG, DAVID
    1960 "Some Recent Developments in American Fertility Research." *In Demographic and Economic Change in Developed Countries,* pp. 137–51. Princeton, N.J.: Princeton University Press.

GOLDSCHEIDER, CALVIN
    1971 *Population, Modernization and Social Structure.* Boston: Little, Brown.

GOODE, WILLIAM J.
    1963 *World Revolution and Family Patterns.* New York: The Free Press.

GUSTAVAS, SUSAN O., and CHARLES B. NAM
    1970 "The Formation and Stability of Ideal Family Size Among Young People." *Demography* 7:43–52.

HAAS, PAULA H.
    1972 "Maternal Role Incompatibility and Fertility in Latin America." *Journal of Social Issues* 28:111–28.

HARBESON, G. E.
    1967 *Choice and Challenge for the American Woman.* Cambridge, Mass.: Schenkman Co.

HARTLEY, RUTH E.
    1959–60 "Children's Concepts of Male and Female Roles." *Merrill-Palmer Quarterly 6.*

HAUG, MARIE R.
    1973 "Social Class Measurement and Women's Occupational Roles." *Social Forces* 52 (September):86–98.

HAVENS, ELIZABETH M., and JUDY C. TULLY
    1972 "Female Intergenerational Occupational Mobility: Comparison of Patterns?" *American Sociological Review* 37:774–77.

HAWTHORN, GEOFFREY
    1970 *The Sociology of Fertility.* New York: Macmillan.

HILL, REUBEN, J. MAYONE STYCOS, and KURT BACK
    1959 *The Family and Population Control.* Chapel Hill, N.C.: University of North Carolina Press.

HILL, REUBEN, and D. KLEIN
    1973 "Relative Economic Status and the American Fertility Swing." In E. B. Sheldon, *Family Economic Behavior,* pp. 167–69. Philadelphia: Lippincott.

HOFFMAN, LOIS W., and FREDERICK WYATT
    1960 "Social Change and Motivations for Having Larger Families: Some Theoretical Considerations " *Merrill-Palmer Quarterly* 6:235–44.

HOLTER, HARRIET
1970 *Sex Roles and Social Structure.* Oslo: Universitet-Forlaget.

HOMANS, GEORGE C.
1961 *Social Behavior: Its Elementary Forms.* New York: Harcourt, Brace and World.

HORNER, MATINA S.
1970 "Femininity and Successful Achievement: A Basic Inconsistency." In J. M. Bardwick *et al., Feminine Personality and Conflict.* Belmont, Calif.: Brooks/Cole Co.

KANTNER, JOHN F., and MELVIN ZELNIK
1972 "Sexual Experience of Young Unmarried Women in the U.S." *Family Planning Perspectives* 4:9–17.
1973 "Contraception and Pregnancy: Experience of Young Unmarried Women in the U.S." *Family Planning Perspectives* 5:21–35.

KAMMEYER, KENNETH
1964 "The Feminine Role: An Analysis of Attitude Consistency." *Journal of Marriage and the Family* 36:295–305.
1966 "Birth Order and the Feminine Role Among College Women." *American Sociological Review* 31:508–15.
1973 "The Effects of Purposive-Rationality, Traditionalism, and Economic Aspirations on the Process of Family Formation." Unpublished paper. College Park: Department of Sociology, University of Maryland.

KATONA, GEORGE
1971 *Aspirations and Affluence: Comparative Studies of the U.S. and Western Europe.* New York: McGraw-Hill.

KELLEY, JONATHAN
1973 "Ideology, Career and Sexuality." Unpublished paper. New York: Center for Policy Research, Columbia University.

KOHN, MELVIN L.
1969 *Class and Conformity: A Study in Values.* Homewood, Ill.: Dorsey Press.

KREPS, JUANITA
1971 *Sex in the Market-Place.* Baltimore: Johns Hopkins Press.

LAURIAT, PATIENCE
1969 "The Effect of Marital Dissolution on Fertility." *Journal of Marriage and the Family* 31:484–99.

LENSKI, GERHARD
1961 *The Religious Factor.* New York: Doubleday.

LIPMAN-BLUMEN, JEAN
1972 "How Ideology Shapes Women's Lives." *Scientific American* (January):34–42.

MASON, KAREN O., and LARRY L. BUMPASS
1973 "Women's Sex Role Attitudes in the United States, 1970." Madison: Center for Ecology and Demography, University of Wisconsin.

MILLER, S. M.
1971 "The Making of a Confused Middle-Class Husband." *Social Policy* (July-August):2:2:33–39.

MILLMAN, MARCIA
1971 "Observations on Sex Role Research." *Journal of Marriage and the Family* 33:772–76.

MITCHELL, JULIET
1969 "The Longest Revolution." In T. Roszak and Roszak, eds. *Masculine–Feminine: Readings in Sexual Mythology and the Liberation of Women.* New York: Harper and Row.

MOBERG, DAVID O.
1962 *The Church as a Social Institution.* Englewood Cliffs, N.J.: Prentice-Hall.

MOYNIHAN, DANIEL P.
1965 "Employment, Income and the Ordeal of the Negro Family." *Daedalus* 94:745–69.

NIE, NORMAN, D. H. BENT, and C. H. HULL
1970 *Statistical Package for the Social Sciences.* New York: McGraw-Hill.

OPPENHEIMER, VALERIE K.
1970 "Demographic Influences on Female Employment and the Status of Women." Unpublished paper. Los Angeles, Calif.: Department of Sociology, University of California.

PARSONS, TALCOTT
1955 "The American Family: Its Relation to Personality and to Social Structure." In T. Parsons and R. F. Bales, *Family Socialization, and Interaction Process.* New York: The Free Press.

PEARLIN, LEONARD I.
1972 *Class Context and Family Relations: A Cross-National Study.* Boston: Little Brown.

PESCATELLO, ANNE
1973 *Male and Female in Latin America.* Pittsburgh: University of Pittsburgh Press.

POHLMAN, E. H.
1969 *Psychology of Birth-Planning.* Cambridge, Mass.: Schenkman.

POLOMA, M. M., and T. N. GARLAND
1971 "The Married Professional Woman: A Study in Tolerance of Domestication." *Journal of Marriage and the Family* 33:531–40.

POPULATION COUNCIL
1970 *Selected Questionnaires on Knowledge, Attitudes and Practice of Family Planning.* Vols I. II. New York City.
1973 Annual Report. New York City.

PRESSER, HARRIET B., and LARRY L. BUMPASS
1972 "The Acceptability of Contraceptive Sterilization Among U.S. Couples: 1970." *Family Planning Perspectives* 4:18–26.

PRINZ, ROLAND
1973 Associated Press Report. In Bloomington, Ind., *Herald Telephone*, July 19, p. 23.

RAINWATER, LEE
1965 *Family Design: Marital Sexuality, Family Size, and Contraception.* Chicago: Aldine.

RIDLEY, JEANNE CLARE
1968 "Demographic Change and the Roles and Status of Women." *Annals of American Academy of Political and Social Science* 375:15–25.

ROSEN, B. C., and A. B. SIMMONS
1971 "Industrialization, Family, and Fertility: A Structural–Psychological Analysis of the Brazilian Case." *Demography* 8:49–70.

ROSEN, BERNARD C., and ANITA L. LARAIA
1972 "Modernity in Women: An Index of Social Change in Brazil." *Journal of Marriage and the Family* 34:353–60.

ROSSI, ALICE
1970 "Deviance and the Conformity in the Life Goals of Women." Unpublished paper, University of Massachusetts, Amherst.

RYDER, NORMAN B.
1970 "Fertility Increase from the 1930's to the 1950's." Unpublished paper. Princeton, N.J.: Princeton University.

RYDER, NORMAN B., and CHARLES F. WESTOFF
1971 *Reproduction in the United States, 1965.* Princeton, N.J.: Princeton, N.J.: Princeton University Press.

RYDER, NORMAN B.
1973 "A Critique of the National Fertility Study." *Demography* 10:495–506.

SCANZONI, JOHN
1965 "Resolution of Occupational–Conjugal Role Conflict in Clergy Marriages." *Journal of Marriage and the Family* 27:396–402.
1970 *Opportunity and the Family.* New York: The Free Press.
1971 *The Black Family in Modern Society.* Boston: Allyn & Bacon.
1972 *Sexual Bargaining: Power Politics in American Marriage.* Englewood Cliffs, N.J.: Prentice-Hall.
1975 "Sex Roles, Economic Factors, and Marital Solidarity in Black and White Marriages." *Journal of Marriage and the Family* 37 (February).

SCANZONI, JOHN, and MARTHA McMURRY
1972 "Continuities in the Explanation of Fertility Control." *Journal of Marriage and the Family* 34:315–22.

SCHEIBE, KARL E.
1970 *Beliefs and Values.* New York: Holt, Rinehart & Winston.

SEGAL, SHELDON J.
1972 "Contraceptive Research: A Male Chauvinist Plot?" *Family Planning Perspectives* 4:21–26.

Sinha, S. N.
  1970 "Men and Women of India Today." In G. H. Seward and R. C. Williamson, *Sex Roles in Changing Society*. New York: Random House.
Steinmann, Anne, D. J. Fox, and R. Farkas
  1968 "Male and Female Perceptions of Male Sex Roles." *Proceedings of the American Psychological Association*, 421–22.
Stolka, S. M., and L. D. Barnett
  1969 "Education and Religion as Factors in Women's Attitudes Motivating Childbearing." *Journal of Marriage and the Family* 31:740–50.
Stycos, J. Mayone, and R. Weller
  1967 "Female Working Roles and Fertility." *Demography* 4:210–17.
Sweet, James A.
  1970 "Family Composition and the Labor Force Activity of American Wives." *Demography* 7:195–210.
Tangri, Sandra S.
  1972 "Determinants of Occupational Role Innovation Among College Women." *Journal of Social Issues* 28:177–200.
Tietze, Christopher
  1970 "Relative Effectiveness of Methods." In Mary S. Calderone, *Manual of Family Planning and Contraceptive Practice*, pp. 268-75. Baltimore: Williams and Wilkins Co.
Tomasson, Richard F.
  1966 "Why Has American Fertility Been So High?" In Bernard Farber (ed.), *Kinship and Family Organization*, pp. 327-38. New York: John Wiley.
Turner, Jonathon H.
  1974 The Structure of Sociological Theory. Homewood, Ill.: Dorsey.
Veevers, J. E.
  1974 "The Moral Careers of Voluntarily Childless Wives." In S. Parvez Wakil, *Marriage and the Family in Canada: A Reader*. Toronto: Copp-Clark.
Weitzman, L. J., D. Eifler, E. Hokada, and C. Ross
  1972 "Sex-Role Socialization in Picture Books for Preschool Children." *American Journal of Sociology* 77:1125–50.
Westoff, C. F., R. G. Potter, Jr., P. C. Sagi, and E. G. Mishler
  1961 *Family Growth in Metropolitan America*. Princeton, N.J.: Princeton University Press.
Westoff, C. F., R. G. Potter, and P. C. Sagi
  1963 The Third Child. Princeton, N.J.: Princeton University Press.
Westoff, Charles F., and R. H. Potvin
  1967 *College Women and Fertility Values*. Princeton, N.J.: Princeton University Press.
Westoff, Leslie Aldridge, and C. F. Westoff
  1971 *From Now to Zero*. Boston: Little, Brown.
Westoff, C. F.
  1972 "The Modernization of United States Contraceptive Practice." *Family Planning Perspectives* 4:9–13.

1974   "The Populations of the Developing Countries." *Scientific American* 231:108–21.

WHELPTON, P. K., A. A. CAMPBELL, and J. E. PATTERSON
1966   *Fertility and Family Planning in the United States.* Princeton, N.J.: Princeton University Press.

WILLIAMS, ROBIN M.
1968   *American Society* (rev.). New York: A. A. Knopf.

WILSON, FRANK D., and LARRY L. BUMPASS
1973   "The Prediction of Fertility Among Catholics: A Longitudinal Analysis." *Demography* 10:591–98.

YAUKEY, DAVID
1969   "On Theorizing About Fertility." *The American Sociologist* 4:100–4.

U.S. BUREAU OF THE CENSUS
1963   "Methodology and Scores of Socioeconomic Status." Working Paper No. 15.
1970   *Current Population Reports,* Series P-20, No. 205, July.
1971   *Current Population Reports,* Series P-20, No. 211, January.
1971   *Current Population Reports,* Series P-20, No. 226, November.
1972   *Current Population Reports,* Series P-20, No. 232, February.
1972   *Current Population Reports,* Series P-20, No. 240, September.
1973   *Current Population Reports,* Series P-20, No. 254, October.
1974   *Current Population Reports,* Series P-20, No, 263, April.
1971   *Current Population Reports,* Series P-23, No. 39, December.
1973   *Current Population Reports,* Series P-23, No. 46, July.
1972   *Current Population Reports,* Series P-25, No. 480, April.
1969   *Current Population Reports,* Series P-60, No. 64, October.

U.S. DEPARTMENT OF HEALTH, EDUCATION, AND WELFARE
1974   *Monthly Vital Statistics Reports,* Volume 22, No. 13. *Annual Summary for the United States, 1973: Births, Deaths, Marriages, and Divorces.*

INDEXES

Index of Names

Index of Subjects